Exhibit Marketing

Exhibit Marketing

A Survival Guide for Managers

Edward A. Chapman, Jr.

President, Sextant Communications
New York, N.Y.

McGraw-Hill Book Company

New York   St. Louis   San Francisco   Auckland   Bogotá
Hamburg   London   Madrid   Mexico
Milan   Montreal   New Delhi   Panama
Paris   São Paulo   Singapore
Sydney   Tokyo   Toronto

Library of Congress Cataloging-in-Publication Data

Chapman, Edward A., Jr.
    Exhibit marketing.

    Includes index.
    1. Exhibitions.   2. Merchandising.   3. Marketing.
I. Title.
HF5845.C47   1987   659.1'52   87-2621
ISBN 0-07-010669-X

1234567890   DOC/DOC   89210987

ISBN 0-07-010669-X

*The editors for this book were William A. Sabin and Esther Gelatt,
the designer was Naomi Auerbach, and the production supervisor
was Thomas G. Kowalczyk. It was set in Baskerville by McGraw-Hill
Xyvision. Printed and bound by R. R. Donnelley & Sons.*

Contents

Preface

It used to be that only people in the health care field had to convene constantly to keep on top of what's new — and that the furniture industry did its purchasing at buying shows. Now it's everyone and every industry. The notion of a convention as a gathering of like-minded people who want to trade information and goods hasn't changed for hundreds of years. But the pace of change has accelerated. Buyers as well as sellers reach personal and professional goals in a shorter period of time at conventions, trade shows, and fairs. Exhibits work for both.

Result: The number of yearly conventions and trade shows in the United States and Canada has practically doubled in the last decade. New and improved facilities in which these events happen have sprouted up everywhere.

Who Manages the Exhibits?

Perhaps the largest group of people managing the exhibits are "first timers" — people doing their first shows. They could be business owners, sales managers, staff people working for a sales manager, or corporate communications people pressed into service. If you fall in this group, you will especially appreciate Part 1 (Chapters 1 – 3) of this book. These opening chapters offer a quick fix to anyone going through the panicky process of handling an exhibit for the first time. In this sense, *Exhibit Marketing* is a true survival guide for all managers.

Another large group of people involved in exhibit marketing are "part timers" — people who perform this function as part of a larger job. They could be sales managers, manufacturers' representatives, branch managers, and small business owners who operate a small-scale exhibit program — about three or four a year. If you find yourself in this situation, you will welcome the coverage in Parts 2 and 3. Part 2 (Chapters 4–10) offers guidance on how to manage an annual program of exhibits, and Part 3 (Chapters 11–20) offers in-depth coverage on all aspects of creating and managing an exhibit.

Finally, there are the "full-timers" — the professional exhibit managers who view their work as a profession. If you are a member of this group, you will find in Part 4 (Chapters 21–23) a discussion of the key issues on the exhibit industry.

Exhibit management professionals like to tell others that their job is difficult, time-consuming, a destroyer of sleep, and a bit mysterious. They never admit that the fun remains. Managing an exhibit is all of these things, including fun — perhaps not in the old-fashioned sense of funny hats and swimming pools but enjoyable nonetheless. Exhibit marketing operations start and finish within time periods we can understand and feel. We know whether we've passed or failed, privately, at least, within short gulps of hours, days, or weeks.

Except for those who spend careers as exhibit specialists, most people never become completely comfortable in the medium. Nonetheless, all managers should be able to use exhibits effectively to great personal and business advantage, an increasingly important plus.

It's unlikely that your first show will require managing one of the exhibit extravaganzas that huge corporations create at their key trade shows. They involve massive amounts of space; heroic and sophisticated structures; graphics and live shows; special VIP events; press conferences; advertising and sales promotion. They are staffed by scores, even hundreds of people. Think of Panasonic or Sony at the Consumer Electronics Show or the National Association of Broadcasters meeting; Carrier Corporation at its major heating and air-conditioning convention; Pepsico at the Food Marketing Institute; AT&T at the International Communications Association meeting; IBM at the Info Show or the National Computer Conference; Johnson & Johnson or Pfizer at any one of several health-care events; Kohler at the home builders' show; or McGraw-Hill at the American Booksellers Association meeting.

Even if you are going to exhibit at one of the well-known exhibit showcases, you'll probably be dealing with a small booth and marketing program. If not, you will be at one of thousands of lesser-known conventions and trade shows. Whether or not your event is known to the public or business community at large, it's known and important to you. You've got to make it work.

The Management Process

Perhaps our key message is that you don't have to depend entirely on subjective feelings in evaluating how you are doing. First, we present hundreds of "how tos," from soup to nuts at different levels. After you get through all that, we give you information that lets you make an objective evaluation of how much, where, and whom — not simply how.

Why are choices to participate delayed until just shortly before an event? Almost instinctively, it seems, many managers wake up to an upcoming show only when time is limited to what's needed to ensure decent physical appearance. Most of us have not been trained in how best to use the medium as a whole. And what's worse, our management doesn't understand it either. Since shows seem to produce at least some reward, nobody asks, "How far is up?"

The Goal

In some companies, exhibit coordination is a no-win task. The boss presumes that the company will look good and that customers will be given VIP treatment (or feels that it doesn't matter since the show only lasts a few days — just get through it). You may complain, but there's little time for finger pointing. You should be aiming for much more than a booth and VIP "TLC," but the show will not delay even an hour if you aren't ready. And there's no time to explain.

Expectations and evaluations can be subjective, and that's a risk. The downside is what happens when the boss is not satisfied. As for upside — because often there is little objective measure, you can gain paltry reward for premium performance. You do well or badly only because the chief thinks so. We try to help you fix that.

Like it or not, exhibit marketing is here to stay. The sooner we comprehend that it costs real cash — and the quicker we learn how to comprehend when we're making that money back as well as waving that flag — the better off we'll all be. Both ourselves and our customers.

Acknowledgments

Few books leap from mind to page without help. Writing a trade text makes one especially dependent on others. These books require reporting what others have said and done as well as the author's contributions.

Many people from the old "Bell System" and "new AT&T" influenced this work; among them, Emery Westfall, Jack Shea, Hal Rohde, Dick Darr, Bill Horton, Ron Hardaway, Al Werner, Marilyn Laurie, Whit Weihe, Sanford Hourigan, Mitch Kirby, Pat Benson, Barbara Paul, Ina Feinberg, Al LeMieux, Jim Strinz, Byron Ware, Ed O'Donnell, Bob Greening, Emily Wheeler, Mike Magnini, Rick Paulson, Cathryn Berry, Jim Merrigan, Vredy Lytsman, Dorothy O'Hara, Janice Dahm, and Tom Claydon.

People who have been involved with politics also helped, since campaigns, like exhibits, are planned and run within time limits: Bill Curren, Craig Thorn, Joe Boyd, Steve Blum, Kit Bingham, George Humphreys, Polly Weber, Frank Gannon, Ron Abney, R. Burdell Bixby, Don Martin, Frank Hess, Margo Marabond, and especially Mary Ann T. Knauss.

Exhibit managers and those who serve them, coast to coast, helped — from Merrimack, New Hampshire, and Carrboro, North Carolina, to Irvine, California, and Bellevue, Washington. Some knew they were helping. Some did not. They are Thob Stiles, Marti Wolf, Bob Dallmeyer, Eric Brierley, Joe Frederico, Ed Van Holland, Jeff Malley, Bill Swem, Ralph Jones, Kathi Raftery, Lizanne Fisher, Lynne Gordon, Paul Semon, Bill Winsor, Diane Weintraub, Jerry Peterson, Darlene Zonca, Lee Knight, Dick Swandby, Skip Cox, Tom Grossman, Scott Gray, Bill Mee, Lew Johnson, Dr. Gary Young, David Sable, Bob LaPrad, Carolyn Cook, Lleona' Kitzing, Alan Sitzer, Cindy Spuria, Amnon Bar-Tur, David Rue, Bob Dottinger, Jerry Lowery, Dutch Antonisse, Peter Neville, Bob Francisco, Don Vaughn, Jack McEntee, Dave Gold, Mort Kuff, Jim Gallo, Jim Bergman, Mark Hubbell, Chris Walker, Tom McCarthy, Larry Hettinger, Eileen Dunn, Dietra Hahn, Rosemary Peters, Mary Barbara Alexander, Ron Fritkin, Joan Carol, Edith Householder, Joyce McKee, Dick Gorbett, Tom Burbank, Chuck Price, Rik Lowry, Bob Land, and Laurel Larson.

Two organizations were of great assistance: first is the Trade Show Bureau; second, the International Exhibitors Association.

At a personal level, Darlene Zonca, Joan Carol, Dave Sable, Scott Gray, Dick Swandby, Bill Mee, Lew Johnson, Lee Terwilliger, and Mitch Fink were early supporters. Two others helped more than I can explain. One is Theresa Bellinghausen, powerful in many ways, a dear friend and congenial teacher. The other is my father. He claims to have retired. That is not true.

Edward A. Chapman, Jr.

PART 1
The Quick Fix

1
Players in the Show: An Introduction

Let's be frank. In business we have two objectives. We want to provide quality products or services and we want to make money doing it. If in so doing we have some fun, the enjoyment is a plus.

To make money, we have to make contact. That's what this book is all about. One of the most cost-effective, proven ways to make face-to-face contact is through exhibits. Whether at the county fair or at a trade show 2000 miles away, a booth is neutral, nonthreatening ground where visitors can see competitors side by side and comparison shop, where buyers and sellers can connect.

Unfortunately, many people lose sight of the money-making goal when they start planning an exhibit. Instead, they get caught up in the machinations of developing and setting up the booth itself, the stage upon which contact takes place. Although this is no easy task, is it necessary to focus all our energy on the booth itself? No. This book will show you how to make that chore easier. And, at the same time, it will help you plan to reach the ultimate goal: making money.

Five-Part Book: Which Part for Whom

Depending on who you are, and your situation, you can pick the parts of the book that will help you most. Even though we're all unique, there are things we share. Each part is tailored for groups facing different but similar problems.

Book Part Summary

- This first part, "The Quick Fix," is designed for those putting together their first exhibits.
- Part 2, "Program Management," is for those who have been producing a few exhibits a year as part of their jobs and want to add new meaning to what they've been doing.
- Part 3, "Creating and Managing an Exhibit," provides reference information for everyone.
- Part 4, "The Industry and Corporate Management," is mainly for professional exhibit managers, those of us who do this every day.

There appears to be less material for the last group. This is not the case. Many full-time professionals find themselves slotted as coordinators, and they are paid that way. The book as a whole is designed to help them become more: managers instead of coordinators implementing other people's decisions.

Retail Exhibitor

Many people in the exhibit industry presume the medium is dominated by business conventions and trade shows. It is not. Newspapers and radio and TV advertisements announce vast numbers of *retail* trade fairs: antique, auto, boat, coin, flea, home, garden, recreational vehicle, ski, and sports. Stamp shows and swap meets take place in almost every city. Retailers can find room for themselves among those we list. In fact, Jerry Lowery, a highly respected convention hall administrator, said, "Retailers at home and garden shows seem to have even more problems than first-time exhibitors at business trade shows."[1]

Exhibiting Close to Home

Exhibitors, regardless of the market, seem to have more problems close to home than far away. When you go on the road, you know you have to plan in advance. Planning doesn't seem so important when the show is in your own back yard, but actually the job is no less difficult.

Experienced part-time exhibit managers and full-time professionals can skip the rest of this chapter and Chapters 2 and 3, or just skim. You may enjoy a refresher.

For the First-Time Exhibitor

How, you might wonder, did you ever get hornswoggled into doing this job in the first place? Perhaps you are asking yourself why you didn't take that job at your uncle's bedspring factory. The sense of excitement we get when doing something new is combined with misgiving. You were probably persuaded into handling the exhibit by hearing something like the following:

"I'm heading up the exhibits committee for our state association meeting this year. Since you sell so much to our company, I was thinking you might like to participate with an exhibit."

"I've just heard that the crowd who opened up out at the shopping center is going to exhibit at the fair, so I signed us up for some space too."

"See this note from the vice president's office? She's going to be speaking at this convention, and they are asking us to support her by having a booth and hospitality suite."

"Our best marketing communications and advertising trainees start in exhibit coordination so that they get a feel for our products and for the people we work with in the field."

In any case, the job in the bedspring factory has been filled. The date for the show has been set and there is not much time.

More than a Physical Presence

Developing, moving, setting up, operating, and tearing down an exhibit can be difficult, time-consuming, and nerve-racking. It can absorb so much energy that you lose sight of the ultimate money-making goal. If you let that happen with your first show, you may continue the pattern in preparing for future shows. Some who claim 5 years of experience really have but 1, repeated 4 times. *The physical process of exhibiting becomes an end in itself.* This kind of person, or "survivor," thinks success is a pat on the back from the boss or partner and never takes real advantage of the opportunity for personal and business growth. Producing an exhibit can become fun, but that ultimate sense of satisfaction is missing. Your assignment now is to read on and deliver the exhibit marketing job of a champion.

Quick Fix Contents

The following two chapters include fast facts about:

- *Small exhibit structures and graphics.* An outline of options and suggested approaches to exhibit design, signs, and other graphics

- *Budgets.* A short budget format to use in gathering and adding up essential costs

- *The exhibitor kit.* A summary of what is to be found in the information packet provided by trade show managers to exhibitors

- *Promotional programs.* Some suggestions for quickly executed and inexpensively produced promotional programs to help increase the number of visitors who will come to the booth

- *New prospects and current customers.* Information on how you can differentiate between searching for new customers and selling current customers

- *Selling hints.* A short list of important selling techniques, dos and don'ts, unique to selling at an exhibit

- *Implementation tasks.* Highlights of what must be done before, during, and after at the site of the show

- *Priorities.* An alert as to what a manager must do first

- *Written plan.* Explanation of what should be included in a written plan and why the plan must be constructed

You should be able to survive and grow with the information in "The Quick Fix." Each of its subjects is also expanded later in the book.

Sales Technique Emphasis

You may have noted that not a single quotation on page 5 cites the purpose of the whole exercise: making money. Few people know that secret. If you define true selling goals, you're likely to take the right steps to reach them. You'll survive and grow, providing the physical exhibit and much more.

So if there is enough time before your first show to pay extra attention to a single subject, it should be personal selling. It is detailed in Chapter 17, "Exhibit Floor Selling." Face-to-face contact is the most important single facet of exhibit marketing.[2] An exhibit is little more than a stage on which players perform. Person-to-person selling is the performance.

2

Three-Hour Planning Process

When you are faced with your first exhibit, it's easy to blunder. Exhibits are meant to be looked at, so you naturally think first about appearance. Unfortunately, that's a mistake. Think first about marketing and sales: the money-making goal. Think about appearance second. Then the decisions become easy.

You have a deadline. The show will start with or without you. This may be worrisome, but it's an advantage. There won't be a lot of time for anyone to look over your shoulder.

The best way to plan an exhibit is by drafting a list of questions to be answered and drawing up a schedule for work completion. You may want to revise your plan as you learn more about the situation; but for a start, go with what you know.

Creating an overall plan should require no more than 3 hours. The rest is implementation. Investing 3 hours up front can save many more hours later.

Written Exhibit Plan

Many exhibits are implemented without a written plan. This may be all right for people with years of experience, but even they can forget important details. What follows is a list of plan elements.

Elements of an Exhibit Plan

- Start with a statement of goals. Be as specific as possible. Relate them to the overall marketing goals of the company. Try to position the exhibit as part of a larger effort.

- Analyze the show. Include an audience estimate, a review of the activity planned, a listing of competing events or seminars. Indicate how company products relate to portions of the audience. Review the physical layout of the facility. Consider the position of your booth in relation to others, and to other activities or events that will take place.

- List the products or services to be displayed or demonstrated. Draw up a preliminary layout showing placement priorities.

- Assemble samples of literature to be distributed, along with sales order and lead forms.

- Set preliminary booth work schedules for each day if two or more people will staff the exhibit.

- Summarize activities if you plan preliminary promotional work (such as letters to customers) or hospitality for VIPs at the show.

- Prepare a cost estimate or budget. (You'll find out how, later in the chapter.)

- Make up a work completion schedule.

- Explain how you will measure the program's success after the show.

You'll find that a plan is written in two stages. The first draft will bring questions to light; the second fills in blanks.

Setting Exhibit Goals

When you try to set goals, consider:

- Making contacts with and getting orders from current customers

- Prospecting for sales leads and orders from new customers

- Developing product and company awareness in the audience and within the industry sponsoring the show

- Learning more about both the industry and the competition

Quantifying Your Objectives

General statements about increasing sales or creating presence are not enough. Specific direction is created when objectives answer the question, "How much?"

How many of your current customers will you meet each exhibit day? How many new prospect contacts can you make each day? Is there an opportunity for press coverage? If so, where? What competitors will exhibit? What will they show? What can you learn about the interests of the attendees or about trends in the industry?

Gathering Facts

To quantify objectives intelligently, try getting information from sources such as the following:

Show Prospectus.   Start with the sales literature and information packet provided by the show's management. Try to learn something about who will attend, the educational program, and the competitors who may exhibit. Remember, the information provided in the prospectus is often inadequate. The audience breakdown may not be included, the educational program may be described only in general terms, and the list of exhibitors may be more wish than reality. A talk with the show manager may get you better information (and may even tell you what the show manager does not know).

Attendee and Exhibitor Lists.   The organizer should be able to provide a list of those who attended the *last* show. See if the audience was broken down by job title, industry, or any other classification. Find out if statistics were developed by an independent outside audit. They would be more credible than figures developed by show management itself. Ask for a list of the last show's exhibitors.

Competitors.   Call competitors. Most are willing to share insights. Ask what they think about the audience and the educational program. See if they had any problems setting up.

Other Exhibitors.   If asking a competitor isn't comfortable, talk with anyone else who exhibited in the past.

Internal Sources.   Compare your customer list with actual visitors to the show. Talk with your own salespeople.

Goal-Setting Procedures

Current Customers.   Write down the number of current customers you expect to see at the show. Back this up with a list of names. Estimate the number of orders you want to write and estimate the average value of each order. This creates a dollar goal.

Prospecting.   The average cost of a personal office sales call is well above $200. At a trade show, the sales call is just over $100,[1] and you can do more prospecting there in a day than in weeks from the office. Use the following guide to create a prospecting goal:

1. How many salespeople will be at the booth at one time? How many hours will the show be open—beginning to end?

2. Presume each salesperson makes *10 contacts per hour* during times *when the show is crowded.* If two people will be at the booth, plan 20 contacts in a busy hour.

3. The show may run for 3 days, 6 hours a day; a total of 18 hours. However, traffic may be slow at times. For instance, you may feel that only 12 of the 18 hours will be busy. So multiply 20 times 12 = 240 contacts. (You're ignoring 6 hours; thus, even if 10 per person per hour seems high, it works out for the show as a whole.)

4. Estimate that *20 percent of these contacts* will result in leads or sales: 240 contacts = 48 sales leads or sales.

5. Because trade show audiences are prescreened, you can expect a high number of the leads to be converted to sales, up to 50 percent. Create a sales goal, including sales closed after the show. In this case: 24.

6. Multiply sales by the average value of an order to establish your prospecting dollar goal.

You can adjust the goal based on judgment—but this procedure is a good place to start.

Awareness.   Your booth, products, and people will be seen by more people than you can talk to. In addition, press representatives attend trade shows. You can set quantified goals several ways, for instance:

- Literature can be distributed. You can plan on the number of brochures or flyers to be passed out.

• News release information can be prepared and given to press representatives. You estimate the number of press contacts and what will appear later.

Learning.   Learning goals should be divided into two parts:

1. *Industry education.*   Exhibitors sometimes ignore educational seminars. Don't. (Exhibit selling can be related to an educational theme.) List sessions to attend and promise reports on them. In addition, listen to questions raised. You can set a goal for prospects to identify in the sessions.

2. *Competition.*   List the competitors you expect to see. Promise a report on what each shows at its booth.

Goal setting is detailed in Chapter 5, including explanation of thumb rules for audience analysis and goal-setting procedure.

Preparing a Cost Estimate

The biggest advantage you gain from budget writing is establishing cost-value relationships—ultimately producing better results.

You'll see a sample budget form for small exhibits in Figure 2.1. It is broken into 8 lines. (Large or complex exhibit marketing plans require more detailed estimates. See Chapter 8.) An explanation for each cost element follows.

Eight-Line Budget

1. *Space.*   This is the rent for booth space.

2. *Structure and graphics.*   Make an estimate, but be prepared to revise it after some investigation. If you are unsure, back up the figure on this line with an additional amount placed in a contingency fund.

3. *Transportation.*   Include transporting the exhibit structure, graphics, demonstration products, supplies, and anything else that must be taken to your show (and brought home). This may cover using your car, a rented station wagon, or commercial transportation.

4. *On-site services.*   This item covers service and rental at the arena or hotel. You may have to pay for setup help or electrical services, even

Cost Tracking		
	Estimate	*Actual*
1. Space rent	$_____	$_____
2. Structure and graphics	_____	_____
3. Transportation for exhibits	_____	_____
4. Services at the site	_____	_____
5. Traffic stimulation promotions	_____	_____
6. Customer hospitality	_____	_____
7. Personal expenses for the staff	_____	_____
Total	_____	_____
8. Contingency and miscellaneous at 10 percent of above	_____	_____
Total show budget/actual	$_____	$_____

Figure 2.1. This relatively simple form will allow you to establish an 8-line budget and later monitor your actual costs.

for a booth you can erect yourself. In addition, you may need to rent plants, arrange for booth cleaning, rent carpeting—all sorts of things.

5. *Preshow and at-show promotion.* The costs range upward from postage to advertising, giveaways, and prize promotions.

6. *Customer hospitality.* If VIPs are coming, food, beverage, taxi, suite rental, and theatrical or sports tickets could be involved.

7. *Personal expenses.* Travel and entertainment expense for yourself and others at the show may not be part of the exhibit budget. They are true costs, however, and should be included in an overall estimate regardless of which budget pays.

8. *Contingency miscellaneous.* There are often unforeseen costs. In addition, it's wise to plan for excess in *structure and graphics* and *customer hospitality.* Add a 10 percent "fudge factor" to the combined total of lines 1 through 7.

It should be easy enough to estimate some lines: travel and hotel, for instance. Sources of cost information for others, such as exhibit structure and on-site service, are included in this chapter and in Chapter 3.

First Things First: Avoiding Problems

There are some tasks that must be done far in advance. And there are some jobs that take longer than others to complete. When time is short, they can affect the plan itself. Here are some warnings.

Hotel and Travel

Make reservations as soon as you can. Even if a show is small, there may be competing events. Book hotels, and sometimes travel, through the show manager if lower rates apply.

Staff Selection and Recruiting

If only you and one or two others will be staffing the booth, don't worry. Otherwise, start selecting and recruiting quickly. It's far easier to recruit salespeople who will be dealing with their own customers. More often, however, the benefits are not direct. Those who work the show may feel it a sacrifice to help others earn compensation. You'll see that it's far more effective to use a small team throughout a show than to split booth duties among different people each day.

Exhibit Structure and Graphics

Many companies own exhibit structures and graphic materials. Even then, there are three potential problems to check on, early in the game:

- Trade shows tend to be seasonal. If the show takes place during a seasonal peak, company booths may be committed.
- The specific signs needed may not be available or may not exist.
- A booth used frequently may require touching up or refurbishing before use, or graphic signs may be battered.

If the company does not have a booth, or if the booth is already booked, immediate fact finding is required. See Chapter 3.

Display Products and Literature

If you know exactly what you will be exhibiting and have display samples, relax. On the other hand, if you need to obtain products and literature from others, do it now. We've heard too many "war stories" about companies filling a customer order with the display sample 2 days before the show. The same thing happens with brochures. Inventories disappear. In addition, whenever complex equipment is involved, make arrangements early for technical help at the exhibit.

Preshow Promotion

If the show requires promotional materials, start the work quickly.

- Show programs are printed in advance. Your listing must be written and sent.
- If the promoter (show manager) offers tickets to the event, order far enough in advance for your own distribution.
- If invitations or letters are to be mailed to customers, text must be written and salespeople alerted to produce them.
- If anything at all is to be designed or printed (a special brochure or giveaway), production must be started quickly. As is the case with an exhibit structure or graphic panel, the physical work may take longer to finish than you realize.

Exhibitor Kit

There are two documents supplied by show managers in addition to the program. First is the show prospectus mentioned earlier. It's a sales piece about the show. The second, referred to as an *exhibitor kit*, is an information packet. It spells out the show's rules and includes information and order forms for on-site services.

Reading the kit can prevent nasty surprises during setup. In addition, the contents can be a big help in planning. It's a checklist of what to think about, including prices to help prepare a budget.

Exhibitor Kit Contents

Some of the services listed below are musts. Others are optional.

Drayage Service. The term *drayage* may or may not be used. The service, however, covers moving exhibit materials into the hall and to the boothspace before a show and removing them afterward. The service is priced per 100 pounds. At most shows, it is a must.

Setup Labor. Most larger arenas and hotels operate with union contracts. Even if you can erect the exhibit yourself, there may be a need for professional help. Costs are shown on the order form.

Electrical Service. The contractor installs electrical circuits and, in some cases, plugs in lights and appliances in the booth. At most shows, local codes make professional service a must.

Telephone Service. In addition to ordering telephone lines, you must make arrangements for telephone instruments.

Other Extra-Cost Services. Virtually all shows offer a number of optional services and products. Among them are:

- Booth cleaning

- Photography

- Extra booth security

- Host and hostess service

- Plumbing or high-pressure air

- Imprinters to register booth visitors if the show supplies them with plastic name badges

- Rigging service to hang materials from ceilings or unpack equipment crates

- Plants and flowers

- Audiovisual equipment and operation

- Extra furniture not included in the space rental package, including such things as smoking stands, wastebaskets, and even the supply of complete exhibit booths

- Custom sign-making service

- Booth carpet

Payment expectations are also found in the exhibitor kit. Sometimes cash is required, and this need becomes part of the show plan. If more details on on-site services are required, see Chapter 15.[2]

Show Rules

The show rules are found in both the space rent contract and the exhibitor kit. They can have an impact on your plan. For instance, most shows publish height rules. A wall at the back of a small exhibit is generally limited to 8 feet. Side walls are lower: 4 feet or less. In addition, you'll see in-and-out timing rules for the show.

You should also check the insurance coverage provided by show management and the facility. It may be necessary to purchase additional coverage from your own insurance company.

Show managers often conduct exhibitor meetings in advance. It can really help to attend. You may learn some unwritten ground rules, and you'll get to know the key people you'll see at setup.

What to Exhibit: A Decision Guide

It's not always an obvious *choice*. Sometimes there are more options than one might think. Of course, if you offer one product line, that's it. Even if you have several lines, familiarity with the show will make your decision easy. Sometimes, however, we don't know the show and there are variable product or service *applications*. Extra investigation is needed. The talk with the show manager that we suggested should produce information about audience interest you can relate to products.

There are times when an important product may not match attendee desires. Your choice is simple: Bow out or shift emphasis to reflect the audience. Otherwise, you'll waste time and money.

Preshow and At-Show Promotions

Your needs and types of promotions will differ depending on the show, what your company plans to offer, and the relative importance of show sales to the company's future.

For instance, a meeting involving 500 attendees and 20 to 30 exhibitors should require little or no activity. Both groups are small enough to make it likely that all attendees will visit all booths. An exception might be a brand-new product or an industry leader position to maintain, a public relations objective.

On the other hand, a show that attracts thousands of visitors and scores or hundreds of exhibitors increases your need of a booth traffic promotion especially for exhibitors interested in only a small portion of the total audience. Buyers and sellers have to find each other.

Traffic-building promotions can be divided into three categories:

1. *Current customers.* At minimum, a letter of invitation should be mailed to each, citing reasons to visit the booth. VIP appointments should be offered, focused on times when the exhibit floor won't be busy. Serious conversations can be conducted in quiet. More new prospects may drop by when the show floor is full.

2. *Internal information.* Company newsletters and any other internal media should be used to promote the show. Salespeople who won't be there should alert their customers who may be attending. (Establish a procedure so these customers get special treatment.)

3. *New customer prospecting.* This is a primary advantage associated with exhibiting. Visitors come to see what's new—in both products and companies. There are ways to help them find you:

   - News releases or advertising.

   - Direct mail: Either the preshow registration name list or the attendee list from the prior year can be used.

   - Promotions at the show can be employed as well. For instance, when visitors stay at a single hotel, invitations can be placed outside room doors or in hotel desk mailboxes.

   - At a large show, if you have a small or out-of-the-way booth, hire hosts and hostesses to walk through the hall passing out fliers that tell visitors where you are.

Time-Line Chart

This is the work completion schedule mentioned earlier. In addition to lots of details, there is work done by others. Time must be allocated.

A time-line chart can be your pathfinder. In addition, it shows others how what they are doing fits. The sample time-line chart in Figure 2.2 illustrates the concept.

Exhibit Measurement

You have to decide how to measure success. Goal setting starts the process. Results can be measured against goals in two ways: cost or value.

Time-Line Chart Illustration

Week 4

— Prepare fundamental plan and budget.
— Make hotel and travel reservations. Book suite for hospitality.
— Check booth and graphics for quality.
— Start recruiting staff members.
— Send in show program listing.

Week 3

— Check display product and brochure supply.
— Start new graphic sign production and have exhibit touched up.
— Start writing customer letters. Prepare suite invitations.
— Complete staff recruiting. Send names to show manager for badge preparation and revise travel reservations.

Week 2

— Complete booth repair and new graphics. Ship to show.
— Mail customer letters of invitation.
— Make preliminary plans with hotel for food and beverage in suite.
— Mail orders for show services.

Week 1

— Confirm receipt of service orders and exhibit.
— Write thank-you letters for use after the show.
— Pack office supplies for show, including copies of mailed orders and shipping bills of lading.
— Travel to site, pick up badges, hire labor, assemble exhibit.
— Greet salespeople and conduct preshow briefing. Outline goals.

During the Show

— Conduct daily meetings to check on goals and make changes.
— Keep order and sales lead paperwork up to date.
— Arrange for postshow shipping.

After the Show

— Prepare preliminary results report.
— Process leads, orders, and thank-you letters.

Figure 2.2. This illustration is based on assumptions that may not apply in every situation. They are: the trade show opens in 28 days; a 20-foot booth exists and will be used; travel to a neighboring city is involved; orders will be written with current customers; customer hospitality will be involved; the show itself is relatively small.

Cost-Related Measurement

With numerical results tabulated, cost comparisons are possible. For instance:

- Cost per current customer met

- Cost per lead obtained
- Cost per order written
- Cost per item of literature distributed
- Cost per news story printed

Value-Related Measurement

This type of measure compares dollar returns in orders written against cost. It can also be used to compare *potential* dollar return against cost by having sales leads evaluated after the show. As a rule of thumb, you should try to obtain at least $10 return—reported actual or potential—for each dollar spent. This process is detailed in Chapter 10.

You may want to choose some but not all of these ways to evaluate your first show. Try to pick a method you can continue. The real value in measurement is comparing one exhibit against others, asking yourself why one does better than another.

Implementation planning is covered in the following chapter. You will also find information to help fill in blanks in the initial plan.

3

Operations Before, During, and After the Show

With a draft for your exhibit plan in hand, you should have a pretty fair idea of what has to be done. Now we focus on implementation planning.

Exhibit Structure

We bet your first exhibit is relatively small, a booth for a space 10 or 20 feet long. Even if it's larger, the same fundamental principles guide decision making.

Your Options if No Booth Is Available

If you already have a booth, consult the *graphic guidelines* beginning on page 23. If not, you have options.

Table and Drape. Show organizers provide the basics in return for space rent. Check your space contract and exhibitor kit; but for the most part, this means a draped back wall and side rails plus perhaps a table and a couple of chairs. A stenciled sign showing your company name and space number will be attached to the back wall drape. Place products on the table and open for business.

Booth Rental.   You can rent extra furniture or an exhibit structure, complete with back wall, counters, and such. You have two sources. The decorating company serving the show is one. Its offerings are shown in the exhibitor kit information packet. In addition, most custom exhibit design and production companies sell, rent, and service one or two lines of already manufactured exhibits. Check the telephone company's *Yellow Pages* under "Display Designers & Producers—Exposition, Convention, Etc."[1]

Already Manufactured Exhibit Purchase.   Scores of manufactured exhibit systems are available. There are two basic types. One is placed on top of a table provided by the show's manager. The other includes its own floor-standing back wall. A *Directory of Exhibit Systems* is published by *Exhibitor Magazine.*[2] Another source is the *National Tradeshow Services Directory* published annually by *Tradeshow Week.*[3] Its 1986 edition lists over 150 dealers nationwide under "Exhibits: Modular/Portable." The custom builders we mentioned will sell these systems as well as rent them, or rent with an option to buy. Another source for already manufactured exhibits is starting to be found in larger cities: specialized stores offering a range of display systems.

Terms.   You'll hear two terms used to describe manufactured exhibits. One is *modular* and the other, *portable*. Most units can be used in multiples, thus modular. Most are relatively light and easy to move, therefore portable.

Custom Exhibits.   Custom exhibit designers and producers offer ground-up design and fabrication, starting with needs analysis and culminating in a structure built to meet your specific requirements. You needn't be big to interest custom designers. They devote much of their time to small units, including customized versions of the manufactured systems. Understand, however, that custom work takes more time and costs more.

Factors to Consider in Making a Decision

The factors to consider in making a rental or purchase choice are product, how often an exhibit might be needed, and cost.

Product Factor.   There are some products and situations that require starting with a custom-designed booth. For the most part, however, manufactured systems exist for different product types. You can start with a manufactured system and wait a few shows before deciding on exactly what you need in a custom unit. There are three basic designs:

- If you are selling a service, or need backdrop for a floor-standing product, there are systems featuring full-wall graphic sign space.
- If you are demonstrating a desktop product, there are systems with sturdy counters, free-standing or attached to a back wall.
- If you need to display small products, there are units with several shelves that fit on a back wall.

Frequency-of-Use Factor.   Should you rent or buy? That depends on how often a unit will be used. If you are thinking about three or four shows a year—buy. But you may not be sure. If that's the case, rent with an option to buy.

Cost Factor.   Floor-standing manufactured systems cost from under $1000 to over $5000, *plus* the cost of graphic signs. Tabletop displays run from $300 to $1300. (These prices are based on units for a 10-foot-wide space.) Price differences are based on durability, shipping cases, counters, and flexibility. (Durability and spare parts availability are important if you'll exhibit several times, especially out of town.)

Custom booth designs cost considerably more. Expect to spend $12,000 to $15,000 for a custom 10-foot booth (including graphic signs).

Figures 3.1 to 3.3 reflect design concepts used in manufactured exhibit units. Figure 3.1 illustrates the use of large graphic signs and Figure 3.2 the display of desktop products. Figure 3.3 offers a sketch of a *custom*-designed 10-foot booth. It illustrates not only custom design but also the third situation—racking small products for display. (As we've said, there are also manufactured systems with this same basic capability.)

Regardless of product, situation, and budget, don't forget that a booth is a shell. It is simply a backdrop for graphics, products, and people. Exhibit design concepts and production are covered in greater detail in Chapter 12.

Graphic Guidelines

Even if you have a booth and it's in good shape, you'll have to check its graphics: New signs may have to be made for your particular show.

Figure 3.1. Some manufactured systems emphasize the potential of: (1) using large graphics to help sell services that can't be displayed or (2) backdropping floor-standing products. *(Sketch courtesy of Joan Carol Design and Exhibits, Suitland, Maryland.)*

Remember that show visitors are bombarded. They see an assortment of attention-getting signs. The result is that most won't read a lot of text.

Graphic Thumb Rules

Rule 1: Try and attract potential buyers only.   Use a few short words to outline what is being offered, who should buy and why. Often a "benefit statement" is best.

Rule 2: Signs at different heights work in different ways.   A large sign placed near the top of a booth is seen from quite a distance. A prospect moving close to the booth no longer "sees" this sign but instead becomes conscious of smaller signs placed lower on the wall or on a counter.

Rule 3: Cut copy. After writing a first draft for sign copy, try to reduce the text by 50 percent. Professional writers follow this approach. Relate words to the audience. Focus on the product with just a few key benefit words to attract attention (new, proven, and so on).

Figure 3.2. If you demonstrate a product, the manufactured system used should place more emphasis on a heavy counter. There is less room for graphic support on the back wall. People, equipment, and counter fill the space. *(Sketch courtesy of Gallo Displays, Inc., Cleveland.)*

Figure 3.3. A number of manufactured exhibit systems provide good back-wall shelving for the display of small products. This unit, however, is a custom design for a legal book publisher. *(Design and sketch courtesy Giltspur Exhibits, Boston.)*

Headline or "Header" Copy

The term *header* describes a panel across the top of a back wall. Headers are set out from the wall, providing a hiding place for lights shining down on wall signs, counters, and products displayed below. The same light shows *through* the panel, backlighting text on the header itself. The text appearing here is like a newspaper headline. (You'll see headers often on custom exhibits; but they are avoided on many manufactured units to save weight and simplify booth setup. In that case, the area near the top of the wall is treated the same way, with spotlights illuminating headline text.)

Some managers try to attract visitors by presenting the company name high on the back wall. It is often more effective to highlight a product feature or name. To create the most effective headline, focus on the key sales message for the show. Rule 1 applies.

Supporting Sign Copy

Text below the headline, or on counters, should also be cut to the bone. Good signs summarize just two or three selling features. Don't try and tell the whole sales story. Signs cannot replace well-versed, exhibit-trained salespeople.

In addition to text, exhibitors use illustrations, photographs, and charts for graphic support. The same rules apply: Artwork should relate directly to the audience and the selling message. Decoration for its own sake wastes space and money.

Graphic Sign Costs

Signs are custom designed and produced. It's really difficult to provide specific cost guidelines. There are simply too many variables. Don't be surprised, however, at spending several hundred dollars for a single large and complex sign. Backlighted signs can be especially costly. There are three ways to save:

- Restrict graphic work to what's needed to tell a simple sales story in good taste.
- Allow as much time as possible for production: Avoid overtime.
- Don't change after production is complete.

Graphic quality standards in the exhibit world are very high, and quality costs money. The key to a fine and effective appearance lies in outlining clear goals first, then spending the dollars required to reach them. Remember signs support but cannot replace sales conversation.

Audiovisual Presentations

Try to avoid using films, video tapes, or slide shows at a small booth. Lighting and sound levels in exhibit halls are too high, and most audiovisual productions are too long. There are too many distractions. Save audiovisuals for room environments in which sound and light are controlled and more time can be spent without distraction.

What to Bring to the Show

Your plan is ready, the exhibit packed, sales team set, customers alerted. Yet there remains much to do. A temporary company sales facility is being established.

There are dozens of details, many related to very ordinary tools and supplies we take for granted. Even if a show takes place locally, it can be inconvenient, time-consuming, or even impossible to obtain what may be needed without advance planning. Some items are obvious, others easy to forget. What follows are two checklists.

Exhibit Structure Checklist

The Exhibit Itself.   A packing list must be prepared, complete with panels, graphics, counters, carpet, and products to be displayed. Include a setup drawing showing how each part fits with others when erected.

A Tool Kit.   Exhibits at arenas are often erected by skilled craftspeople who have tools. Many shows, however, are in small facilities. "Do it yourself" then becomes the byword. Either way, you need a tool and supply box.

What follows is a short list of tools and supplies suitable for most small exhibits. A trip to your hardware store should be enough to locate most everything. An expanded list appears in Figure 3.4.

- The specialized tool that may be required for assembling a manufactured unit and spare fixtures or connectors unique to it

- Hammer and nail selection

- Pliers and wire cutter

- Screwdriver set and screw assortment

- Knife

- Industrial tape

- Tape measure (25-foot)

- An industrial quality extension cord (25-foot) with a commercial electrical outlet box at one end

- Indelible felt-tip marking pens

- Touch-up paint in exhibit colors, small brushes

- Spare light bulbs (same as used on exhibit)

- Plastic sheets to cover carpet during setup

- Cleaning cloths, spray cleaner, and a portable vacuum cleaner

---

EXHIBITOR'S TOOL KIT

With knowledge of exhibit and products, you should edit this list.

- Hammer
- Selection of nails and nail puller
- Pliers and wire cutter
- Screw assortment and screwdrivers, regular and Phillips head
- Scissors
- Tape: rug, strapping, masking, double-faced, Velcro (fabric loop)
- Staple gun, staples
- Tape measure (25-foot)
- Flat extension cords (25-foot)
- Waber strips, 4-way electrical outlet boxes
- Indelible marking pens
- Shims (wooden, for leveling)
- Fire extinguisher (ABC type)
- First-aid kit
- Hot-wire tester
- Touch-up paint for exhibit colors, small brushes
- Cleaning solutions (lighter fluid)
- Plexiglass repair kit and polish
- Spare light bulbs (same size and "color" as used by exhibit)
- Saws (small, wood and metal)
- Allen wrenches and a ratchet set
- Flashlight, utility light
- Wire (bailing)
- Chalk, string, plastic sheets to cover carpet during setup
- Cleaning cloths, spray cleaner, and a portable vacuum cleaner
- Spare fixtures, unique to a manufactured system

The list is extensive, suitable for a large exhibit installation. If there is any question of whether or not an item should be packed, take it along. Expect the unexpected, especially when stores are closed or you are in a strange city.

Figure 3.4. An extensive list of the tools and supplies suitable for a large exhibit installation. (Courtesy Exhibitor Magazine, vol. 1, no. 10, 1982; by Ina Feinberg and Michelle Neuman.)

Office and Sales Supplies

Office supplies and company forms are necessary. You will find a complete list in Figure 3.5. It's possible to purchase some things after you arrive at a show; but time will be short, the show may open on aweekend when stores are closed, or you may have to hunt for a stationery store. Be sure, regardless of all else, to bring business cards, sales lead and order forms, and traveler's checks or cash to pay for emergency purchases.

In addition to standard items, there are things directly related to individual shows that must be brought along. They, too, are listed in

---

EXHIBITOR'S SALES AND OFFICE SUPPLIES

Office supplies and company forms can be forgotten. Start with:

— Sales lead forms and carbon paper, order and contract blanks
— Office letterhead and notepaper
— Folders for temporary files
— Inexpensive paper staplers (several) and staples
— Staple remover
— Business cards
— Ballpoint pens (several) and marker pens
— Calendar
— Leather-bound appointment book to use for formalizing customer appointments at the booth
— Leather-bound guest book for VIP sign-in at a hospitality suite
— Cellophane tape and paper clips
— No. 10 standard office envelopes and 9 by 12 envelopes
— Traveler's checks and cash for on-site payments
— Note on where copying service can be obtained near the show
— Portable typewriter or note on rental sources near the show

In addition to general supplies, specific show items can include:

• Bills of lading for commercial transportation
• Exhibitor kit, including contract and order forms, and copies of orders sent in advance
• Telephone set (if a line was ordered)
• Travel tickets, hotel and rental car confirmation numbers
• List of all staff members, complete with home telephone numbers
• Copies of product brochures and fliers, press releases
• Name badges if sent to you in advance by show management
• Show tickets left over from those provided in advance by the show

---

Figure 3.5. A complete list of office supplies, company forms, and other items to bring along to the exhibit.

Figure 3.5. The most important are transportation bills of lading, show contracts, and reservation confirmation numbers.

Exhibit Transportation

It can be just as exasperating to move an exhibit across town as across the nation—if the movement is not planned. Some of the most vexing problems can arise in the exhibit hall itself.

Transportation Methods

There are three methods used to transport materials to a show:

- Shipping commercially to a *drayage* contractor appointed to handle moving into and out of the exhibit hall. Exhibits are sent to a warehouse and concentrated for delivery to the arena.

- Shipping commercially direct to the loading dock at the show site.

- Bringing the exhibit to the show yourself.

Although you may bring your own exhibit to the hall, most show managers insist that their drayage contractor move materials to the booth space. Rule: If you can't carry it under one arm, don't try. (Touched on in Chapter 2, the term *drayage* describes a function: storing exhibits before the show, moving exhibits into the hall, storing crates during a show, and moving exhibits out after a show is over. Charges are per 100 pounds of weight, and there are minimums for small boxes.) Order forms in the exhibitor kit will help you estimate cost.

Saving Time and Money in Transportation

Here are some ground rules. They can ease the process, decrease the potential for losing things, and, for the most part, lower cost.

- Concentrate as much material in as few boxes or crates as possible. Write a thorough inventory of the items in each box.

- Reduce the number of individual shipments as much as possible. It is far less confusing to receive all crates and boxes at one time.

- Mark each box clearly on top and on two sides. Mark the delivery address clearly, including the name of the show and the *booth number* in large print. (Count the boxes or crates being shipped, and mark each one, "1 of 4," "2 of 4," and so on.)

- Find out in advance where unloading can be accomplished if you are bringing things in yourself.

- Try to reduce the number of times each crate is handled. This lowers damage risk. For instance, an air freight shipment may be handled up to 10 times.

- Remember that packing materials will have to be used again after the show. Sheets of plastic bubbles are easier to handle than loose balls of protective material.

- Don't rely on cardboard boxes alone. A drayage contractor stores sturdy *crates* during a show. Most times the contractor can't accept cardboard boxes. Place them inside a larger, more substantial crate. If you don't have a crate, ask an exhibit neighbor at the show. Nothing is uglier than cardboard boxes tucked under a table in the booth.

Setup at the Show

You may not understand the complexity of installing a trade show or consumer fair. Scores or even hundreds of exhibits are moved and erected in a short time. Until shortly before opening, a trade show floor looks like a maelstrom of confused activity. Plan to arrive early, and understand that there are rules to follow.

Service Contact Points

There are three primary contact points:

1. *Show management office.* This is the place where overall coordination takes place. Solve serious problems there.

2. *Service desk area.* A separate desk for each contractor is set up at the edge of the hall. People there take orders, accept payment, and assign work. It's best to order services in advance, but they can be revised or initiated at the show.

3. *Exhibitor registration booth.* This is where exhibitor staff badges are either held on a will-call basis or typed when you arrive. It's the place to pick up your show packet: The convention program, event tickets, and general information about the city. You must wear your badge to get into the hall during setup and the show. The registration booth may not be open if you arrive early. In that case, you can obtain temporary work passes in the show management office.

Exhibitor Kit Contracts

We pointed out, in Chapter 2, that the exhibitor kit contains order forms for an array of services. Compare the list in Chapter 2 with the order forms in your kit to ensure that nothing has been left out.

Booth Setup Procedure

There is a logical sequence to setting up a booth:

1. Check the location. Measure the space and make sure that no pipes or columns that were not on the floor plan have sprouted. See where electrical connections have to be made.

2. Move your exhibit materials to the edge of the space.

3. Lay carpet *after placing electrical cables* on the floor if they must run out into the space—to feed power to a counter, for instance. Slice the carpet to pull cables up in the right spot.

4. After the carpet has been taped to the floor, cover it with plastic sheets to keep it clean during setup.

5. Erect the booth, making electrical connections afterward.

6. Place signs, graphic panels, and products.

7. Touch up nicks and scratches on structure and graphics.

8. Unpack and place literature and office supplies.

9. Place plants or flowers. Clean and polish booth panels. Remove plastic carpet covers and vacuum. (Even covered, rugs get dirty.)

During unpacking, crates are marked with "empty" stickers supplied by the drayage service desk. Mark your company name and space number clearly.

Exhibit transportation and setup are covered more extensively in Chapter 15. A suggestion: At least for your first show, consider hiring an exhibit house to manage show setup. This can cost extra, and you *can* do it yourself, but it steals time from getting ready to sell.

Operations

If a show is scheduled for an afternoon opening, there is a temptation to delay your arrival until the morning of the first show day. Those who do are frantically hanging graphics and unpacking literature with 20 minutes to go before the opening. Their first show day is a waste. They are not fresh and adjusted to the situation.

Preshow Meeting Agenda

Even if you'll only have two or three people with you, there is need for a formal meeting. What follows is an agenda:

- *Goals for the show.*   Assign each person individual goals for each show day.
- *Products and services.*   Remind everyone of key selling points.
- *Lists of key customers.*   Compare and share. Plans for out-of-hours VIP customer entertainment and selling must be confirmed.
- *Booth work.*   Decide on work schedules. (Booth staff people must never sit. One person should be expected to work only 4 hours in a day.)
- *Coverage of seminar sessions.*   Announce assignments. In addition, assign people to learn what competitors are showing.
- *Demonstration practice.*   If you must demonstrate a product, practice doing so while talking, spelling out sales points.
- *Social hour.*   Even if people know each other, interrelationships change at shows. Let this happen before you open for business.

Selling Techniques

Regardless of where you put it on the agenda, the main part of your preshow staff meeting *must* be a review of selling techniques at the booth. Even experienced exhibit salespeople serving a few times a year need refresher training each time. A list of dos and don'ts to use in a solid sales training session appears in Figure 3.6. There are, however, some essentials in that list to emphasize:

- Wear business dress for the industry and region even if the show is at a resort, and wear comfortable shoes.
- Never say, "Can I help you?" Ask open-ended questions that can't be answered with a simple yes or no.
- Spend the first minute qualifying a visitor. Then make your presentation or end the contact, depending on what you learn.
- Ask for an expression of buying interest within 5 minutes.

Hints on Prospecting at the Booth

- Wear business dress standard for the industry and region, even if attendees will visit the trade show floor informally clothed.

- Wear older, very comfortable shoes.

- Arrive at the booth 15 minutes before start time each day.

- Never start a conversation with, "Can I help you?" Instead, create an open-ended question that encourages visitors to indicate a bit about who they are and what they do. Rehearse openings. Don't memorize, but do have a stream of conversation in mind.

- Use the first minute of conversation to "qualify" a true prospect before starting demonstration or discussion. Then make a conscious decision to continue or back off.

- Ask about buying interest within 5 minutes. Try to complete contacts as quickly as possible while remaining polite, friendly.

- Speak clearly and slowly. Show floors are noisy.

- Do not carry on conversations with other booth staff members, even during quiet periods. Stay on the alert, at the edge of the aisle, giving attendees an impression of your willingness to help.

- Do not sit, smoke, eat, or drink in the booth.

- Body language is important. Stand with hands at sides or cupped below the waist. Folding arms across the chest looks defensive. Hands in pockets imply, "I don't care."

- Wear your name badge on the *right* side, so that it can be seen during handshaking introductions.

- Use care in writing down particulars about the prospect and what is of interest for follow-up. Don't depend on memory.

- Remain professional and businesslike. Exhibits are not for the shy, but at the same time a huckster's approach does not work.

- Avoid indiscriminate distribution of sales literature or giveaways, unless a goal is education or overall awareness.

We suggest this list be copied and distributed.

Figure 3.6. A list of dos and don'ts to use in a sales training session.

Hints on Current Customer or VIP Contacts

- *Preshow appointments.* Contact current customers and VIPs in advance to make appointments at the show. Try to schedule appointments when traffic on the floor will be low. This reduces interruption and avoids missing potential new customers on the floor.

- *At-show appointments.* If a customer arrives unannounced during a hectic moment, try to schedule an appointment for a quieter time. Use a leather-bound appointment book to show serious intent.

- *Key account list.* A list of important customers should be drawn up before the show and kept at the exhibit, along with the staff work schedule. If a key customer arrives when his or her account representative is not on duty, an appointment can be scheduled.

- *Closing rooms.* At medium-sized and larger trade shows, try to write orders away from the hustle and bustle of the booth.

- *Hospitality.* Food and beverage services provided depend upon the time of day. A degree of formalization is required. A hospitality suite is a place for business, not play.

Learning at Seminars and from Competitors

Conventions are ideal places at which to learn, both about visitor interests and how competitors are approaching the market. You can even use your exhibit for research, asking attendees to evaluate products or suggest new applications.

Competitors. It's natural for you to search out competitors. Don't stop with that. Find out what each competitor emphasizes at the show. Prepare a report.

Seminars. Technical sessions or seminars offer subjects of interest to visitors. See which are of interest to you and attend them. You can gain insight for future product modifications or new applications. Again, write reports. Added value comes from listening to questions from the audience. You may spot prospects to whom you can introduce yourself afterward.

Daily Show Operations

You have to prescribe a work pattern for each day. There are too many things to do and too little time. The essentials can be lost.

- Sales orders and leads must be written up and reviewed each day.

- A short meeting must take place after each day, or shift, to compare sales experiences and pass along information.

- Work schedules may have to be revised to meet needs, such as a VIP customer appointment.

Postshow Operations

Getaway day is frantic. And the first day back in your office is catch-up time, equally frenzied. Both days require preparation.

Exhibit Tear-Down and Removal Procedure.   Organize your departure in advance, during the show. The steps are the reverse of installation. They include:

- *Dismantling.*   Placing orders for people to dismantle and pack
- *Rentals.*   Confirming pick-up of rental items—including desks, counters, audiovisual equipment, and plants
- *Transportation.*   Making arrangements for transportation or storage of exhibit crates after the show
- *Reservation.*   At popular shows, making a preliminary space rental reservation for the following year.

The moment the closing announcement is made, drayage people start delivering empty crates to booths. During tear-down:

- Organize materials to be packed by shipping crate.
- Check each display product, exhibit panel, and graphic for nicks or damage so it can be repaired before the next show. A checklist is required, noting where each damaged piece is packed.
- During packing, make sure new shipping labels are clear.

Don't leave the hall until freight has been picked up and shipping papers obtained. Shipments stay lost if bills of lading don't exist.

Paperwork.   Exhibit professionals tell horror stories about opening crates and finding sales orders from the *last* show inside. Paperwork, an evil tolerated in daily business, seems to be less well accepted at a show.

- *Orders and leads.*   Do not store these documents at the booth. Put them in your pocket.

- *Learning notes.* Notes written about competitors and seminars should be the responsibility of one person.

- *Thank-you notes.* Your sales team members, vendors, and customers respond favorably to notes of appreciation. Write text for them *before* the show. Build name lists daily.

Your first day back in the office is an extension of the show.

- Sales leads and orders must be processed.

- Costs must be tabulated.

- Exhibit damage notes must be written up and repairs ordered.

- Short papers should be prepared on competition and seminars.

- If photographs were taken, the film must be sent for processing.

The preliminary evaluation report called for in Chapter 2 must be developed immediately. Memory fades quickly. The paper serves as an excellent guide to the future.

The subjects covered in "The Quick Fix" are expanded on in later chapters. Pay special attention to three: Chapter 12 focusing on exhibit structures and graphics; Chapter 15's coverage of transportation and services at shows; and especially Chapter 17's expanded discussion of selling technique. If you have time for just one of them, flip to Chapter 17. When all is said and done, making money is our purpose. Face-to-face selling achieves it.

PART 2

Program Management

4

Preparing an Annual Exhibit Plan

If you are a part-time exhibit manager, Part Two is for you. You've been in and out of the arenas, experienced the problems. You want the jobs done with as little fuss, money, and time invested as possible. For the most part, the process runs on automatic pilot: The shows come and go—except that you are always in the middle of a squeeze play. Look good where management is interested, but spend less overall. People down the ladder want more support, more than you can give.

There are other scenarios. For instance, there are a few shows a year that are musts, so automatic that nobody really thinks about them any more. Or, you are going into a new market and nobody remembers that you can use exhibits to introduce the company. Most vexing are those who call with that great idea about a show they've heard about and want you to go into—three weeks away. Tie all this in with the rest of your job, and you have a full plate.

There is an annual plan of sorts, but nobody pays vast attention to it. Your time is nibbled away all year long. The people you talk to think this part of your job is spending money, arranging to put up exhibits, and making hotel reservations.

Whatever the specifics, making money with exhibits has not been an issue. Instead, exhibits equal cost. Just as important, they are thought about *one at a time*, not as part of a program.

A changed perspective is what you can bring to the table. This chapter explains how to write an annual plan. The balance of Part Two,

"Program Management," helps you define and defend individual shows in that program. Use this material and those around you will change *their* perspectives about exhibits and your role.

Marketing Mix and Annual Exhibit Planning

An exhibit is both a temporary sales office and an advertisement. An exhibit *program*, however, is part of something larger: sales and marketing strategy, and a company's communications effort. When you develop a show list, position it as part of that overall marketing strategy and show how it relates to sales goals. In addition, tie it in with advertising and other sales promotion activities. Include all three—marketing strategy, sales goals, and advertising tie-in—even if your program is for a local office or division of a national company.

Marketing Communications Mix

Don't dwell extensively on marketing communications media. However, including an overview in your plan document helps to position exhibits in the mixture. Break marketing communications into three major divisions: advertising, media or press, and sales promotion.

Advertising.   Advertising is used to reach several goals. It creates and maintains awareness. Advertising presents key selling arguments and provides information that acts as a backdrop for selling. Advertising can be directional or response oriented, telling prospects where to buy or providing a way to order immediately.

Media or Press.   Press coverage is a backdrop too. Your company may have a great reputation. In spite of this, when a third party—the paper, trade magazine, TV, or radio station—presents your information, greater credibility is gained. Readers or listeners expect, presume, that reporters and editors screen and evaluate. If your product were a movie, they'd be your reviewers.

Sales Promotion.   This is a catchall category for more "tactical" marketing communications tools and activities. Booklets, brochures, fliers, newsletters, point-of-sale displays, bill stuffers, and many other devices are thought of as sales promotion. They reinforce and expand advertising or press coverage. Several layers of sales promotion can be involved with an individual product. For instance, a simple brochure may be backed up by a more extensive booklet for those who show serious buying interest. Both may be related to an information package provided after a sale is made.

Special events are part of sales promotion. The company can sponsor an event, sports or cultural. Or you may tie in with an event sponsored by others, bringing VIP customers and providing hospitality. As a sponsor, you may reach press and advertising goals. Even if you don't, inviting VIP customers puts you in a position to know them better.

Exhibit Fit in the Marketing Communications Mix. An exhibit can be synergistic, involving all the media. It often acts as a focal point. As advertising alone, however, nothing is more costly than an exhibit. Mass media ads are more cost-effective in developing product awareness. Booklets and brochures are more cost-effective in putting information into the hands of prospects. Exhibits are the most cost-effective way of establishing personal contact. See note 1 for Chapter 2.

When you write your annual program, show how exhibits fit as the face-to-face payoff.

Exhibit Value. The time spent in prospecting, presenting, objection answering, closing, and ordering is compressed. An average you can quote: The number of sales calls required to close an industrial sale is *reduced almost 80 percent* when the process starts with an exhibit lead.[1]

Exhibit Role in Reaching Overall Sales Goals

The exhibit plan should also be targeted to sales goals. Starting in Chapter 5, we show you a way to quantify projected exhibit results. Develop a preliminary projection for each show, add the projections together, and you have an estimate of sales assist value for the program. Compare this to total office or company sales objectives. The result is a plan that shows not only how exhibits take advantage of other marketing communications but also how they directly support money making.

Exhibit Role in Corporate Planning

For most of us, an exhibit plan should be positioned as direct sales assistance. Some, however, use exhibits to reach other goals.

Nonselling Exhibit Goals

Product evaluation and professional audience research are two nonsales goals. Three others are community, industry, and stockholder relations improvement.

Product Evaluation. Large and small companies alike use show audiences as sounding boards. Many major corporations tuck product prototypes into private rooms. Nondisclosure statements are signed by potential customers asked to evaluate them. At the other end of the size scale, a consumer fair manager from Vancouver, British Columbia, tells how a husband-and-wife team did the same thing, on the show floor, with their invention: a rolling cart to move logs from the family woodpile to fireplace.

The couple rented a space at a spring "home" show, hardly a time to sell firewood carriers. The pair asked visitors to evaluate the design. That fall, a revised carrier was introduced. Sales? Excellent. The couple even found retailers who ordered for their stores.

Audience Research. It can be costly for research companies and their clients to find and interview people with defined interests. Since trade shows attract defined audiences, they are efficient places to capture interviews.

Company Relations. Improving public relations with important groups, such as community or government leaders, can be a worthwhile corporate goal. The goals are both education and establishing presence. Shows and conventions can play a part, and deliver quantified results. There may be no immediate dollar returns, but research can measure attitude changes and you can count the number of VIPs reached.

Corporate Policy Impact on Exhibit Program Plans

The nature of an exhibit plan depends on who buys and how they buy. Its *effectiveness*, however, owes much to company policies and practices. You should deal with both in your plan.

Sales Compensation

If salespeople work on commission and territories are assigned geographically, it may be difficult to recruit the best to work at national or regional exhibits. Visitors come from all over. Shows in a salesperson's own territory are another story.

Fight it or not? To make more money, you may choose to plan less for the big shows and put more behind local events.

Corporate Organization

Are you completely responsible for exhibits? Or is another department a partner in the process? If two groups are involved, you already know that each sees things from its own vantage point. Dollars from somebody else's budget seem *less* important. Each sees its role as *more* important. An annual plan should surface and settle differences for the year; this is better than following a by-the-show approach that wastes time.

Convention Market Analysis

Exhibit planning is driven by opportunity. Some industries meet more often than others. For instance, if tire or auto manufacturers are a target, there are few industry-specific conventions for their executives. On the other hand, if you sell to the financial, medical, or retail gift industries, there are lots of shows. A program aimed at industries sponsoring few meetings will take a different form.

Nontraditional Exhibit Programs

You have several options if industry shows don't match your needs:

- Private, by-invitation-only meetings for top executives.

- Exhibiting at shows attracting specialists. For instance, data processing experts in auto and rubber companies may attend computer and automation shows.

- Exhibiting where target companies themselves exhibit, at their selling shows where top executives attend to support salespeople. For instance, though there is no specific convention for tire *makers*, there is an important show for tire *dealers*.

Types of Trade Shows

All of us tailor sales operations to traditional buying methods in the industries we serve. Exhibit plans reflect this. Your shows should fall under one or two of the following categories:

- *Reseller order-writing shows.* Buyers are purchasing inventory for resale.

- *End-user business shows.* Buyers are businesses searching for products and services to use themselves.

- *Retail sales shows.* Buyers are consumers.

Overall Exhibit Plan Coverage

A properly prepared exhibit marketing plan should report up to three layers of activity:

- Large national shows
- Regional shows
- Local shows

If your program is for the local or district office of a large company, it is especially important to spell out how it relates to the other shows sponsored by the company.

Timing Implications

A show schedule should be positioned in context with the timing of other factors:

1. Seasonal buying patterns in the industries served

2. A projection of when your new products may be introduced

3. The timing of major advertising programs and other, larger shows sponsored by the company

4. An estimate of when competitors will be introducing new products or taking other initiatives

Budget Development

One of our most difficult chores is providing budget guidance. The number of variables is immense. For instance;

Products. The size, weight, and complexity of your products can impact substantially on exhibit costs. If your products are small, light, easy to pack and carry, cost is lower than otherwise.

Booths. If your shows require a simple 10- or 20-foot standard booth, the cost is far less than for providing custom, big-space units.

Graphics. If your product line is limited, and changes take place infrequently, the cost for sign production is minimal.

Corporate support. If your company provides a booth, your budget will be less than if you to have to get one.

Building-Block Budget Writing

The best way of building a budget for the year is to develop the budget for each show: Then add them up. Chapter 8 provides a method of building individual show budgets, and a short form is part of Chapter 2.

Annual Budget-Writing Shortcuts

We've warned you about variables. But there *are* guidelines to use in estimating annual cost without writing detailed budgets for each show. Try the following methods,[2] which are based on a major research study:

Space Cost Method

- *If you must include cost for a booth.* On the average, the cost for space rent represents about 20 percent of total out-of-pocket. If, for instance, booth space for a show costs $1000, you can estimate total out-of-pocket at $5000. This includes a portion of the cost of the booth itself, divided over several shows. It does *not* include expenses for people.

  If, however, personnel expenses for the staff are part of your budget, project about 35 percent *added* to the total. If out-of-pocket is $5000, add $1750 for personnel.

- *If you don't have to include cost for a booth.* Space rent should represent about *one-third* of total out-of-pocket. If the space is $1000, project $3000 as total out-of-pocket, excluding staff expenses.

  If, however, personnel expenses are part of your budget, project about 50 percent *added* to the total. If out-of-pocket is $3000, add $1500 for people. (The staff expense projections don't exactly match. Both are estimates. That's why we say "about.")

Direct Cost per Square-Foot Method. The Trade Show Bureau is responsible for the research that produced our space cost method and the two which follow. The first is direct cost per square foot, excluding personnel costs. The figures spread the cost of an exhibit structure across several shows.

Direct Cost per Square Foot, Average: 1983–1985

Type of booth	Total direct	Space	Without space
Back-wall	$58/ft^2	$12/ft^2	$46/ft^2
Island or peninsula	$63/ft^2	$13/ft^2	$50/ft^2

A 10-by-10-foot booth space, 100 square feet, produces an estimate of $5800 of direct cost, including an allocation to pay for the booth over several shows.

Direct Cost per Linear Foot Method. The other measurement provided in the study is direct cost per linear foot. Back-wall type booths alone can be measured in this fashion. The 1983–1985 *total direct cost per linear foot* average was $1012. A budget for a 10-foot-wide space would be $10,120 following this method.

The data for all three methods comes from questionnaires answered by medium and large exhibitors. The average space used by respondents was 800 square feet. This does not represent the truly "average" exhibitor. *Tradeshow Week* publishes an analysis of the largest 200 trade shows each year.[3] Over 100,000 companies appear at these shows, and the average space rented is closer to 300 square feet than to 800. The rent per square foot for space was in the same range but somewhat lower than the Trade Show Bureau study work. Try all three methods and modify based on your experience.

Illustrations Using Shortcut Methods

Presume your program will involve a half-dozen shows and that you will use three 10-by-10-foot spaces in a back-wall configuration at each: 300 square feet per show or 1800 square feet for the program.

- *Direct cost per square foot method.* At $58 per square foot, program cost is $104,400 plus staff expense.

- *Direct cost per linear foot method.* Calculating the same program using this method results produces a far different estimate: $182,160.

Three spaces per show, times six shows, equates to 180 linear feet, and this is multiplied by almost $1012 per foot.

- *Space cost method.* Presume space rent will represent 20 percent of direct costs. Exhibit structure dollars will be involved. In addition, use $12 per square foot as an average space rent charge.

Our six-show illustration involves 1800 square feet. Rent is $21,600. If this is 20 percent of total direct cost, the program estimate is $108,000. We can also estimate the personnel costs. If 35 percent is added, the total program budget becomes almost $145,800.

Check the actual space rent for the shows in which you'll participate. The range is wide, from $1 to over $20 per square foot. You can adjust the percent that space should represent of the total.

Budget Development Judgment

You may have difficulty accepting the cost of exhibiting. You may want to operate on a shoestring, taking every step possible to reduce investment and yet be at the show. Be warned. There is no more competitive place in the business world than an exhibit hall. Competitors face each other in a miniworld where visitors make instant evaluations. You may even think you are having a good show, because you have nothing with which to compare it, but be losing, in the long range, based on what people see as they walk by.

Sales managers drive costs too low to maximize immediate return. Advertising people, trained to reach longer-range goals, push too high.

Industry Averages

It's useful to have some background on industry cost averages; not to prepare a budget but to defend and administer it. *Tradeshow Week* conducts an annual reader survey to spot trends.[4] The managers who subscribe are from companies with established exhibit programs.

- *Budget.* Allocation of dollars to exhibiting is on the rise. Over three-quarters of the companies in the surveys are increasing their investments or at least staying the same: up 18 percent in one year even after inflation is eliminated.

- *Space rent.* Exhibitors are renting more space. Almost half of those who respond are increasing the space they rent.

- *Percent of the promotional pie.* About half of the companies say the percent of marketing communications expense allocated to exhibiting is stable. Within the *other* half, however, companies increasing almost double those reducing emphasis on exhibits.

Building a Show List

You may know exactly which shows make sense for you. If you do, skim past this section. If, on the other hand, you sell to a broad spectrum of industries or are entering a new market, selecting a show can be difficult.

Show Fact Sources

There are a number of information sources. Directories published for the exhibit industry are listed in Chapter 19. Your Visitors and Convention Bureau keeps track of what's going on locally. And, of course, industry association offices will fill you in. They often sponsor shows on a state or regional basis, as well as nationally.

Regional and Local Events

Don't discount regional and local shows. The sales potential of trade shows classified as "regional" is the same as that for "national" meetings.[5] In either case, eight out of ten attendees are ultimate decision makers or buying influences for the product lines at the show. Regional conventions allow you to concentrate geography. Four of ten visitors travel *less* than 50 miles to get there. At national shows, six of ten travel *more than 400 miles* to attend.

"First-Year" Show Warning

Be cautious about new, "first-year" shows. You could be buying a show manager's prayer. Check the following:

- Specifics on the promotion program: Don't be satisfied with vague statements such as "advertising" and "direct mail." Find out who and when and what schedule. Ask to see samples of ads.

- Specifics on the educational program: Don't be satisfied with general statements. Ask to see a syllabus, and call some of those who are scheduled to make presentations.

- The financing and track record of the show organizer.

Older events must also be evaluated with care. Audience data is often presented in very general terms. Talk with the show manager and make an evaluation of audience makeup to see what part of it should be interested in your products. Overall, eight of ten visitors can make or influence buying decisions, but this is for *all the products at a show combined*. The percentage that counts for you is less.

Vertical and Horizontal Shows

You can estimate audience potential using industrywide research statistics. Shows are classified by type, and a standard measurement called the *audience interest factor* is used. The AIF is the percentage of visitors who stop to talk or obtain literature from at least 20 percent of the exhibitors.[6]

Vertical Sellers' Shows. Exhibitors specialize in products for an individual market, function, or industry. Within this broad group, there are two kinds of shows:

1. *Vertical buyers.* These are shows at which attendees are just as specialized. The Operating Room Nurses meeting (AORN), the National Retail Merchants Association Electronic Data Processing conference (NRMA-EDP), the Home Builder show (NAHB), and the Radiological Society of America convention are examples. You are offering specialized products at shows attended only by your specialized buyers.

   The AIF for vertical buyer shows is higher than for other categories: 57 percent.

   Vertical buyer shows provide a highly concentrated group of prospects. Because the audiences are so specialized, however, total attendance can be relatively low. In addition, attendees may come from broad geographic areas.

2. *Horizontal buyers.* Specialized exhibitors offer their wares to visitors from many industries or job functions. Examples of shows falling into this category include: the INFO show, Wescon/Electro, and the ASW welding show.

   The AIF is somewhat lower: 48 percent.

   Shows tend to be larger, in terms of both exhibitors and audience size. Buyers come from several industries, and geographic coverage may be more regional or local.

Horizontal Sellers' Shows.   This is the second category. Exhibitors represent a wider variety of products and industries, instead of the narrow focus at vertical shows. There are two kinds of shows here as well:

1. *Vertical buyers.*   Although exhibitors are diffused, visitors represent a common industry or function. The Offshore Technology conference, for instance, offers exhibits from many industries, but the buyers all come from the oil industry.

   The competition for attention is quite brisk at these shows. And as you might guess, the audience interest factor drops off to some extent. Only 39 percent of the audience visits 20 percent or more of the exhibits. However, a show of this kind may be an excellent place to try a new market.

2. *Horizontal buyers.*   This last group features not only widely disparate sellers buy buyers from different functions or industries as well. The Design Engineering and the Plant Engineering and Maintenance shows are illustrations.

   Sellers reach a broad spectrum of buyers representing different functions. Because both the audience and exhibitor groups are diffused, the AIF is lowest of all, 35 percent.

The study work was done at national and large regional conventions. You can also use the same logic in evaluating the potential of state and local business shows, and for consumer events.

For instance, if you are thinking about special group shows—such as those aimed at insurance, banking, or health care—check last year's exhibitor list. See if the exhibitor group is focused or diffused. Broader business interest shows, such as the San Diego or Detroit Business shows, Portland Office Products, or Long Island Loves Business in New York, seem to fall into the last category, horizontal buyers and sellers.

Regardless of the show type, one of the most interesting research findings is that, on the average, over 8 out of 10 visitors to a company's exhibit have not been called on by a salesperson from that company for over a year.[7] This does not mean that the *company* has not been called on. It does mean that important people you don't know visit trade shows. Thus, trade shows can be added to your list to deepen sales penetration inside current customer organizations.

Consumer Shows.   AIF guidelines can be applied to consumer shows. Shows aimed at collectors of stamps, coins, and other specific items would tend to fall into the vertical-vertical group with narrow-interest buyers and sellers together.

Public shows aimed at special interests such as antiques, flowers, boats, and recreational vehicles provide a greater degree of variety but remain focused. Exhibitors are not quite so specialized.

General-interest home and garden shows, plus state and county fair expositions, would seem to be horizontal-horizontal.

One additional factor is visitor admission price and the degree to which the promoter will discount that price. If a price is quoted but it is easy to obtain low- or no-cost tickets, the audience may be inflated with lookers instead of more serious potential buyers.

Annual Plan Document

The goals of a formal plan document are twofold:

- First and most important is defining or refining your own thinking as you write the plan. You'll gain even if you are familiar with the shows.

- Second is providing information to others, soliciting support for the program. A well-documented, carefully prepared annual plan elevates the exhibit program and helps to assure support.

Elements of a Planning Document

- *Overall marketing goals.* As specifically as possible, state the overall goals of the company in the upcoming year. (Financial, new product, organizational, and anything else that might impact on an exhibit program.)

- *Sales goals.* State them, even if they are well known.

- *Marketing communications program.* Outline the advertising and sales promotion program, even if your program is for the local office of a large company and advertising is companywide.

- *Exhibit program and costs.* Present a summary of the exhibit program, whether it be 3 shows or 30, as a single unit. Don't name the shows at this point. Show the total cost and value of the program as a whole. Spell out how it will be measured. Make sure to relate it to other activities, such as a seasonal sales push or new product introduction.

- *Related exhibit programs.* If your company does exhibits at national, regional, and local levels, include reference to all.

- *Show participation list.* List individual exhibits with as much detail as possible. At the minimum, indicate overall goals and costs for each

SAMPLE TIME FLOWCHART

January
- New companywide advertising program
- National show

February
- Local advertising start
- Our first trade show of the year

March
- National show
- Our second show of the year
- End-of-quarter sales results report

April
- Two national shows and one regional show in our area

May
- New product introduction at national show
- New product national advertising and promotion program released

June
- Local new product advertising
- Local new product introduction at our third show of the year
- End-of-quarter sales results report

July and August   National and local advertising only

September
- One regional trade show in our area and one national show
- End-of-quarter sales results report

October
- Two national shows
- Special local private show for top customers
- Our fourth local trade show

November
- Two national shows
- Our fifth local trade show

December
- Holiday open house for customers
- End-of-year sales results report

Program summary: five trade shows and two special customer events

Figure 4.1.   This illustration presumes you are planning a program for the local office of a national company.

show. Summarize related activities such as advertising, pre- and at-show promotion, VIP hospitality, and media relations factors.

- *Time chart.* Product a simple flowchart to show how the exhibits fit together into a unified activity flow involving advertising and other sales planning. Figure 4.1 illustrates an annual time chart.

Reasons for an Annual Plan

You'll accomplish three goals, two for you and one for the company. You'll elevate the importance of what you are doing. You'll save time explaining things in the months ahead; and the performance of the company at its exhibits will improve. You'll start managing instead of implementing. The company will make more money and so will you.

5

Establishing
Goals for
an Exhibit

Ten or fifteen minutes with a pocket calculator can transform an exhibit goal from "waving the flag" to making the money. It will surely change your perspective and shift viewpoints among those around you.

In Chapter 2, we summarized goal setting for first-time exhibitors. Now, and in the chapters that follow, we expand on it. General statements such as "increasing sales" or "establishing presence" are not enough. You start to develop a set of targets only when you try to answer the question, "How much?" Aim points can have a dramatic influence on what you do.

This book devotes more pages to goals than to any other topic. Billion after billion is spent every year by companies large and small, and at least half of the companies can't tell you *why*—at least not in any way that a logical businessperson should accept.

The newsletter *Tradeshow Week* conducts an annual reader survey and finds that between one and two out of ten corporate exhibitors set no goals at all.[1] The rest claim to set objectives; however, only half report trying to quantify them. Trade Show Bureau research produced similar findings. Although seven of ten exhibitors count leads, only half trace them to sales.[2] Companies want to sell but don't say how much. They want to establish awareness or presence but don't define what that means. They have no basis upon which to evaluate and improve performance.

The situation is probably a lot worse than the surveys say. The newsletter's circulation is relatively small compared to the scores of thousands of businesses using the medium. Subscribers are from companies that exhibit frequently.

Probe a manager as to why no specific goals are set, and you'll hear things like, "If we announce a sales lead goal, our people won't pay attention to the quality of the leads. They'll just get the numbers." Another says, "If I set an objective, the staff will stop working after we reach it." A third said, "If we set a goal and don't make it, my boss will come down on me."

There's another reason, which doesn't surface very often. We don't like admitting we don't know how.

Four Exhibit Goal Categories

Exhibit goals are broken into four categories:

1. Prospecting goals

2. Awareness development and image enhancement goals

3. Current customer selling and positioning goals

4. Learning goals

List them under these categories, and you can start to put numbers beside each.

Prospecting Goals List

Aim points run the gamut from booth contacts to leads or orders written. The raw numbers can then be converted to dollar return and compared to cost.

- Number of selling contacts at the booth
- Number of qualified sales leads to take at the booth
- Number of leads converted to sales after the show
- Number of orders to write or sales to close at the show
- Total revenue from sales
- Expense-to-revenue ratio, an index comparing cost to return

Awareness Development and Image Enhancement Goals List

Distributing brochures, presenting a live show or educational seminar, issuing a press release, or conducting a news conference: These activities increase awareness or establish an image. You can count the number of people to be reached and compare this with cost. Or you can sponsor professional research to find out how many remember a message or see how attitudes have changed, a measure of accomplishment.

- Number of brochures, samples, or giveaway promotional items to be distributed

- Number of visitors exposed to live or audiovisual shows

- Media coverage: number of stories, column inches, "mentions" in printed stories or on radio/TV

- Awareness increase or attitude shift from professional research

Current Customer Selling and Positioning Goals List

The people with whom you do business already can be counted, even named. You can sit down and spell out what you want to accomplish, as a group and individually. You want to write orders or introduce new products? How many and what? Later you can compare returns with cost.

You may want to cement your relationship with VIPs or get to know new people who work for client companies. Hospitality suites, food and beverage services, theater or sports tickets—even formal dinners for dealers—can be involved. Quantify goals and compare cost.

- Number of VIP customers, association, or media executives to be entertained

- Number of specific sales to be initiated or closed with current customer organizations

Learning Goals List

Shows provide three ways to learn. One is finding out what the competition is presenting. Second is learning more about the concerns of attendees by attending their seminars. Third, buyer concentration provides an arena for product evaluation research. Opportunities can be quantified and compared to cost.

- Number (and names) of competitors at the show and list of products or services emphasized
- Number (and names) of key seminars to attend
- Attendee surveys or research programs on products or services

Value of Quantified Goal Setting

The number goals we propose are not bottom-line measures. They shouldn't be that. Exhibits assist in reaching the bottom line. They can't take all the credit. Even so, there are three advantages that come to those who set quantified goals.

- They drive the planning process, resulting in a more powerful, more effective exhibit marketing program.
- Postshow evaluation provides clues to improve future exhibits, especially when shows are compared with each other.
- Everybody from company president on down starts thinking about exhibits the same way they think about the rest of the business.

How to Establish Goals

We present a procedure. Make judgments and tap a calculator. Then compare results with your feelings about a show. The process is not as precise as some would like. It won't replace judgment: It refines and defines. Risk is inherent but becomes calculated.

Audience Analysis Concept

Show names create a mental picture. The name Gift Show conveys the notion that wholesale or retail gift buyers attend. The National Computer Conference implies computer buyers. We presume home owners go to a Home and Garden Show. Some exhibitors make decisions to participate based only on a show's name and a total audience promised by its promoter. The mental picture may be accurate, but even so we must look more closely to find our specific audience.

There are *no* shows where your products are appropriate for the entire audience. In Chapter 4, we defined audience buying interests at four types of gatherings. The audience interest factor (AIF) at even the most powerful, narrow-interest convention is less than 60 percent of attendance. Four out of ten visit less than 20 percent of the booths.

Does this mean you should not exhibit? Certainly not. You must, however, isolate that part of the audience which should be yours. You'll learn what to put on your signs. You'll see how big your space should be to reach your market.

Many professional show management companies and association managers provide audience breakdown figures from past shows. The information is gathered from visitors when they register and from outside researchers auditing the events.

A warning: In part, show managers are in the real estate business. To increase profit, it's natural to provide as few services as possible in return for rent. There remain a number who feel that statistics don't help to sell booth space. (They think we are looking for reasons not to exhibit, and they want to keep their costs low: So no research.) They don't fully understand that, increasingly, we use statistics to help *aim* our effort, that basic values are accepted.

Show managers are going through a maturing process. The situation is improving. Exhibitors are not as concerned about space cost as they are about audience quality. Research investments can be passed on to exhibitors in higher space rent. Show managers are finding that audits help *keep* exhibitors. (We never have a bad exhibit. We blame the show, not ourselves. Show managers are finding that audience data can point the finger back at us. We change the approach and stay the next year.)

Audience Analysis Procedure

If your show prospectus does not include a detailed audience analysis from the past, talk to the show's manager and other exhibitors. Try to answer the following questions:

Business Trade Show Questions

- What percent of the total audience is spousal? (How many husbands or wives attend with the buyers?)

- Are other exhibitors included? How many?

- Does the audience include press, seminar speakers, or students? How many?

- How many different business come, as well as people?

- What job titles are represented?

- What segments of the industry attend?

- What geographic spread is expected? How many local attendees? (Even "national" shows tend to have regional attendance. It's one of the reasons why associations change convention locations.)

Consumer Show Questions.   Audience questions can be asked about "public" consumer shows:

- What is the average income level expected?

- How many family units attend?

- What percent are apartment dwellers?

- What percent will be renters and what percent owners?

- How far will people travel to the event? How many family units will stay overnight at a hotel to attend the fair?

- What is the admission price and how will it be policed?

- What percent of the visitors own specific kinds of products (boats, antiques, etc.)? How many subscribe to related magazines?

If outside research developed a show manager's estimate, the data is more persuasive. If not, you'll have to use judgment on how much faith to place in what is said. Ask competitors or other exhibitors their opinions. Exhibitors are family and share noncompetitive viewpoints.

Check the audience estimate against the seminar and show advertising programs. Will the seminars attract the audience? Is the advertising targeted to the same audience?

Answers to the questions may result in *deductions* from the audience promised by a show's promoter. After deductions are made, you are left with your own target audience. The exhibit should be sized and creatively aimed at reaching only that audience.

State Exhibit Illustration

Throughout the next five chapters we explain planning procedure with the help of two hypothetical exhibit marketing programs. (Look for these gray page sections.) First is the "State Exhibit Illustration." Assumption: You are interested in a statewide industry meeting. The sponsoring association says will it will attract 3000 visitors.

Individual Show Analysis Audience Deductions

As a result of reading the promotional literature and talking with the show's manager, competitors, and your own salespeople, you make the following deductions from the projected audience:

Spouses	600
Other exhibitors	300
Press, guests, students	100
Total	1,000

This leaves 2000 people who deliver buying potential at the show.

The next deduction should reflect the potential interest in your products among the 2000. (Remember, it's unlikely your products will be of interest to all.) The show organizer association may have figures breaking down the show audience. It may not. If not, you probably *do* have some feeling about the way your lines match with the industry as a whole. Failing all else, use that.

State Exhibit Illustration (continued)

For sake of the illustration, assume the association does *not* have figures available on past shows for analysis. Experience tells you, however, that your products are used in about 25 percent of the industry. Divide 2000 into quarters. Your target audience is 500 people who are interested in your products.

Exhibit Industry Standard Method

There is an alternate method. Research has been done over a period of two decades related to the AIF study work outlined in Chapter 4.[3]

The average percent interest in a single product is 16 percent of the total audience (before deductions). You can adjust the figure, depending on the type of show. If you are selling a specialized product at a specialized show, the percentage should be higher. If the show attracts diverse exhibitors and audiences, move the percentage lower.

State Exhibit Illustration (continued)

We're sticking with 16 percent for the illustration. The total audience estimate of 3000 translates to a target audience of 480 interested in your products, slightly lower than the target derived through show analysis.

Estimating the Number of Decision Makers

There are lots of attendees who are interested but don't have any say in purchasing. The most frequently quoted figure in exhibit industry research is that four out of five business trade show attendees are decision makers or people who substantially influence purchasing. This reality is what makes the medium powerful.

That's all well and good, but you are an individual exhibitor and this figure doesn't count for you. The research finding is for *all* products and services offered at an average show.

Percent Decision Makers or Buying Influences for a Single Product

On the average, *45 percent* of those who have an interest in a product actually influence purchasing. For working purposes, round up to half. We call it the *50-percent rule*, half of the 16 percent interested.

State Exhibit Illustration (continued)

We estimated 480 out of 3000 would be interested in the products. Apply the 50-percent rule and 240 attendees are both interested *and* influential.

If you're inclined to mathematics, you have spotted a shortcut. Calculate 8 percent of the *total* audience. You get the same result.

Averages can mislead. You and your show are unique. If you don't have a lot of research to back you up, apply judgment *after* running the math. Use experience. Talk with others about the show.

The calculation provides a frame of reference, an underpinning. Your judgment is no longer a raw guess.

Waste Factor

If you've ever sold at an exhibit, you know that lots of people who drop by are not at all interested in buying what you're selling. Some are curious. Others are competitors. Sometimes we pick out the wrong attendee to introduce ourselves to. Often a gimmick attracts the wrong people. We make time to talk to VIPs from our own companies. From a selling viewpoint, these are wasted contacts. Try and cut down waste, but plan for it when setting goals.

There is no industrywide study. However, one large company surveyed over 40 national and regional exhibits. It found that the average waste was 25 percent of the total number of contracts, one out of four![4] Individual shows varied considerably, some more than 100 percent above the average and others more than 100 percent below.

Use this waste factor unless you have something better. If you've sponsored professional exhibit research in the past, the data may be there already, hidden in the questionnaires answered. Ask the research company to investigate. Regardless, evaluate and adjust if you don't feel comfortable with the result.

The rule of thumb: *Add one-third to the target audience estimate to cover waste.* (For every three conversations with interested prospects, add one.)

Illustration of Waste Factor

State Exhibit Illustration (continued)

Our target audience is 480 interested prospects, 240 of them the actual buyer market. To reach the 480 (and thus the 240), we'll have to plan on meeting *one-third* more: 480 × 1.33 = 638. Rounded off, the exhibit plan should reflect the need to speak with 640 people.

Conversion to Sales

You've developed a goal for talking with people. What is it worth? Can you translate it into dollars? You can, by making some assumptions and then testing, adjusting.

How many prospects drop by the wayside during the selling cycle? Four out of five? Two out of three? If you have this experience, you can apply it—but with some modification because exhibit selling is so effective. Prospects have screened themselves. They have made an effort to be at the show. They are serious buyers.[5]

The same logic applies to retailers who exhibit at a consumer fair or "public show." These exhibitions are temporary shopping malls, but consumers make a special effort to visit; they pay a price to be there.

Contact-to-Lead Conversion

We used research done for a private company to give us a bench mark in estimating wasted contacts. That same research provided a bench mark for the number of qualified leads to anticipate, as a percent of the number of people we talk to. On the average, *two out of ten* exhibit selling contacts resulted in qualified sales leads.

Ten-Contact Breakdown

Contacts with people not actually interested	2
Contacts interested but not buyers	4
Contacts with buyers but no leads	2
Contacts with buyers and leads taken (the pay-off)	2
	10

You can sponsor research to see how your company differs. But we have to start someplace, and the *20-percent rule* is that place. Use it and modify, based on experience, instinct, or research. The rule of thumb: *20 percent of total contacts will be qualified leads or sales at the show.*

Revenue Goal Establishment

Estimating dollars is a two-step process. First, project how many ultimate sales will be made from the leads. Second, apply an average value for each sale.

Lead-to-Sale Conversion

By the time a lead is taken, a prospect has already moved through a number of the steps toward purchasing. This results in a very high sales close rate after the show.

Trade Show Bureau research tells us that *40 percent of show attendees report purchasing* at least one of the products offered within 3 months. The size of the purchases ranges from a few hundred dollars to as high as $10 million, and 43 percent of the orders are greater than $10,000.[5]

Rule of thumb: *For planning purposes, estimate that one out of two leads should result in a sale.*

Dollar Value of Sales Objective

Just multiply the number of sales by an average value. What products will be at the show? How much do you charge for them? How many are sold on an average order? Develop a rough estimate, and multiply by the projected number of sales.

This is a simplistic approach, short-range and conservative. Customer relationships that are started at exhibits can extend for decades. Most fairs and trade shows take place annually, however, and each year's exhibit should stand on its own. Evaluate the impact of an exhibit by measuring what happens in the one year following.

State Exhibit Illustration (continued)
Assume that:

- Two kinds of products will be displayed. One costs $20,000. The other, $4000.

- Of the orders, 10 percent will be for $20,000 items. The balance, 90 percent, will be for the $4000 product.

The sales goal in our illustration is 64. If 10 percent of the orders will be $20,000 each, the dollar value will be $128,000: 64 × .10 = 6.4 × $20,000 = $128,000.
The balance, 90 percent, will be $4000 each. This translates to $230,400: 64 × .90 = 57.6 × $4000 = $230,400.
Combining the two figures produces a goal of $358,400.

Figures 5.1 through 5.3 illustrate blank forms to use in going through this process for your exhibits.

Audience Analysis		
Total estimated audience		_____
Deductions		
Spouses	_____	
Other exhibitors	_____	
Press	_____	
Students	_____	
Total deductions		−_____
Total buying audience		_____
Percent of market served		×_____
Target audience		_____
Exhibit industry average (alternate method)		
Total estimated audience		_____
Average percent interest in a single product line		×___.16
Target audience		_____

Figure 5.1. Planning form—audience analysis for goal setting.

Waste Factor Calculation	
Target audience (from Figure 5.1)	_____
Waste factor	×___1.33*
Total exhibit contact goal	_____
*From a study of 40 exhibits by one large company.	

Figure 5.2. Planning form—waste factor projection (with target audience determined).

Subjectivity in Goal Setting

What we've outlined produces a conservative set of objectives. At each step, you should apply a test for reasonableness. Does the result match what you or others consider reasonable? If not, change the factor that seems suspicious and recalculate.

Figure 5.4 lists exhibit goals and includes the figures developed for the state exhibit illustration.

Nonsales Goal Setting

Because the primary goal for most exhibitors is selling, we pay it greatest attention. However, you can establish goals in other areas. If you need to increase awareness or educate, quantify how much. Be specific. Audience analysis is the path to follow. If a major goal is learning from attendees or competitors, spell out exactly what you need to learn.

In this chapter, we've set goals by looking at the show and ourselves. We've ignored time. We've ignored space. In the next chapter, we deal with time and space. How much time do we have to do the job? How much space should we rent to reach our aim points? Read on.

Sales Goal Projection

Sales lead goal

Total exhibit contact goal (from Figure 5.2)	———
Less: waste contacts	———
Target audience contacts (from Figures 5.1 and 5.2)	———
Percent buyers and purchasing influences	✕___.50*
Total interested *and* buyers	———
Lead generation rate in this group	✕___.50†
Sales lead goal	———

Current customer show order goal

Number to contact	———
Percent of them to place orders	✕___
Current customer show order goal	———
Sales lead goal (from above)	———
Percent sold within 1 year	✕___.50
Total sales goal from sales leads	———
Plus: current customer show order goal (from above)	———
Total sales goal	———

Dollar sales projection

Product ————————————————	
Total sales goal (from above)	———
Percent of sales orders for this product	✕___
Sales goal this product	———
Average value each sale this product	$___
Sales goal this product (from second line above)	✕___
Dollar sales projection this product	$___

(Repeat for each product and combine for dollar total. Percent of sales orders for all products combined should total 100.)

Dollar sales goal for the exhibit	$___

*Rounded up from an average of 45 percent.
†Research from 40 exhibits sponsored by one company.
  Cross-check by estimating 20 percent of all projected contacts at the booth.

Figure 5.3. Planning form—sales lead and dollar goals.

Overall Exhibit Goals
<u>Selling</u>

<u>Prospecting for New Customers</u>

Selling contacts at the exhibit	640*
Sales leads	128
Sales closed at the exhibit	_____
Follow-up sales	64
Dollar sales	$358,400

<u>Current customers and other VIPs</u>
(Exhibit or hospitality suite)

Customers and other VIPs	_____
Names: _____	_____
Selling contacts	_____
Sales orders	_____
Dollar sales	$ _____
Sales leads for follow-up	_____
Follow-up sales	_____
Dollar sales	$ _____
Total selling contacts	_____
Total orders and leads	_____
Total dollar sales	$ _____

<u>Awareness and Image Development</u>

Giveaways/brochures/samples distribution	_____
Attendees at live or audiovisual show	_____
Seminar presentation audience	_____
Press coverage (number of stories, column inches, or radio/ TV mentions)	_____
Exhibit-related advertising	_____
Awareness or attitude shift from research	_____

<u>Learning</u>

Competitors   _____
   Name:_____ Exhibiting:_____

Seminars to attend   _____
   Names:_____ Covering:_____

Product evaluation   _____
   Names:_____ Covering:_____

*Figures from State Exhibit Illustration.

<u>Try to quantify as many goals as possible.</u>

Figure 5.4. Exhibit goals.

6
Time, Productivity, and Space

A student's progress is measured in half and full semesters. Business report cards are published monthly, quarterly, and annually. An exhibit marketing program operates in days, half days, and hours. Fail and you wait a year for another chance at the show.

The hours during which an exhibit will be open each day are spelled out in the show's literature. Added together, they form an outside jacket of the time we have to do what we want to do.

Impact of Time

How much selling time will you have? How fast can you work? Figure these out, and you'll know how much space you must rent to reach everyone you want to reach.

Slack-Hours Analysis

Restaurants and stores, depending on traffic flow, know all about rush hours and slack times when traffic is light. How many cash register ring-ups will there be and when? They plan for their fast and slow times, and sales projections reflect this. Exhibits are the same, but even experienced retailers often forget this when they are at a show. It's a whole new world to industrial sellers!

There are hours during which show floors are filled with prospects. At other times, a cannon shot wouldn't hit a soul. You have to estimate when this will happen and how much of it you'll see. A slack-hour estimate will tell you when you and your team can do other things. The analysis will help you set productivity goals for the show.

If you are familiar with a convention, you probably know when these periods occur and how many of them can be expected. If not, take a look at its program, for the event upcoming or the last year's, and compare trade show hours with other, competing activities.

Typical Slow-Hour Periods

1. The first and last hours of each day may be slow. Ask yourself, "Are attendees staying in hotels close to the convention hall? How do they commute? Where do they eat breakfast? Are there lots of private parties or special events in the evening?"

2. The first day may be slow if exhibits open during the afternoon and attendees come in from out of town. It can be especially so if day 1 is Sunday.

3. If a full slate of educational seminars are taking place when exhibits are open, the crowd in the exhibit hall will be small.

4. See if attendees get lunch as part of their fee for attending the convention. If so, midday will probably find the show floor empty. (In contrast, a show drawing a local audience may experience heavy lunchtime traffic.)

5. Is a prominent outside speaker slated at a formal luncheon or dinner meeting? If the exhibit hall is open at the same time, don't count on many visitors.

6. If attendees travel home, the last afternoon of a show may be dead. There are planes to catch and hotel checkout times to meet.

Show Management Traffic Stimulation

See if the show organizer is planning anything special to encourage traffic in the hall (coffee service between technical sessions, breakfast or a cocktail reception on the show floor). You may estimate some slow periods that turn out to be quite busy.

For instance, the National Cable TV meeting and many other conventions have started with an afternoon cocktail reception held right on the trade show floor. Meetings of the State and County Officials Association have opened with a Sunday morning breakfast in the exhibit area. The International Exhibitors Association convention has served-lunch to attendees right on its trade show floor. Show managers are sensitive to the slack-hour problem. They try to help overcome it.

Some promoters try to provide attendee incentives to help stimulate traffic in the exhibit area throughout the show. Each visitor is provided with a card to be stamped by exhibitors. Those who turn in full cards win a prize or are entered in a drawing. Except at shows that bring together narrow-interest buyers and sellers, considerable time can be wasted in stamping cards for people not interested in the products you offer. These promotions are less helpful than special events aimed at stimulating traffic in slow hours. An exception: Trade shows with exhibits in several different halls. The card-stamp promotion encourages visitors to visit all of them.

After considering the time schedule for each day and estimating the impact of travel, competing convention events, and show management promotions, you should be able to project the number of potential slack hours during a show and know when they'll take place.

Active-Hour Calculation

Why bother with slack-hour analysis? There are two reasons. First, you can plan for different numbers of salespeople at different times. Staff members can be freed for private appointments or to attend seminars. If the last day is going to be light, some can go home a day early. Second, and more important, you can estimate the number of *active hours* and from that calculate prospecting goals.

Illustration of Active-Hour Calculation.   In Chapter 5, we started an illustration, a state exhibit for an overall audience of 3000. We projected a need to talk with 640 attendees, of whom 480 will be interested in our products; 240 of these will be buyers. We figured on 128 sales leads and 64 ultimate sales valued at $358,400. How many hours do we have to talk to 640 people?

State Exhibit Illustration (continued)

The meeting will last four days. It takes place out of town for most attendees. The program from last year and discussion with the show manager let us predict when slow hours can be expected.

1. The convention will start Sunday afternoon, with the exhibit area open from 2 p.m. to 6 p.m. A welcoming cocktail reception on the show floor is planned from 4 p.m. to 6 p.m. Although the show stays open 4 hours, we eliminate the first 2 hours as slack and presume 2 active hours. Out-of-town visitors will be checking into the hotel and probably will not arrive until the reception starts.

2. Days 2 and 3, Monday and Tuesday, require exhibits to open at 9 a.m. and stay open until 6 p.m.: 9 hours each day. For Monday, however, a well-known speaker has been engaged for a "general assembly" luncheon. Thus, we should deduct 2 hours from the middle of that day. On Tuesday, an "awards dinner" takes place in the evening and several large exhibitors schedule cocktail parties beforehand. We deduct 2 potential slack hours at the end of the day. Two 9-hour show days shrink to 14 active hours.

3. On the fourth and last day, Wednesday, the exhibits again open at 9 a.m. However, the show will close at 3 p.m. Total hours: 6. Because attendees will be checking out and driving or flying home, the afternoon period should be light. Deduct 2 hours. The active-hour total on the last day becomes 4 hours.

Time Factor Analysis

Exhibits open	From–to	Hours	Deduct	Active hours
Day 1, Sunday	2 p.m.–6 p.m.	4	2	2
Day 2, Monday	9 a.m.–6 p.m.	9	2	7
Day 3, Tuesday	9 a.m.–6 p.m.	9	2	7
Day 4, Wednesday	9 a.m.–3 p.m.	6	2	4
Total		28	8	20

This table appears in the Appendix as a form, Figure A.8. As we plan this exhibit, figure 20 hours to make 640 selling contacts. We must prepare to meet with 32 people per active hour:

$$640 \div 20 = 32.$$

Take one more step and you can produce hourly and daily goals. The sales lead objective is 128. This equates to 6.4 sales leads per hour:

$$128 \div 20 = 6.4.$$

Goals per Hour and Day

Day	Active hours	Contacts per hour	Contacts per day	Leads per hour	Leads per day
Sunday	2	32	64	6.4	12.8
Monday	7	32	224	6.4	44.8
Tuesday	7	32	224	6.4	44.8
Wednesday	4	32	128	6.4	25.6
Total			640		128

This table appears in the Appendix as a form, Figure A.9.

This approach lets you track progress each day, making adjustments to reach overall targets. We've pointed out that our goal setting procedure is conservative. For goal setting purposes we ignore what can be accomplished in slow times or during evenings.

Appointments with Current Customers

Slack-hour analysis delivers an added benefit. Slow times, once identified, are the times to arrange appointments with current customers. If a good customer arrives during a busy period, you will be able to suggest a specific time to get together when things will be less hectic. (Use a leather-bound appointment book at the exhibit for this purpose. It formalizes the arrangement, and most customers will arrive back at the booth on the dot.) It's difficult to give special treatment to good customers in a hubbub. It's far more effective to use those times for prospecting and to meet people you know in more relaxed circumstances.

Booth Sales Staff Productivity

A well-trained, hard-working salesperson should be able to average 10 contacts with potential prospects for each active hour at the booth. Many of these will be short. Generally, a solid selling job should produce 2 sales leads from the 10 contacts.

Estimating Team Size

Simply match the contact productivity goal for each salesperson with the number of selling contacts required each active hour. You will be able to see how many people must work at the booth at once.

State Exhibit Illustration (continued)

The statewide exhibit program requires us to make 32 contacts each active hour. The contact productivity for each salesperson is 10 per active hour. Thus, we have to plan 3 on duty during active hours: $32 \div 10 = 3.2$. Round down to 3 people.

Estimating Booth Space

Many of us are preconditioned to rent space without reference to audience analysis, market potential, or the products that must be shown. We are captives of tradition. First-time exhibitors talk about "renting a booth" and presume listeners know they are talking about 10 feet of linear space.

Inexperienced show planners sometimes think of space purely in terms of the products they plan to display. They pack a space with more product than it warrants and lose sales as a result.

It's a lot smarter to decide how much space to rent *after* you've set goals. Space size, in addition to time and productivity, controls how well you'll do.

People-Space Requirement

Products don't make sales. People make sales. Early in this book, we pointed out what's been learned through 20 years of research: Buyers credit conversation with salespeople as their primary learning source.

Lots of study has been given to how people crowd at exhibits. Much of it involves photography to help establish traffic flow patterns and crowd density limits. People are willing to stand close together at a live show or audiovisual presentation. They will *not* group themselves tightly in conversations with salespeople.

The ground rule to follow is: *49 square feet* of space, in which semiprivate conversations can take place with one or two prospects,[1] should be allocated to each salesperson. This does not include space required for physical properties. If you happen to be reading this book at a typical 6-foot desk, visualize it a bit longer and as a square. Or think about a king-sized bed with two or three people standing in that size space carrying on a semiprivate talk.

Product-Display Space Requirement

You must also accommodate counters, tables, smoking stands, perhaps a free-standing product display and a back wall upon which signs are placed. There is a guideline for estimating this requirement as well as one for people space.

Unless your product is bulky—like a steamroller, helicopter, or large machine—*one-third of your people space*, added to that estimate, produces your overall space requirement.[2]

On the average, each demonstration station will require *65.3 square feet of space* for salespeople, product, furniture, *and* customers.

Space Relationship to Goals

You know how many contacts you have to make to cover the market at the show. You know how many you have to make an hour. You know how many people must be on duty to accomplish this. Now we know how much space must be allocated for each of these people to work in. Simply multiply the size of the team on duty by 65.3.

State Exhibit Illustration (continued)

To cover the market, we need 640 selling contacts in 20 active hours. To do the job, 3 salespeople must be on duty.

People-Space Factor

If three salespeople are on duty at once, we allocate 49 square feet for each: total, 147 square feet of space for people.

Product-Display Factor

We're not selling steamrollers or helicopters. Take one-third of 147 and add it to the space for people. One-third of 147 is 49. Add 49 to 147, and the overall space requirement then becomes 196 square feet.

Figure 6.1 presents on one page all the calculations for our state exhibit illustrations. A blank form, Figure A.10, for making your own calculations is in the Appendix.

1. Total sales contact goal	640
2. *Divided by* total active hours	20
3. Total contacts per active hour	32
4. *Divided by* contacts per active hour per salesperson	10
5. On-duty sales staff (rounded)	3
6. *Times* people-space factor (49 square feet)	147 square feet
7. *Plus* one-third of people space (49) for product display	49 square feet
8. Total required	196 square feet
9. Rounded to nearest rentable space amount	200 square feet
Booth spaces to rent __2__	

Figure 6.1. Space size estimating—completed from calculations used in the state exhibit illustration shown in Chapters 5 and 6.

Rounding Off Rent Units to Space

Promoters price their space on a per-square-foot basis but rent by units. Most often, the standard is an 8-by-10-foot or a 10-by-10-foot unit. Round off your space need to the nearest multiple. In our state exhibit illustration, we round *up* from 196 to 200, presuming that space is rented in 10-by-10-foot lots: 100 square feet each.

Had space been offered in blocks 10 feet wide by 8 feet deep, we would have rounded *down* from 196 to the nearest multiple: two spaces at 80 square feet each, 160 square feet. Either way, we end up with a 20-foot-long linear booth with three demonstration stations, one for each of three salespeople.

Variable Factors

Your personal situation may lead you to change the factors that drive the calculations we've made. You may be selling a steamroller, and you've got to fit it in. Or you may think that asking salespeople to make 10 contacts an active hour forces people too hard.

Be careful, especially about accepting a lower productivity goal. The 10-contact-per-active-hour productivity pace recognizes goals for the show as a whole and presumes slack hours that are not part of the calculation. What would happen if we accepted a more relaxed six contacts per active hour in our state exhibit illustration? Five salespeople would have to be at the booth instead of three; almost 350 square feet of space would be needed. The cost of exhibiting would skyrocket to reach the same objectives.

Be subjective, but follow this procedure so that you'll see the impact of your decisions. Exhibit planning remains a bit of an art form; but as we break the process into its parts, results become more predictable. Your exhibit report card will look a lot better.

7

Setting Goals When Space Is Already Set

For a lot of us, the targeting and space-planning process in Chapters 5 and 6 is Utopian. It doesn't matter what we *should* do. The amount of space we rent is limited by the company or the organizer. It's rare to have the opportunity of planning an exhibit based purely on marketing and audience analysis, starting from scratch.[1]

List of Limiting Realities

An exhibit planner's limiting realities can include:

- The space contract has already been signed.
- Two departments share exhibit responsibility, and the other group decides on how much to rent.
- The company provides a standard booth, and space requirements have to match it.
- The show sells out, and its manager rations how much you get.
- Exhibit budgets are set on "high," and top managers don't really want to listen to your logic.
- The company's financial position forces a limit on expense, regardless of longer-range potentials.

- Your status in the company doesn't allow you the freedom to do what should be done without a major internal effort.

None of this lowers value of or diminishes need for quantified objectives; however, the process is no longer aimed at reaching a market potential. Instead, it projects limits. It also helps to establish direction and provides guidance on where dollars should be spent. Fixing aim points provides the basis for ultimate results evaluation. They can be the start of new direction leading to a more Utopian approach. If you read Chapters 5 and 6, you'll see that we use the same principles here, but in reverse.

Space-and-Productivity-Planning Assumptions List

- An average 49 square feet of people space is required for each salesperson.
- One-third must added for products and other physical properties. One selling station requires 65 square feet.
- The productivity standard is 10 contacts an active hour for each salesperson.

Use of Planning Assumptions

With space fixed, you can estimate the number of salespeople (and selling stations) at the booth. With the team size and individual productivity known, you can estimate the number of selling contacts that will be achieved in an active hour. (Multiply people on duty by 10.) With active hours estimated, you can forecast how many selling contacts will be made during the show.

Goal-Setting Illustration When Space Is Already Established

In Chapters 5 and 6, we developed a state exhibit illustration demonstrating how to set goals and determine the amount of space required to reach them. Ultimately, that helps figure out how much we'll need to do to reach 100 percent of the market. Now we introduce another illustration, one that starts with the space already set.

Regional Exhibit Illustration

The company in the state exhibit illustration is now going to exhibit at a larger, regional trade show; 20,000 attendees are expected. This time, however, the company has already booked a 20-by-30-foot island space. Direction must be established. Goals must be set. We must estimate our potential market penetration at the show. We must be prepared to measure results with a view toward changing our space the following year.

Sales Team Size. A 20-by-30-foot space equals 600 square feet. Dividing 600 by the average of 65 square feet for each salesperson produces 9.23 selling stations: $600 \div 65 = 9.23$. We'll round up and fit in 10 selling stations.

Productivity per Hour. Each salesperson should make 10 selling contacts in an active hour. With 10 people on duty, the crew should generate 100 contacts during each active hour.

Active-Hour Calculation. This larger convention operates in exactly the same way as the statewide meeting in Chapters 5 and 6. The exhibit hall is open for business 28 hours over 4 days; but there are 8 hours during which little traffic will appear on the floor. The active hour total becomes 20. So, multiply 100 selling contacts in each active hour by 20. This results in a sales contact goal of 2000 for the show as a whole: $20 \times 100 = 2000$.

Contact Goal with Space Fixed

1. Square feet of exhibit space		600
2. *Divided by* average space per selling station		65
3. Number of selling stations (rounded up from 9.2)		10
4. *Times* selling contacts per person in an active hour		10
5. Number of selling contacts in an active hour		100
6. Total hours open	28	
7. *Less* slack hours	8	
8. *Times* active hours		20
9. Total selling contacts for the show as a whole		2,000

Target Audience Calculations

In Chapter 5, we focused on finding target buyers within an overall show audience, a prelude to figuring out how big a booth space is needed to reach them. Now we face a limit regardless of how large our target group is. Target audience calculations are used to find out if the space buy was correct or not, and they are used to define goals.

Target Audience Planning Assumptions

- In Chapter 5, we introduced the *waste factor*. One large company researched exhibits and found that 25 percent of its contacts were with people who had no interest in buying its products. If you estimate a total number of exhibit contacts, presume that one-quarter of them will fall into the waste category.

- We also introduced the 50-percent rule. Industrywide research tells us that almost 8 out of 10 visitors at an average show are influential or ultimate buyers for all its products and services *combined*. The average for any individual product or service being offered is 45 percent. We round off to 50 percent.

- Private research also provided a working guideline for the number of sales leads to expect. Out of 10 contacts, 2 (20 percent) should result in quality sales leads.

- Finally, we estimated that half of the sales leads taken will result in orders, many within 3 months after the show.

Regional Exhibit Illustration (continued)

Our 600-square-foot booth, staffed by 10 salespeople, should generate 2000 contacts.

Waste-Factor Calculation. We assume that 25 percent of 2000 booth contacts will be with people who have no interest in buying the products offered. So, 75 percent of 2000 (1500) should represent our target audience: $2000 \times .75 = 1500$.

Percent of Decision Makers of Purchasing Influences. Using the 50-percent rule, we cut 1500 in half. This leaves us 750 selling contacts with people who are both interested in what is offered and in a position to influence purchase of these products.

Sales Leads Percent. We assume that 20 percent of our contacts will result in leads. Our regional exhibit will produce 400: $2000 \times .20 = 400$.

Sales Percent.   Presuming a 50-percent conversion rate from this point, 200 sales will result.

Target Audience Analysis Illustration

9. Total selling contacts for the show as a whole	2,000
10. *Less* .25 percent waste factor	500
11. Target audience	1,500
12. *Less* 50 percent (not decision makers)	750
13. Decision makers or purchasing influences	750
14. *Times* sales lead conversion (20% of total contacts)	2,000
15. Qualified sales leads to take at the booth	400
16. *Times* sales conversion ratio	.50
17. Sales to close during or after the show	200

Revenue Projection

The last step, ultimate revenue projection, is based on your pricing. Simply multiply sales by an average value for an order.

Regional Exhibit Illustration (continued)

We stay with the assumptions made for the state exhibit illustration. Of the orders, 10 percent will be for $20,000 products and 90 percent for $4000 products: $200 \times .10 = 20 \times \$20,000 = \$400,000$; $200 \times .90 = 180 \times \$4000 = \$720,000$.

Combining the two produces a total revenue potential of $1,120,000 for the show.

Revenue Conversion Illustration

18. Average value of sale for 10 percent (20) @ $20,000	$400,000
19. Average value of sale for 90 percent (180) @ 4,000	720,000
20. Total projected revenue	$1,120,000

The table is displayed on one page as Figure 7.1. It also appears in the Appendix as a blank form, Figure A.11.

1. Square feet of exhibit space		600
2. *Divided by* average space per selling station		65
3. Number of selling stations (rounded up from 9.2)		10
4. *Times* selling contacts per person in an active hour		10
5. Number of selling contacts in an active hour		100
6. Total Hours Open	28	
7. *Less* slack hours	8	
8. *Times* active hours		20
9. Total selling contacts for the show as a whole		2,000
10. *Less* .25 percent waste factor (.25 × line 9)		500
11. Target audience		1,500
12. *Less* 50 percent (not decision makers)		750
13. Decision makers or purchasing influences		750
14. *Times* sales lead conversion (20% of total contacts)		2,000
15. Qualified sales Leads to take at the booth		400
16. *Times* sales conversion ratio		.50
17. Sales to close during or after the show		200
18. Average Value of sale for 10 percent (20) @ $20,000		$ 400,000
19. Average value of sale for 90 percent (180) @ 4,000		720,000
20. Total projected revenue		$1,120,000

Figure 7.1. Goal setting with space fixed for regional exhibit illustration covered in this chapter.

We have to apply a test of reasonableness after going through the estimating exercise. It is, however, far more exacting to apply judgment *after* going through the exercise than before.

Market Penetration Estimate

Was 600 square feet enough space to rent? Or are our projections too high because we have more space than we need to cover our market? The only way to find out is by looking at the total audience, as we did in Chapter 5, and estimating our target audience.

Market Penetration Planning Assumptions

To recap, there are two approaches:

- With the help of the show manager, last year's registration statistics, and discussion with other exhibitors, calculate deductions from the total audience and arrive at a target audience. See Chapter 5.

- Use the industrywide average—.16 percent of the total audience as interested in one product line—described in Chapter 5.

Regional Exhibit Illustration (continued)

We've indicated that 20,000 attendees are anticipated at the show. Using the 16-percent method, we assume that 3200 attendees should be interested in the products offered at our 600-square-foot booth. By following through, we get these results:

- Of 3200, about half (or 1600) should be not only interested but also influential in purchasing. This converts to a potential for 480 leads and 240 sales.

- To reach all 3200, we'd have to plan on talking with one-third more people: the waste factor calculation to use when starting with the target audience as the "known." The exhibit program would have to be planned to include talking with 4266 people, twice the maximum potential of the booth.

The regional exhibit did well, but it reached less than half its potential market.

Other Exhibit Objectives

The most important part of preshow planning is determining the nature and size of the audience anticipated, matching it with what you can offer. We have illustrated how to use the process in setting prospecting objectives.

There are a number of other points of aim for exhibit marketing. In addition to prospecting for new customers, and selling old customers, measurable goals can be achieved in awareness development, image enhancement, and customer positioning and learning.

Program Elements and Trade-Offs

In addition to establishing prospecting goals, it is possible to set targets for orders to be written and for related dollar volume. You might want to take some of this work away from the booth itself, however, saving it for prospecting. This is where a separate closing room or suite can pay its way.

There are numerous situations in which product or company awareness must be a show goal. For instance, the illustration developed in this chapter led us to understand that we'd have time to talk with only half of our market. A number of measurable techniques can help us make an impression on the other half.

One possibility is a trade-off. Sacrifice one or two selling positions at the booth, and the sales leads generated, and produce a small live show in the space. This would attract and inform more visitors. Other techniques involve literature distribution, advertising, and news releases. You could also sponsor an educational seminar as part of the convention. These are all measurable.

It is redundant to focus great attention on all the goals in this chapter. They have been touched upon in Chapter 4 and in Part One, "The Quick Fix." You should, however, approach planning for each one in the analytical fashion used in this chapter.

What you do away from the booth can be as important as the action that takes place there. This is especially so when space has already been purchased and you have to wedge too much into the booth or it is too small to reach your market.

In all cases, try to quantify what you want to accomplish. Later on, you can compare this with how much the activity cost, making sensible value judgments. This holds true for everything from hospitality suites to seminar attendance, from product research to competition analysis and more. Count the beans, and you'll learn and improve.

8
Exhibit Budget and Company Costs

The budget format in this chapter is an "explosion" version of the 8-line budget in "The Quick Fix," Chapter 2, with an added wrinkle. If you're running a program, you don't have the luxury of using a budget as simple as the 8-line. Too many dollars are involved.

Exhibiting costs have risen virtually 400 percent in the last 15 years. This is hardly remarkable in itself. Lots of things have gone up that much and more. At the same time, however, the number of trade shows has doubled. In addition, companies find themselves steadily increasing exhibit expense in contrast to what they invest in other marketing communications media. Serious money is being spent at a time when everyone's profit margins seem to be narrowing.[1]

Exhibit managers should be value managers. Our bosses, however, have never been more concerned about raw cost, never mind the return. In this chapter we identify expense areas and present a method of overseeing them. Stewardship has never been more important.

Total Company Exhibit Costs

The wrinkle: Often the *hidden* costs of exhibiting are higher than those identified and evaluated. Various departments absorb portions of the expense in large and sometimes amorphous budgets. One Fortune 500 company pays for exhibit transportation in its product delivery freight budget.[2] In addition, lots of large companies don't have the foggiest idea about what local groups spend on exhibits. Even when asked, these offices don't have the records. Many small firms don't have exhibit budgets at all. And almost nobody tries to identify total company investment. Industry cost surveys reveal an iceberg's tip. If we're talking about your company, stand by to become a hero.

Cost Area Accountability

Some costs fall to you naturally. Others do not. Some are clear and easy to understand. Some aren't so easy to understand.

- *Space.*   If you have any kind of exhibit budget, space rent is part of it. Sometimes, however, advance rent is paid in the year prior to a show and is forgotten when the bills are added.

- *Structure and graphics.*   For the most part, the exhibit budget pays. Your company may stock standard units, however, and all you cover is modification and special signing.

- *Transportation.*   This covers exhibit structure, demonstration products, supplies, and anything else that must be carried to and from a show. You probably pay these costs, but you probably do *not* pay all the costs for transporting people to the shows.

- *On-site services.*   This is a natural. A number of vendors are involved and, traditionally, one of our responsibilities is show setup. We budget for it.

- *Preshow and at-show promotion.*   This one may elude us. Sales promotion and advertising managers sometimes get involved and pay costs. Sometimes cooperative work is involved. Creative work may be in one place, with money for ad space or postage someplace else.

- *Customer hospitality.*   Hospitality operations can be a big item, and often costs are diffused. Sometimes professional events managers are employed. Responsibility and budget authority are not always given to the exhibit manager.

- *Personal expenses.*   Most times, "travel and entertainment" expenses of those working at a show are not part of exhibit budget. A lot of money is involved. A study by the Trade Show Bureau shows staff salary and expense add half again more to the *direct* costs of exhibiting.[3]

- *Press contacts.*   The costs for news conferences, press packages, and entertainment may be absorbed by a media relations group.

- *Speaker support.*   If you provide a seminar speaker, dollars for slides and handouts may come from the speaker's own department.

- *Display product cost.* Product inventory costs money. Do you charge it to the exhibit budget? How about installation and repair?

- *Time cost.* Your largest hidden expense is time: sales hours and days that could be used doing something else for the company.

Budget Management and Show Cost Tracking

To be a hero, keep two sets of books. The first is for your budget. The second estimates costs absorbed by others or somehow "lost" in the company. Together, they form show cost: *the true comparison with return.*

Methods of Allocating Show Cost

Show cost allocations can come from three places:

- Direct charges to the show from your budget

- Direct cost paid by others or otherwise absorbed in the company

- Indirect expense from your budget (fixed dollars devoted to exhibits generally but not influenced by a single event)

Here are examples of each type, along with ways to allocate:

- *Exhibit structure.* You pay once for a new booth. However, you should spread the expense over the number of shows at which you expect to use the exhibit. Let's say you spend $20,000 and plan to use the booth 4 times a year for 3 years, 12 shows. It is not fair to tag the first show with all $20,000. A value manager wants to compare shows with each other on even footing. It's not fair to figure that the other 11 are "free." So, divide $20,000 by 12. Impose an artificial charge for each show of $1666: $20,000 ÷ 12 = $1666.

- *Disposables.* You may supply sales literature or promotional giveaway items for shows. Regardless of which budget pays, you should project a unit cost and allocate depending on quantity used.

- *Exhibit operations costs.* There are fixed costs that can't be attributed directly to a single show. Exhibit storage bills, office rent, utilities, your salary and benefits support exhibit activity. Each show should be debited a fair share. Add up and divide by the number of shows you anticipate. Allocate an amount to each.

- *Display product cost.* The manufacturing cost of display products should be included. They may not cost you a dime, but the company has paid. Impose an artificial charge for each show, the same way we recognize investment in a booth. How long will the product be used on the show circuit? How many shows will be involved? Split the cost.

- *Staff time.* We've said that time can be your biggest hidden expense. Estimate staff time and plug it into each exhibit. Here's how:

    Estimate the average cost of a salesperson's time in your company, including compensation, benefits, and office. Divide by the average number of workdays a year. Then multiply the dollar figure by the number of person days devoted to the show.

    An example: Presume an average salesperson makes $50,000 a year. Add 25 percent to cover benefits plus 15 percent for other costs— office space, electricity, and the like. This person *costs* $70,000 a year: $50,000 × .40 = $20,000 + $50,000 = $70,000.

    With weekends, holidays, vacation, and some sick days removed, we can be left with as few as 220 workdays in a year. Divide $70,000 by 220, and an average salesperson *costs* $318 per day: $70,000 ÷ 220 = $318.

    Finally, multiply $318 by the number of person days devoted to an exhibit. For instance, if 6 people spend an equivalent of 4 days each at an exhibit, you've spent 24 person days. The result is $7632 in time cost: $318 × 24 = $7632.

We have a two-level budget management job. We must watch our own dollars and at the same time look out for the company's overall investment in exhibits.

Value of Show Cost Bookkeeping

There are three advantages. First, the higher cost revealed will inspire you to make a greater effort to measure corresponding value. Second, show planning will be improved, leading to more and more cost-effective exhibits. And third, because of stringent measurement, you will inspire greater management confidence in your judgment.

Exhibit Budget Itself

Exhibit budgets are difficult to manage. One reason is that most company accounting practices don't match needs. Operating budgets are organized by work group and traditional budget "lines." They track such things as rent, salary, travel, and office expense. In most, one line is set aside for "projects"; this is appropriate because the dollars are relatively few. In an advertising or exhibit department, however, this one line can be larger than all the rest put together. The project lump is not manageable as a lump. It combines diverse costs.

Some companies break projects down by traditional budget line. An example is the exhibit-hauling cost mentioned a moment ago. Or, exhibit space rent is flowed into an overall rent line and exhibit travel costs are part of overall personal travel. Freight is freight. Rent is rent. Travel is travel. The procedure conspires to obscure rather than reveal, making exhibit expenditures difficult to manage.

Project Budgets

Because of these accounting practices, we all develop our own "project" budget formats. There are dozens. They differ, depending on our specific exhibit responsibilities and the extent to which clerical support is available to create records.

We said we had a two-level budget management job, that we must keep two sets of books. It's really *three*: first, our own informal project format to control expense; second, the same dollars as they flow into official company budget lines; third and most important, we must know show cost to manage use of the medium itself.

Exhibit Budget and Show Cost Elements

To help show how the method works, we carry forward the two hypothetical exhibit marketing plan illustrations developed in Chapters 5, 6, and 7. Notice how we can keep track of our own expenses and at the same time estimate the costs of others.

Each cost category important to an exhibit is treated separately. You can relate each to an appropriate "official" budget line in your company, if that's necessary.

Exhibit Space

Assume, in both illustrations, that rent is $10 per square foot.

State Convention Illustration. In Chapters 5 and 6, we described a statewide convention attracting 3000 visitors. To reach 100 percent of the market required two 10-by-10-foot booth spaces, a total of 200 square feet. At $10 per square foot, the space rent was $2000. It was paid during the year of the show; no advance payment was required.

State Convention Illustration

Budget item	Exhibit manager's current budget	Another budget contribution	Show cost allocation
1. Space rent			
a. Space (current year)	$ 2,000		$ 2,000
b. Deposit (last year)			
c. Deposit (next year)			
d. Total space	$ 2,000		$ 2,000

We will be building this 3-column format by adding additional budget lines throughout the chapter.

Regional Convention Illustration. The illustration in Chapter 7 was for a larger regional trade show attracting 20,000. A 20-by-30 "island" space was rented. At $10 per square foot, this 600-square-foot booth space cost $6000.

A 50-percent deposit, $3000, was paid last year. It is shown under "another budget contribution" and carried over to "show cost allocation." The balance, $3000, was paid from the current budget and is also carried over to show cost allocation. The total is $6000. When the exhibit's results are measured, they'll be compared to show cost allocation.

Remember, from Chapter 7, that larger space was justified in the future? Assume that a decision was made to go up to 800 square feet. The cost will be $8000, of which half must be paid now. The budget shows $4000 as current *budget* expense but does *not* allocate the prepayment to this year's show cost. When you evaluate this exhibit, it would not be fair to include the $4000.

Regional Convention Illustration

Budget item	Exhibit manager's current budget	Another budget contribution	Show cost allocation
1. Space rent			
a. Space (current year)	$ 3,000	$	$ 3,000
b. Deposit (last year)		3,000	3,000
c. Deposit (next year)	4,000		
d. Total space	$ 7,000	$ 3,000	$ 6,000

Exhibit Structure, Graphics, and Display Products

Lots of things fit on this line. A new exhibit with new graphics is one. Refurbishing an older unit, touching up signs, could also be involved. Sometimes a new setup drawing is the only current cost.

There are two expense areas. One is for doing work directly related to the current show, and it comes from the current budget. The other is a fair share of the investment in exhibit materials expected to last for a time. We have already outlined the method for figuring this. It appears under "another budget contribution." Both amounts are part of show cost.

As we said before, use the same concept to recognize company cost for display products. Project how often a sample will be exhibited before the company changes lines or is replaced. Divide and apply.

State Convention Illustration. Two 10-foot exhibit units provided by the company are used at this show. Product graphic signs are part of the package. The cost to the company was about $8000 for each 10-foot unit, including signs, packing cases, and setup drawings. The total was $16,000. The units are expected to last for 2 years and be used at 4 shows a year. A show cost allocation of $1000 for each unit is appropriate, resulting in $2000 for use of two units: $8000 × 2 = $16,000 ÷ 8 = $2000.

There will be some out-of-pocket cost as well. For this show, two special signs are to be made at $500 each: $1000. Some refurbishing, to remove nicks from a counter, will cost $500. Floor carpet must be replaced and it will cost $1000; though it will be used again, we decide to allocate the cost to this show.

State Convention Illustration

Budget item	Exhibit manager's current budget	Another budget contribution	Show cost allocation
2. Exhibit structure, graphics, and display products			
a. Design	$	$ 2,000	$ 2,000*
b. Building/refurbishing	$ 1,500†		$ 1,500
c. Graphics	1,000‡		1,000
d. Total structure	$ 2,500	$ 2,000	$ 4,500
e. Display products			
f. Total structure, etc.	$ 2,500	$ 2,000	$ 4,500

* Allocation of initial exhibit production cost.
† Refurbishing, $500; carpet, $1000.
‡ Two signs at $500 each.

The products on the exhibit are also used by salespeople for other demonstrations; incremental cost allocation is not worth the trouble.

Regional Convention Illustration.   The larger regional convention is the scene for a new product introduction: a new, modular booth with 10 selling stations and all new graphics to go with a new advertising program. The investment is $80,000, or $8000 per selling station. (This includes $8000 for design, $62,000 for construction, and $10,000 for graphics.)

We must pay in the current budget, but we will use the booth, or a substantial number of the selling stations that are part of it, in at least 6 shows a year for 2 years: a minimum of 12 uses for each selling station. Dividing $8000 per selling station by 12 uses produces a show cost allocation of $666 for each station. Since we're using all 10 at this show, the allocation is $6666: $80,000 ÷ 10 = $8,000 ÷ 12 = $666 × 10 = $6660.

We're given two product samples for this show and for five subsequent shows over its first year of product life. The manufacturing cost is $12,000 each, a total of $24,000 spread over six shows. The $24,000 is shown under "another budget contribution" and the show cost allocation will be $2000 for each of the two units. Since both will be used at the introduction, the show cost allocation will be $4000: $12,000 ÷ 6 = $2000 × 2 = $4000.

Regional Convention Illustration

Budget item	Exhibit manager's current budget	Another budget contribution	Show cost allocation
2. Exhibit structure, graphics, and display products			
a. Design	$ 8,000		
b. Building/refurbishing	62,000		
c. Graphics	10,000		
d. Total structure	$ 80,000		$ 6,660[*]
e. Display products		$ 24,000[†]	4,000[†]
f. Total structure, etc.	$ 80,000	$ 24,000	$ 10,660

[*] Allocation of initial exhibit production cost.
[†] Estimated manufacturing cost absorbed by the factory for two display units, to be allocated for 1 year as a show cost at $2000 each for every show.

Promotions and Presentations

This is our third major cost group, after space rent and exhibit structures. It includes activities to stimulate booth traffic and draw special attention to products or key benefits. These activities could be:

- Preshow direct mail
- Preshow and at-show advertising
- At-show premiums or giveaways
- Special literature for the show
- Standard product literature for show distribution
- Live or audiovisual shows at the exhibit
- Special group presentations in private rooms or seminars
- Preshow press releases and at-show press packages
- At-show news conferences
- Trade show program listing

The budget format we present is long. When you copy the blank from the Appendix, edit. *We have eliminated lines from the form in our illustrations. You'll see that each line is identified by a letter and some letters are missing. All lines are shown in Figure A.12 in the Appendix.*

State Convention Illustration. The program is modest and aimed at reducing wasted exhibit visits, telling visitors what is being featured to stimulate traffic *only* among those interested in the products offered. The program includes:

- A letter and brochure mailed to 2000 potential visitors
- The same brochure distributed to hotel room mailboxes
- A preshow press release sent to the association's trade magazine for the convention issue
- Several copies of a press package placed on a table reserved for this purpose in the convention pressroom
- A listing in the convention program highlighting what is being featured (at no cost)

Except for paying the hotel for distributing brochures to mailboxes, all the costs will be absorbed by the advertising and media relations departments of the company.

State Convention Illustration

Budget item	Exhibit manager's current budget	Another budget contribution	Show cost allocation
3. Promotions and presentations			
a. Direct mail creative	$	$ 750*	$ 750
b. Production/printing		750*	750
c. Postage/handling		800*	800
g. Special literature creative		See above	See above
h. Production/printing		See above	See above
i. Handling	100†		100
j. Product literature		200‡	None
r. Preshow press relations		$ 100¶	$ 100
s. At-show press package		$ 100¶	$ 100
w. Total promotions	$ 100	$ 2,700	$ 2,800

* Creative and production cost is covered by company promotion budget. Postage and handling cost is covered by sales.
† This is the cost of paying the hotel for mailbox distribution.
†† This *estimates* printing paid from the sales promotion budget for 200 copies of an extensive product booklet for selected visitors.
¶ This is an *estimate* of the out-of-pocket cost to the media relations department for reproducing, packaging, and mailing the press release and the kit for distribution at the show.

Our illustration contains more detail than you'll really need. When you do this yourself, think about major cost areas. Provide just enough detail to feel confident in measuring exhibit returns against cost later.

Regional Convention Illustration.   This show will require more activity to reach its goals. A new product is to be introduced along with a new advertising campaign. The promotions and presentations program will include:

- A direct mail program similar to the smaller convention but with 5000 units mailed
- Advertising placed in the key trade magazines and in a "convention daily" newspaper introducing the new product
- Two hostesses hired to distribute copies of the brochure enclosed in the direct mail program, just inside the entrance to the show floor, for the first 2 days of the show
- In addition to preshow press releases, a breakfast press conference held in a hotel conference room on the first morning of the show
- This same room used later for private group presentations about the new product to key customers

In the illustration few of the costs are absorbed in the exhibit budget. A reminder: In the illustration we have eliminated lines not used. The complete form is presented in Figure A.12 in the Appendix.

Regional Convention Illustration

Budget item	Exhibit manager's current budget	Another budget contribution	Show cost allocation
3. Promotions and presentations			
a. Direct mail creative	$	$ 900	$ 900
b. Production/printing		1,000	1,000
c. Postage/handling		1,400	1,400
d. Advertising creative		3,000	3,000
e. Media buy		2,800	2,800
i. Handling	500		500
j. Product literature		1,500	1,500
p. Preshow slides; etc		$ 2,000	$ 2,000
q. At-show rent, etc.	750		$ 750
r. Preshow press relations		300	300
s. At-show press package		300	400
v. At-show rent, etc.	500		500
w. Total promotions	$ 1,750	$ 13,300	$ 15,050

Customer Hospitality

Activities away from the booth, from closing rooms and hospitality suites to formal dealer dinners, all fit under the umbrella of customer hospitality.

State Convention Illustration.   The exhibit is planned without a special program. Just a few salespeople are involved. It is economical to accept higher than average expense statements for informal customer entertaining.

Regional Convention Illustration.   The audience is bigger. The company's team size is greater. A new product is being announced. A press conference is planned along with private demonstrations. A daytime "closing room" and display center becomes a hospitality suite at night.

Regional Convention Illustration

Budget item	Exhibit manager's budget	Another budget contribution	Show cost allocation
4. Customer hospitality			
a. Suite/room rental	See press conference		See press
b. Food/beverage, day	$ 600		$ 600
c. Food/beverage evening	2,500		2,500
d. Decor/flowers	200		200
e. Host/hostess	300		300
i. Invitations	200		200
m. Outside management fee	700		700
n. Total hospitality	$ 4,500		$ 4,500

Transportation

This cost group includes the movement of goods, not people, to the site of the show and back.

State Convention Illustration. Only 20 feet of structure are involved, 6 or 8 crates. Display products are added, plus odds and ends. The exhibit budget pays.

State Convention Illustration

Budget item	Exhibit manager's current budget	Another budget contribution	Show cost allocation
5. Transportation			
a. Shipping to, by truck	$ 1,500		1,500
d. Shipping from, by truck	1,500		1,500
h. Total transportation	$ 3,000		$ 3,000

The figures used in these illustrations are hypothetical. Do not assume that they can be considered typical. And, as before, we've eliminated lines not applicable to the illustration. See complete form, Figure A.12, in the Appendix.

Regional Show Illustration. This exhibit is substantially larger. In addition, new product samples will come from another location by air. The exhibit budget pays, except for the air freight, which is covered by the factory.

Regional Convention Illustration

Budget item	Exhibit manager's current budget	Another budget contribution	Show cost allocation
5. Transportation			
a. Shipping to, by truck	$ 3,500		3,500
b. Air freight		1,500	1,500
d. Shipping from, by truck	4,000		4,000
h. Total transportation	$ 7,500	$ 1,500	$ 9,000

Field Service On Site

This cost covers virtually everything required in services and rentals in the hall itself. It can include drayage, labor for setup and tear-down, electrical costs, telephone, projectionists, security, booth cleaning, plants and flowers, photography, furniture, carpet, audiovisual rental, plumbers, riggers, emergency exhibit repairs, and sign making. Exhibitor kits are filled with contracts.

State Convention Illustration.   The exhibit is not large or complex. It should take three or four craftspeople no more than a few hours to set up. Based on that, here is what the budget might look like.

State Convention Illustration

Budget item	Exhibit manager's current budget	Another budget contribution	Show cost allocation
6. Field service on site			
a. Drayage into hall	$ 800	$ $	800
b. Drayage out of hall	800		800
c. Labor up	600		600
d. Labor down	500		500
e. Electrical costs	150		150
g. Rental of plants, etc.	200		200
j. Booth cleaning	100		100
m. Total show service	$ 3,150	$	3,150

Regional Convention Illustration.   The exhibit for this show is substantially larger: a new exhibit set up for the first time. The exhibit budget absorbs the cost.

Regional Convention Illustration

Budget item	Exhibit manager's current budget	Another budget contribution	Show cost allocation
6. Field service on site			
a. Drayage into hall	$ 2,000	$ $	2,000
b. Drayage out of hall	2,000		2,000
c. Labor up	1300		1300
d. Labor down	900		900
e. Electrical costs	700		700
f. Telephone	200		200
g. Rental of plants, etc.	400		400
h. Photography	200		200
i. Security	400		400
j. Booth cleaning	200		200
k. Other services/ miscellaneous	250		250
l. Management fee/ expense	2,000		2,000
m. Total show service	$ 10,550	$	10,550

Some exhibitors use outside managers to supervise setup and teardown. Exhibit houses provide this, and there are specialist firms.

Exhibit Staff Personnel

This is where we try to keep track of people cost, even if it's not part of our own budget.

Calculating the Value of Time. Earlier, on page 92, we outlined the procedure: *average annual loaded compensation divided by workdays times person days at the show.* See what the figures might be in your company and develop a cost per person per day. By the way, when you add up person days at a show, don't forget yourself.

Out-of-Pocket Costs. Even if out-of-pocket costs for travel, hotel, and food are paid from another budget, you should estimate them so the expense is part of the exhibit's evaluation equation.

Training Cost. At all but the smallest shows, everyone needs preshow training. Extra time and cost are involved, and these must also be counted in. Conference room rental, food, and audiovisual support may be required.

State Convention Illustration.   For this illustration *and* our regional illustration, we'll assume the $318-per-day cost worked out earlier as average compensation of $50,000 a year.

The state convention requires 3 people on duty at the exhibit. Because of the long hours, 2 teams will work the show. A supervisor will also be present, along with yourself: a total of 8. The show lasts 4 days and we must add a 5th day to cover travel and training. Thus, we estimate 40 person days: 5 days × 8 people = 40.

At a time cost average of $318 per day, the show cost allocation is $12,720: $318 × 40 = $12,720.

Out-of-pocket must be estimated too. The exhibit budget covers you; others charge their own offices. Either way, travel costs are not high since all drive their cars to the show, which takes place in the state. Hotels and food should average $100 per day for 4 nights, or $400 per person. Add $100 for travel. The total estimate comes to $500 each.

You, however, rent a suite, increasing your out-of-pocket expense to $750. The suite serves double duty. In addition to providing sleeping quarters, it is used as a clerical center and a place to have both training and postday show critique meetings.

Seven people spending an average of $500 each means $3500: $500 × 7 = $3500. You spend $750, raising the total to $4250. However, you split expense between personal, $500, and training support, $250.

State Convention Illustration

Budget item	Exhibit manager's current budget	Another budget contribution	Show cost allocation
7. Staff Personnel			
a. Time value of staff		$ 12,720	$ 12,720
b. Personal expense	$ 500	$ 3,500	4,000
c. Sales training/ clerical	250		250
d. Total staff expense	$ 750	$ 16,220	$ 16,970

Time value estimates are an especially good management tool. "Is it worth $17,000 in time, plus the rest, to gain $350,000 in gross revenue, the show goal?" Can the people prospect, present, and close more ultimate business during 5 days at home?

Regional Convention Illustration. We follow the same guideline. The team size is larger. There will be 10 salespeople per shift: a total of 20. In addition, a sales manager will be required, along with a technical expert for the new product and yourself: a team of 23. Time value will be 23 × 5 = 115 × $318 = $36,570. Expenses will be larger too. Some people must fly to the show. We estimate $800 out-of-pocket expense per person for the 4 days: $800 × 22 = $17,600 + $1150 (for yourself, including training room expense) = $18,570.

Regional Convention Illustration

Budget item	Exhibit manager's current budget	Another budget contribution	Show cost allocation
7. Staff Personnel			
a. Time value of staff		$ 36,570	$ 36,570
b. Personal expense	$ 800	$ 17,600	18,400
c. Sales training/ clerical	350		350
d. Total staff expense	$ 1,150	$ 54,170	$ 55,320

Research

The last significant cost category is research. There are three types. One is informal, asking customers to evaluate products and applications. The second is an audit sponsored by show management (at no cost to you). The third is professional research that you sponsor.

We assume no research for the state convention exhibit. However, a new product was introduced at the regional convention. A private research firm is employed to produce professional results on the awareness created.

Regional Convention Illustration

Budget item	Exhibit manager's current budget	Another budget contribution	Show cost allocation
8. Research			
b. Professional	$ 3,500		$ 3,500
c. Total	$ 3,500	$	$ 3,500

At the end of this chapter we've summarized and totaled both our state and regional exhibit cost estimates. In each case, we add 10 percent as a contingency. To find out what we've spent, see Figures 8.1 and 8.2.

Budget item	Exhibit manager's current budget	Another budget contribution	Show cost allocation
1. Space rent		
d. Total space	$ 2,000	_____	$ 2,000
2. Exhibit structure, graphics, and display products		
f. Total structure, etc.	$ 2,500	$ 2,000	$ 4,500
3. Promotions and presentations		
w. Total promotions	$ 100	$ 2,700	$ 2,800
4. Customer hospitality		
No program. (See Figure 8.2 or blank form in Appendix.)		
5. Transportation		
h. Total transportation	$ 3,000	_____	$ 3,000
6. Field service on site		
m. Total show service	$ 3,150	_____	$ 3,150
7. Staff personnel		
d. Total staff expense	$ 750	$ 16,220	$ 16,970
8. Research		
No program. (See Figure A.12, a blank form in the Appendix.)		
9. Total	$ 11,500	$ 20,920	$ 32,420
10. Contingency (10 percent)	$ 1,150	$ 2,092	$ 3,242
11. Grand total	$ 12,650	$ 23,012	$ 35,662

Figure 8.1. Budget summary for state convention illustration.

Creating Your Own Format

In Part One, "The Quick Fix," we presented the simple 8-line budget. In this chapter we have expanded, perhaps too much for you. So we prepared an alternate, in-between version. You'll find it as a blank form, Figure A.13, in the Appendix. It may be just right.

International Exhibitors Association Standard. The International Exhibitors Association (IEA) has developed an excellent budget format that is even more detailed than the one we present in this book. For instance, it breaks down exhibit design and construction into 3 cost lines: design, materials, and construction. In addition, it offers somewhat more detail

Budget item	Exhibit manager's current budget	Another budget contribution	Show cost allocation
1. Space rent			
d. Total space	$ 7,000	$ 3,000	$ 6,000
2. Exhibit structure, graphics, and display products			
f. Total structure, etc.	$ 80,000	$ 24,000	$ 10,660
3. Promotions and presentations			
w. Total promotions	$ 1,750	$ 13,300	$ 15,050
4. Customer hospitality			
n. Total hospitality	$ 4,500	$	$ 4,500
5. Transportation			
h. Total transportation	$ 7,500	1,500	$ 9,000
6. Field service on site			
m. Total show service	$ 10,550		$ 10,550
7. Staff personnel			
d. Total staff expense	$ 1,150	$ 54,170	$ 55,320
8. Research			
c. Total	$ 3,500	$	$ 3,500
9. Total	$ 115,950	$ 95,970	$114,580
10. Contingency (10 percent)	$ 11,595	$ 9,597	$ 11,458
11. Grand total	$ 127,545	$ 105,517	$126,038

Figure 8.2. Budget summary for regional convention illsutration

in the show services area. If your exhibits are large or complex, we recommend it. The association uses this format in context with an annual cost survey. You can get the material from IEA or, each year, *Exhibitor Magazine* publishes the form along with an analysis of cost changes.[4]

Double Value in Budget Management

One of our prime responsibilities is stewardship. All of these formats give you that capability, especially when you start comparing cost lines in different shows. You'll spot differences and wonder why.

By adding nonbudget cost estimates, you'll achieve another goal: developing better information to use in making participation decisions. You can compare estimates with goals, asking, "Is it worth it?"

Start Point for Individual Exhibit Budget Building

In Chapter 4, we detailed methods for developing program budgets. What follows here could be used as an alternate approach, but it may be even more valuable if you're starting from scratch to develop a budget for a good-sized individual show. It's a summary of cost breakdowns based on industrywide statistics.[5] Everyone's situation is unique; but if you keep these figures in mind, you'll have a solid base.

Cost group	Percent
Exhibit space rental	21
Exhibit construction	21
Refurbishing	12
Show services	21
Transportation	13
Special personnel	5
Speciality advertising	2
Miscellaneous	5
	100
Personnel expenses added	34

All you have to do is figure out your space rent. Multiply that by 5 to approximate total cost, excluding personnel expense. If personnel cost is part of your budget, multiply by 7.

Actual Versus Budget

After shows are over, you'll have to track actual expenses against the budget. Duplicate our blank forms, Figures A.12 and A.13, and change their titles. Many of the figures in the center column will remain estimates, but you'll have a way to manage both the medium and your budget.

We've identified each budget line by number and letter. You may decide to computerize the form or you may need a shorthand system to help clerical associates in your office. If you want to computerize, most spread sheet programs for personal computers can be adapted to the work. In addition, if your budget is compressed into 2 or more official company budget lines, entries on "unofficial" lines can be folded into the proper company budget category at the same time.

We've looked at objectives and cost estimates in Chapters 5 through 8. In the next two chapters, we bring them together and find out how well we're doing. We become *value managers.*

9

Evaluating Exhibits Based on Cost

Like it or not, most of us don't manage value. We're coordinators or cost managers. We worry most about what's *spent* for space, structure, graphics, freight, drayage, setup, electrical equipment, telephone, food, beverage, and storage. The list goes on. This is even true in Fortune 500 companies. At least one such company provides exhibit service to its divisions through an in-house group working as a profit center competing with outside vendors the divisions can employ if they wish. This very professional group is more involved with process than result, more with cost than corporate return.

At least one other Fortune 500 corporate exhibit group worries only about design and design-related economics. Management of the medium itself is assigned to divisions and field offices. The corporate group is restricted to image making: all well and good if the others know about exhibit money-making. That is not always the case.

Regardless of your company's size or organization, the path to becoming a *value* manager starts with becoming a better cost manager. You have to lead the way, convincing bosses as you grow.

Reasons for Cost-Management Focus

Exhibits started emerging as an expensive part of the marketing communications mix 2 decades ago. (Before, conventions were thought of as occasional activities that meant little.) During this formative period, there was little information upon which judgments could be made except cost. Managers were struggling to find ways of measuring, to justify expense bubbling up in their companies.

In addition, exhibit results can be fuzzy. Of course, there are some order-writing shows in which business written can be compared to cost. For the most part, however, results are not clearly and quickly defined. This is the second reason for emphasizing cost evaluation.

Cost-Data Methods

By the end of the 1960s, enough people were compiling cost facts to start providing industrywide measurement. Two methods evolved that you can use to evaluate expense.

Industry Cost-Average Method

The cost annual cost surveys we mentioned in Chapter 8, produced by the International Exhibitors Association, can be compared with experience. (See note 3 for Chapter 8.) After establishing a "base," you can compare changes in your costs with those experienced in the industry as a whole. You may run lower or higher than the average in different cost areas, but the rate of change should be consistent.

At the end of Chapter 8, we outlined industry averages that help you build a budget. These same averages can be used for cost-evaluation purposes. (See note 1 for Chapter 8.) See how you fit:

Cost group	Percent
Exhibit space rental	21
Exhibit construction	21
Refurbishing	12
Show services	21
Transportation	13
Special personnel	5
Speciality advertising	2
Miscellaneous	5
	100
Personnel expenses added	34

Cost-Per-Exhibit-Product Method

Most of us find this method easier to work with. The physical "products" produced by an exhibit can be compared to cost. The concept started with industrywide data on cost, combining it with audience research.

Trade Show Bureau studies tell us the industrywide average cost for an exhibit selling contact. For 1985, an exhibit selling contact averaged $106.70. (See note 1 for Chapter 8.)

On the surface, you'd think it easy to count the number of people you talk to and then come up with your own per-contact cost to compare with the average. It isn't. One large company tried. The industry figure is produced through audience research, a more precise method than our people-counting. Visitors remember and report even short contacts, including quick visits to pick up literature. We tend to remember and take note only of longer selling conversations.

You can, if you wish, try to estimate the number of contacts you make based on the private company research we reported in Chapter 5 (see note 4 for Chapter 5). The lead-to-contact ratio is 2 sales leads for every 10 contacts. For instance, if you obtain 50 leads, assume 250 contacts and compare to cost. To beat the $106.70-per-contact industry average, your exhibit would have to cost less than $26,675 ($106.70 × 250 = $26,675).

It is more practical to apply the concept to work production that you can count with accuracy. You can count such things as leads, orders, brochures distributed, VIPs entertained, seminar attendance, news releases, and competitors. Develop internal cost standards. First establish benchmarks and then compare future shows against them.

Internal Measurements

You can compare cost with each of the four major sets of exhibit goals. The complete list appears in Chapter 5.

Selling goals
  Cost per selling contact
  Cost per sales lead
  Cost per order written

Awareness-development and image-enhancement goals
  Cost per item of literature or sample product distributed
  Cost per viewer at a live or audiovisual show
  Cost per story or column inch for media coverage
  Cost per visitor at company-sponsored seminars

Customer-positioning goals
  Cost per VIP visitor reached

Learning goals
Cost per competitive evaluation
Cost per seminar attended
Cost per research program implemented

Select goals important to you and start storing data. To stay consistent, always compare with the *total* cost of the show. Don't try to segregate specific costs for specific projects. Judgments from show to show will skew results. The "cost per" expense in some categories looks high. Don't worry. The value of this measure emerges only later, when first show results are compared with a second, third, or fourth show. Look for differences, not the total. You'll ask yourself, "Why?"

If you write orders at shows, there is some industrywide research that *may* help, even though it measures the cost of converting a lead to a sale afterward. We mention it because 54 percent of show leads are closed without an additional personal call. It's not the best measure for order-writing shows, but it's better than nothing. The average cost of booking an order that starts with an exhibit lead is $290.[1] The presumption of an order-writing show is that sales are closed without personal call follow-up. Per-order cost should be under $290.

Cost-Measurement Illustrations

In Chapter 5 we started two illustrations. One is for a state convention with an estimated show cost of $32,420, including the value of time spent at the exhibit by the sales staff. The second, a larger regional show was projected to cost $114,586.

State Convention Illustration

Round off the cost to $32,000. Acitivity goals included 640 selling contacts: 128 sales leads, 64 follow-up sales, 2000 direct mail letters, one preshow press release, and one press package at the show. We have some goals for cost-per measurement.

Selling Goals

- *Cost per selling contact.* Divide $32,000 by 640, and the result is $50 per visitor, well below industry average.

- *Cost per sales lead.* Divide $32,000 by 128, and the result is $250 per lead. Store the figure to compare with the future. There's no industry average.

- *Cost per order written after the show.* Divide $32,000 by 64, and the result is $500 per order. This cost can be compared with future shows or the $290 industry average.

Awareness-Development and Image-Enhancement Goals

- *Cost per item of literature or sample product distributed.* A direct mail program is planned for 2000 prospects. Ignore its budget. Simply divide 2000 into $32,000. Cost for each is $16. Again, store the figure for future show comparison.

- *Cost per story or column inch for media coverage.* A news release is to go before the convention, and there will be another at the show. Press relations people attempt to measure productivity. One is by "column inches" of coverage. We can measure in *three* ways, all against the total cost of the show: $32,000.

- Two stories were produced, so a cost per story of $16,000 serves as a benchmark for the future.

- Presume three trade news outlets, two for each story. Six translates to a story cost per outlet of $5333.

- If 120 column inches of press are printed, the cost per column inch would be $266.

Our coordinates in advertising, sales promotion, and press relations may take umbrage that we measure what they produce against *total show cost.* Tell them we need an easy-to-use and consistent cost base. This does not measure the value of their direct mail or news releases. That value may be far more than the cost of the show.

Regional Convention Illustration

This exhibit was larger, more expensive. Round the cost to $115,000.

Selling Goals

- *Cost per selling contact.* The goal was 2000 contacts. Based on

$115,000, this means $57.50 each—more than the state convention but still below the industrywide average.

- *Cost per sales lead.* The show goal was 400. Dividing this into $115,000 produces a cost of $287.50 for each—somewhat higher than the $250 per lead at the state convention.

  Note: Even at this point we can ask, "Why the difference?"—a question a good manager asks of himself or herself. This time the added cost is because of the new product and VIP programs.

- *Cost per order written.* The show goal is 200 sales. Dividing this into $115,000 produces $575 per order—larger than the $500 state exhibit cost for the same reasons.

At the regional exhibit, literature was distributed, a news conference was held, VIP customers were entertained—all tied in with introducing a new product. The cost-per-unit-of-production measure can be used for all of these activities.

Cost-Measurement Summary

For most of us, the cost of a sales lead or show order is the best productivity measure—but there are companies in which the most important goals can be awareness development, VIP contact, or something else. Select the goals consistently important to you and start tracking costs, show by show. The cost-per measure evens things out, allowing you to compare, even though some exhibits cost more than others.

If you become a good cost manager, you're more than halfway home to developing a reputation as a value manager. To complete the process, read the next chapter.

10
Measuring a Return on Investment

To be a value manager, you have to measure value. This is where most of us fall down. We reported that half of *Tradeshow Week* readers, responding to publication surveys, say they don't set quantifiable goals.[1] Of course, it's possible to count results without setting objectives in advance. It seems unlikely, however, that those who don't set goals first would measure value later in any kind of coherent fashion. Too many of us live or die by the sword of subjective management opinion instead of by measured results to help improve our own performance.

Advertising Industry Measurement

Advertising professionals plan with cost in mind. The basis of media planning is expenditure compared with exposure to readers, viewers, or listeners—"cost per thousand" and so on. The agencies and their clients don't stop with exposure cost. They make an attempt to measure impact as well, awareness development and attitude shifts. Except for direct response advertising, however, where order dollars can be compared with expenditure, it's not easy to measure return. Nonetheless, advertising yardsticks do provide a basis for sensible decisions and a method for evaluating personal contributions of managers.

Our yardsticks are behind the rest of the marketing communications community; that holds for all of us in show and facilities management but especially those in exhibit management. Our place in the marketing mix is more closely allied to direct support of sales, and measurement can be more complex.

Of course, we do use research—similar to that of advertising—to measure impact upon show audiences, including awareness development, image change, and exhibit effectiveness. Show organizers use research to evaluate audiences, but many shows and exhibits are relatively small. We're inclined to sponsor studies only for larger events.

It is fairly easy, though, to evaluate dollar return yourself, easier than for most other forms of marketing communication. You can do it far less expensively than by sponsoring a large number of professional surveys. "Sweat equity" can produce good yardsticks.

Impact of Distribution Methods

The ease with which you can measure return on investment depends on what you're selling and the purchasing traditions in your industry.

Order Evaluation

Sales orders are written at shows. Some shows are more conducive to buying than others. Retail events—stamp, coin, boat, auto, and home fairs—encourage show purchases. Business buyer shows, which are part of the wholesale and retail distribution chain, also emphasize exhibit ordering. The housewares and consumer electronics industries shown are among them. The Toy Show in New York is an illustration, along with scores of gift shows around the nation. Some follow-up may be needed, but the dominant purpose is to fully complete the purchase process at the show. Immediate dollar returns can be counted and compared to exhibit cost.

To a somewhat lesser extent, businesses place firm orders at trade shows for things they use internally. For the most part, these are products not modified to meet individual buyer needs: an off-the-shelf computer program, office furniture, surgical instruments, tools, or perhaps a copy machine. Again, show orders can be compared to cost.

Lead Evaluation

Envy the few who know how much money is coming in at the end of a show. Most of us don't. Follow-up sales leads are our primary product. After a "home" show, the aluminum siding dealer may have to visit prospects' homes to price jobs and obtain signed contracts. The business buyer faces complications. Companies set dollar buying limits by management level. The show attendee's boss may have to be sold, too. More than one department may be involved. Lots of things have to be customized. Both buyer and seller have to do some homework before making a final decision. Often, executives use trade shows simply to winnow out the number of vendors with whom they later want to talk in detail. In any case, the ultimate sales close must wait and the dollar value of an order emerges only later. Sometimes even the product itself changes from where things started at the booth. It is difficult to measure dollar return that starts with an exhibit lead.

If your products aren't customized, the yardstick can remain pretty accurate. One computer terminal maker uses company order numbers to identify exhibit sales leads. Later, the accounting department reports business written under those order numbers. The exhibit manager totals and compares to cost.

Indirect Exhibit Marketing

At some shows, selling is not permitted. For instance, certain conventions for medical professionals prohibit floor selling per se. (Hypocrisy exists. Often, buyers and sellers get together off the show floor, in a suite or hotel bar, to finalize purchases.) Sometimes, however, an exhibitor never sells directly to the trade show visitor, regardless of the show's rules. The goal? Education: Inspiring purchase through intermediaries or influencing visitors to specify a product (for example, getting doctors to specify an ethical drug). This mirrors consumer product mass media advertising paid for by the manufacturer to help move products off supermarket shelves. Exhibit value measurement is quite difficult.

Measuring with Value Estimates

Exhibit managers at big companies claim complexity as a major reason for not attempting dollar return evaluation. They correctly point out that there are too many variables. Results, if published, would not be considered accurate enough. Many of these managers are trying too hard, trying to make measurement too perfect. Without realizing it, they search for perfection so exhibits can "take credit" for sales. Exhibits in themselves don't sell a thing.

You can and should be able to take credit for *assisting* in the selling process. Measurements should make it clear, however, that you are simply trying to measure your own effectiveness and the worth of your exhibits. They are small businesses inside a bigger business. Measurement should be used in the same fashion production and quality indexes that evaluate departments which are not bottom-line profit centers are used.

Measure Exhibits within Themselves

We don't really have to worry about whether or not exhibits in general produce results. They've been around for centuries. And the body of work produced by the Trade Show Bureau over the last decade makes an impressive statement that they are very effective indeed today, with every indication that they'll be even more important tomorrow.

You are probably beyond the stage of having to justify the exhibit concept to management. If you are, it's enough to measure exhibits within themselves. Even if you're not, the two problems should be kept separate. Build one body of information that produces management understanding, another that helps you manage better. All you really need for that are comparisons. It is not necessary to create a perfect bottom-line value measure. Thus, *estimates* of the dollar value of individual leads suffice for value measurement, as long as the same procedure is used from show to show. Simply ask those who are following up to report sales or estimate the potential value of a lead after meeting the prospect.

You don't even have to hear about all the leads given out. If you get feedback on a goodly number, say above 30 percent, you'll probably have enough information to make comparisons from one show to another.

Estimate Short-Term Results

Estimates should be restricted to what happens inside a year, or a first sale. Yes, a lead can be the start of a long-term relationship. You might feel it unfair to measure exhibit performance on the basis of only a first sale. True, but wrong. You decide on shows annually. Long-term benefits should take a back seat. They should not be ignored, any more than you would ignore public relations value; however, each show, each year must stand on its own feet. Estimates and shortterm results are sufficient for our purpose—to evaluate what was right or wrong, to figure out how we can improve.

Third-Party Estimates

Try to avoid having lead quality estimates made by those who unknowingly might perpetuate the past. Estimates must be objective. For instance, if your show is at a resort and salespeople follow up their own leads, there's always concern their estimates may be inflated by the desire to go back next year. To the extent possible, leads should be followed up and evaluated by third parties, by people who did not take them—even if a sales commission split has to be negotiated.

Expense-to-Revenue Ratio

The best method for measuring value is comparing dollar return with cost, developing a ratio or index that can be used from show to show, comparing performance.

Figuring the ratio takes us back to school days. What grade were we in when we learned how to reduce fractions to their lowest common denominator? In this case, however, we round numbers so that one-half of the fraction, "expense," will always be the figure 1. The ratio will always be expressed 1 to x, with x representing dollar return. Its meaning: For every single dollar of expense, x number of dollars came in. If $2000 of cost returns $10,000, the expense-to-revenue ratio is 1 to 5. On your calculator, simply *divide return by cost*. The resulting number is the *right* side of the ratio, revenue return.

There is another way to express the cost-value relationship. Reverse the way in which the ratio is presented and you can claim 5 to 1 revenue to expense, or a 500-percent return. Don't do it. It sounds too good. Right or wrong, many companies consider exhibits an added cost in distribution. (Exhibits substitute for other distribution expense, *reducing* cost of sales; however, this is not yet commonly understood.) Because of divided responsibility, authority, and budgeting, it is almost always necessary to use estimates on *both* sides of the equation, cost and return, to calculate an expense-to-revenue ratio, or E to R. Internal challengers accept a conservative expression of value more readily.

Expense-to-Revenue Goal Setting

If we assume exhibits as added company cost, the ratio goal should be far higher than 1 to 5. If that's all you get, you're probably losing money at shows. In fact, if an exhibit produces a ratio lower than 1 to 10, it is likely you're losing.

We don't propose eliminating traditional values. We don't propose automatically eliminating shows that don't deliver a 1 to 10. There remain reasons for exhibiting that can't be measured; however, the E to R makes you look more closely at exhibit plans. It helps build a new sense of discipline.

Expense-to-Revenue Ratio Illustrations

Throughout Part 2, we developed hypothetical exhibit marketing program plans. One was for a state convention, the other for a larger exhibit at a regional show.

State Convention Illustration. The revenue goal is $358,400. Total show cost, including an estimate of sales staff member compensation, was projected at $32,420. The expense side of the ratio will always be the figure 1. So the calculation requires us to divide the expense projection into the revenue projection: $358,400 \div $32,420 = 11.05. Round 11.05 down to 11, and the expense-to-revenue ratio is 1 to 11.

Regional Convention Illustration. The cost allocation to this exhibit was $114,568. The projection of return for the show was $1,120,000. The calculation: $1,120,000 \div $114,568 = 9.77. The expense-to-revenue ratio is 1 to 10.

Although the ratios do not differ significantly, you can still figure out why there's disparity. Was there any product or customer divergence? Were there productivity nuances? What cost distinctions can be observed? There were contrasts:

- The state convention offered only existing products. The regional show served as the platform for introducing a new product.

- The new product created the need for a press conference and a formal VIP customer program at the regional convention, and there were higher incremental costs associated with training the sales staff for the show.

- A new booth was built for the regional show; however, it was charged only with its fair share cost. The new booth was *not* a significant added cost from a show evaluation viewpoint.

Using E to R helps to stabilize thinking. Without it, lots of us would remember only how costly the regional show was. Using E to R, we can compare the two on equal footing.

Actual Versus Projected Results

We have dealt with goal setting and cost projection. We've seen how we can project value return. Planning is, however, a two-stage process. After each show, actual results must be compared to those projected.

Like it or not, you often exceed your budget. Fortunately, more often than not, results are greater than anticipated. We tend to be conservative on both sides of the equation. And because of the press of the next project, we often fall down on keeping track of what really happened after the last show. We sacrifice half the learning we could have gained by failing to find out what happened.

Keep measurements simple. Pick a few key goals and work only with them. You're more likely to follow up. Overdo and the program is like one more diet that doesn't work. To be a value manager, you have to measure. To measure value, you have to stick with it.

PART 3

Creating and Managing an Exhibit

11

Managing Time

From here on, most of the chapters are optional reading. Pick what you need. There's only one we think everyone should focus on, and this isn't it. (It is Chapter 17, devoted to selling on the exhibit floor.) Before you turn pages, however, realize that time management is not just for the first-time exhibitor.

Reasons for Time Management

Lots of us who have been planning exhibits for years leave planning until too late. Unfortunately, perhaps, *the exhibit medium works so well that we don't know when we've failed*. Results are produced, but we don't know how high is up. Our problem is time, energizing both ourselves and those around us to make decisions early enough so that an operation can reach its crescendo at least cost and most return.

Expanding the Time Envelope

You don't need more time or more people. You just have to expand the time envelope, for others and yourself. You and those with whom you work in the company must decide what you want to do early and stick to it. The outside people with whom you work then have to plan their work flow better.

It's not just your exhibit house, transportation company, or advertising agency. Time is critical for many inside the company as well: sales managers, production staff, and even financial people.

Of course, you see and feel time pinch readily with the outside firms helping you. It'll cost you, and pocketbook pain hits right away. The internal price may not be as clear; but the ultimate cost in lowered results that stems from a hastily chosen product or sales team can be much more. Lowered sales resulting from a lackluster or nonexistent preshow promotion may never surface.

Your exhibit doesn't exist in a vacuum. Lots of other things are going on inside your company at the same time. Your outside team has other work, too. And some physical production chores take time, no matter how much money you pour on a catch-up fire.

Exhibit Production Work Lumps

Regardless of the size of your time envelope, you'll find work compressed into three lumps. The first is at start-up, fundamental decision making and planning. The second lump is spread out a bit, driven by a series of "drop dead" dates you sense as time moves on. The third covers a period from just before the show to just after.

There is another way to look at work flow:

1. Fundamental planning
   Audience analysis and goal setting
   Display product requirements
   Exhibit structure and graphic needs
   Sales and technical staff requirements
   Pre- and at-show promotional needs
   Budget development

2. Execution planning
   Travel and hotel reservations
   Creative development—exhibits, graphics, and promotions
   Shipping arrangements
   Exhibit hall and hotel services
   At-show training and clerical operations
   Budget revision

3. Postshow planning
   Sales lead and order processing
   Exhibit materials and display product movement
   Staff recognition
   Results evaluation

The list looks neat and clean, but the work can be complicated. For instance, your initial exhibit plan should be prepared with budget blinders on. The estimate should reflect cost to do the job as well as possible, based on sales needs. Then, if the dollars are more than you can afford, program reductions can be made; but you can keep it in balance. If you plan for a preordained expense limit, you focus more on cost and less on need. For instance, you might ignore preshow promotion instead of reducing throughout to include it. You'll not be managing the medium but be acting instead as a cost manager.

16-Week Time Line

It's presumptive to say you should start planning 16 weeks in advance. For some exhibits, you should start almost a year ahead. Others can be ignored until 6 or 8 weeks before the opening. However, with experience the teacher, a good average is 4 months if you already have a booth. A 16-week time envelope lets you fold the job in with other things and gives others time to do what they must.

In medium and large companies, there's another value in starting 4 months in advance, even for a small show: the boss. Most bosses have internal alarm clocks—but they often go off too late. The show comes to mind with just about enough time left to produce an appearance. This seems to happen with about 6 or 8 weeks to go. At that point, it's too late to think things through with care or to save money. On the other hand, for most, a 6 month lead time is too much. People won't focus on the plan and make decisions.

Let's say space in a show at the end of April was reserved a year ahead. Everyone "knows" about it but it's wintertime, January. Instinctively, most bosses won't focus on what should be done until late February or even March. Program development will run on overdrive from then on. You should surface an exhibit plan in mid-January, becoming proactive rather than waiting for March and being reactive.

Prototype 16-Week Time Line

As you go through the 4 months, there are checkpoints to help keep you on track. Of course, at the end—just before the show—the exhibit train is rumbling forward on its own. Get on and hold tight!

Weeks 16 and 15

- *Input meetings.* Pull interested people in the company together. Decide, in general terms, what you want to accomplish and what you may have to do to get there.

- *Audience analysis.* By yourself, take a look at the results of the past show and all the information you can get about the projected audience. You may have to talk to the show organizer or other exhibitors. Figure the time you'll have at the show. Translate your general goals into specific aim points.

- *Exhibitor kit.* If the show packet has arrived, read it with care. Make sure your exhibit house gets a copy of the show rules and the schedule for getting things into and out of the hall. Split up the order forms by who is going to fill them out. For instance, the hotel housing form may have to filled out by one person, the orders for services in the hall by another.

- *Rough draft plan.* Rough out a basic plan. Cover everything from the exhibit and graphics to preshow promotion, news releases, VIP hospitality, and sales staff needs. Try to put some numbers against results goals and estimate a price tag for all of it. You'll want to refine this, but start from a loose sketch of the program.

- *Revised plan and budget.* Polish the plan so everyone involved can take a look. You may have to develop *two*: the first based on only need and audience, plus an alternate that reflects cost limits.

Weeks 14 and 13

- *Preproduction meeting.* Review your plans with all the interested people inside the company. Get agreement or revise the program to solve problems that surface. Make sure everyone knows, when the meeting is over, that basic direction is set. Changes can be made, but there should be no revisit of fundamental goals and program content.

- *Final plan and budget.* The document that all will follow can now be prepared and distributed. Set up a series of checkpoint dates for yourself and others who may be doing work, including the exhibit house, show service representative, technical support personnel, advertising department, and promotional or media relations people.

- *Sales staff recruiting.* Success or failure depends on the sales team itself. Start selecting and recruiting right away. Make sure all the salespeople and their managers see the plan and understand that the exhibit is not a flippant exercise.

Weeks 12 and 11

- *Work start/finish.* Confirm work start and completion dates with those who may be working on parts of the plan. Stay "in the loop" with others and you'll stay in the driver's seat.

- *Production process.* Make especially sure that anything which will require physical production is in the works. In addition to exhibit structure and graphics, this can include speciality advertising give-aways, audiovisual shows, invitations, or brochures that will have to be printed.

- *Arrival and departure days.* If the show is out of town, you may be able to save dollars by plotting exactly when different people arrive and depart. For instance, part of the sales team may not have to stay through the last day. You may find that more technical help is needed to install products than remove them.

- *Exhibit staff advisory package.* At some point well before the show, each staff member should be given a packet of information that includes an outline of the exhibit operation, goals, products, promotions, and the rest, including an analysis of the audience and what is planned for the convention as a whole. Some "housekeeping" information should be included, such as work schedules or travel arrangement if the show is out of town. Start assembling now.

Weeks 10 to 6. Regardless of how long a time line you run, there will be a period in the middle when you're not too busy with the show. All you have to do is follow up with others to make sure things are happening.

The exhibitor kit we mentioned before may not have arrived by the 3- or 4-month mark. By now, however, it should have come in and work should have started with it. If not, call the show organizer.

The kinds of things you may need to check in this period are:

- *Recruiting.* Make sure the correct people have been identified and will take the assignment seriously. Some people feel they can cancel at the last minute because of a customer appointment.

- *Production.* Make sure completion dates are still firm.

- *Budget.* By now, your external sources should have been able torefine cost estimates. Put them all together and compare with your initial budget. Some adjustments may be necessary. If there are any unanswered cost questions, you'll at least identify them in advance.

- *Show program listing.* Your text for the show program may have been sent in when the plan was prepared. If not, now is the time.

Weeks 5 and 4.   The problem: We don't know what it is, but you'll have it. At every exhibit there is one nagging problem to deal with. It could be getting the prototype of a new product that is supposed to be introduced. It could be approval for an audiovisual show or getting the right speaker from the company to appear. Now is the moment to recognize and solve that problem. If you fail, this one issue will affect the rest of the preshow production process.

Among the other items to check at this point are:

- *Display product and literature.* Check and confirm availability and delivery, along with technical support if it is needed.

- *Hotel and travel reservations.* Make sure sales staff names are given to hotels and travel reservations take advantage of the lowest fares. Confirm reservations for suites and for hospitality and conference rooms.

- *Seminar speaker support.* Make sure your company speaker's talk is being written and slides, or audiovisual support, are being produced.

- *Preshow notices.*   Advertising, promotion, and direct mail programs should be ready for release on schedule.

- *News conference or press release.* Plans should be reconfirmed.

- *VIP guest programs.* They should be finalized at this point, except for some names of key customers who are invited. There will be last-minute changes in this area.

- *Visitor information.* Obtain pertinent local information from the city where the show takes place for the exhibit staff advisory package.

- *Show service orders.* Make sure they have been sent. File copies for use at the show.

Weeks 3 and 2

- *Final shipping list.* Prepare list of items to move to the show and develop a freight concentration program for delivery.

- *Exhibit staff advisory package.* Complete this and send it to everyone who will be at the show.

- *Production check.* All production should be ready before materials move to the show.

- *Preshow training programs.* This program and support materials should be finalized.

Week 1

- *Travel office.* Put together all shipping way bill numbers, exhibit setup drawings, copies of show labor orders, name and telephone number lists, sales order and lead forms, and anything else that has been developed in the planning program.

- *Personal tool kit.* Prepare one for emergency use at the show, plus basic office supplies required for on-site operations.

- *Cash and checks.* Obtain everything required for on-site payments.

- *VIP customer list.* Be sure you include this.

Preshow Operations at the Site

- *Confirm orders* for onsite labor and rentals and meet with hotel personnel on hospitality operations. Confirm arrival of all materials.

- *Execute setup* and conduct preshow training program.

During the Show

- *Conduct daily staff meetings* to mark progress and to make changes to meet goals.

- *Make arrangements for postshow* take-down and materials dispersal.

- *Reserve next year's space* on a preliminary basis.

Show: _____   *Opening date:* ____ / ____ / ____

Item status	Week 10	Week 9	Week 8	Week 7	Week 6	Week 5	Week 4	Week 3	Week 2	Week 1	Week 0

▪ _____
- Start
- Check
- Check
- Complete

▪ _____
- Start
- Check
- Check
- Complete

▪ _____
- Start
- Check
- Check
- Complete

▪ _____
- Start
- Check
- Check
- Complete

▪ _____
- Start
- Check
- Check
- Complete

▪ _____
- Start
- Check
- Check
- Complete

▪ _____
- Start
- Check
- Check
- Complete

Once this chart is complete, you may wish to copy items to your Job List for the Week sheet.

Figure 11.1. Show production time line.

After the Show

- *Manage take-down* and postshow packing operation.
- *Distribute sales leads and orders* from the show.
- *Prepare preliminary evaluation* of all aspects of the show.
- *Send thank-you letters* for exceptional performance, in and outside the company. They are important.

Work Forms Explanation

You'll find two blank forms, Figures 11.1 and 11.2, you can use to write your own time line. Figure 11.1 is filled in backwards; it is a countdown chart that will show you the entire flow of activity at a glance. You leave time between the start date of each job and the time you need to check or complete the task. Figure 11.2 is filled in second, to warn you each week about jobs to be started, checked, or completed.

There's a hidden, personal reason to use these forms. Of course, as advertised, they'll help you keep on track and in the driver's seat and convince others you are running a professional operation. Not advertised is that they'll help you define and refine your own thinking. You'll feel far more comfortable as the opening date comes closer. There really are "drop dead" decision points along the way, and you'll know when they are about to arrive.

Show: _____	*Opening date: / /*	
Week starting on Sunday, _____. There are ___ weeks to opening.		
Jobs to start		
▪ _____	Check date: /____	Complete date: /____
▪ _____	Check date: /____	Complete date: /____
▪ _____	Check date: /____	Complete date: /____
▪ _____	Check date: /____	Complete date: /____
▪ _____	Check date: /____	Complete date: /____
▪ _____	Check date: /____	Complete date: /____
Jobs to check		
▪ _____	2d check: /____	Complete date: /____
▪ _____	2d check: /____	Complete date: /____
▪ _____	2d check: /____	Complete date: /____
▪ _____	2d check: /____	Complete date: /____
▪ _____	2d check: /____	Complete date: /____
▪ _____	2d check: /____	Complete date: /____
Jobs to complete		
▪ _____	Check okay: /____	If not: /____
▪ _____	Check okay: /____	If not: /____
▪ _____	Check okay: /____	If not: /____
▪ _____	Check okay: /____	If not: /____
▪ _____	Check okay: /____	If not: /____
▪ _____	Check okay: /____	If not: /____

Figure 11.2. Job list for the week.

12
Exhibit Design: Structure and Graphics

It's a good bet that neither you nor I can draw a straight line, much less design an exhibit. Design-trained managers are rare, even in large company exhibit groups. Professional designers work for exhibit builders or with marketing communications design firms.

It's an equally good wager that most professional exhibit designers didn't start commercial art careers in this business. Many came from industrial design backgrounds. Others arrived with architectural degrees and experience. A smaller number started by designing printed-flat graphics: brochures, magazines, advertisements, and the like.

In any case, it takes partnership between you and your designer to produce an effective exhibit. This chapter's goal to help improve what you bring to that partnership.

Visual Quality Control

The president of a large and well-regarded firm specializing in printed-flat graphics design and corporate identity said, "Each brochure, ad, letterhead, bill head, postsale instruction, business card, film, exhibit, or store display is created to reach a tactical goal. But at the same time, each builds an impression of the corporate culture it represents."[1]

Symptoms of the Problem

Most would agree with that design manager's statement. However, we miss when it comes to appearance at trade shows. Sales managers and even business owners can lose sight of a need to maintain their visual quality standards when it is time to exhibit.

- Within large and ostensibly sophisticated corporations, some local managers exhibit with little more than a tablecloth and a hand-stenciled sign. These same managers toss out poorly printed brochures and won't pen in a new phone number on business cards.

- At a home or garden show you'll see retailers who take justifiable pride in the appearance of their home stores but present exhibits that look a mess. Often these are quality companies offering quality products at quality prices. They just *look* cheap when searching for new business at the show.

- If you work for a big company, you've seen managers spend extraordinary time and money developing an internal management presentation but let their own employees use old, nicked, and scratched exhibits to help prospect for new business.

- You've seen managers who will take a full hour discussing and revising the menu for a VIP customer dinner but never give a thought to how the company will look to hundreds, or even thousands, who will pass its exhibit at the same trade show.

Causes of the Problem

Lots of people don't understand how to use the medium best, its competitive nature, or how to work with exhibit designers and producers.

- Sales-trained managers think first about the customers they already have. They are less sensitive to prospecting potential at shows.

- Many forget that their booths are side by side with competitors. Instant impressions are made but seldom articulated. Shows are here today, gone tomorrow. What isn't understood is the remarkable memorability of exhibits, proven again and again by research programs conducted up to 8 weeks after an event.[2]

- Big companies face bureaucracy and out-of-sight, out-of-mind problems. The advertising department looks at ad proofs and television commercials in the office and sees them later in the media. Brochures are passed around and inspected. Direct mail advertising quality control is checked by adding in-company people to the mailing list. Exhibits can't be dealt with in this intimate a fashion. This is especially so when small exhibits are supplied to local offices. Quality control becomes an issue only every few years when the old booths fall apart completely and upper management starts to complain.

There is another malady. Often there is little understanding as to how a company *should* look when it appears on a show floor. This problem is combined with lack of knowledge about how best to take advantage of a professional exhibit designer's skills and talent.

Have you ever said, "Make our exhibit look like an office." Or like a factory, warehouse, home, or golf course? You might be right, especially if you sell office furniture, warehouse equipment, kitchens, or golf course grass. On the other hand, you might be wrong even if you do sell these things. We fall into a trap: dictating design solutions instead of thinking harder, explaining our marketing and sales problems, and letting the designer come back with an idea.

Marketing Goals and Audiences

Our part of the designer-company partnership requires us to ask ourselves some questions and provide our designers the answers.

Questions to Ask Yourself

- Is my most important goal prospecting or is it closing sales with today's customers at the booth? Can I prospect at the exhibit and close sales someplace else?

- How important is educating large numbers of show visitors, or supporting dealers by encouraging large numbers of visitors to specify a product purchased through intermediaries?

- Are the products themselves are so inherently attractive that curiosity seekers will fill the booth, leaving little room for buyers, or are they of interest only to a select audience?

- Are my shows relatively small, with a clearly defined audience, most of whom should be interested in what I sell? (For instance, I could be offering products purchased by nurses and I could exhibit at the convention of operating room nurses.) Or are my shows large, with but a part of the audience interested in my lines?

- Looking at this question from a different angle: Do I supply a specific industry with a key product? Or are my goods used in a number of industries? (Computer and communications equipment vendors are secondary suppliers to a large number of industries. On the other hand, a manufacturer of medical instruments focuses on subgroups in the medical field.) The answer to this question can mean a lot to a designer. It influences how many shows I'll be in. The designer will have to worry less about the economics of transportation and show setup if I participate in fewer shows.

- Are my products "big ticket"? Are they sold "as is" or is there a degree of customizing required to meet user needs?

- Is my company a dominant, well-known supplier? Or are we relatively unknown? Are products well known or do I have to build awareness? There are times when a designer might suggest sales point emphasis instead of highlighting company or product names.

Designer Responses to Your Answers

The essential design will reflect your answers to the questions posed above. For instance:

- If your primary goal is prospecting, the design will be open and inviting, allowing easy movement to demonstrations or displays. If the goal is closing sales, the design will tend to restrict the free flow of people. In large-space booths, some privacy areas may be provided, especially if you sell the same things to competitors.

- If your company or products attract too many curiosity seekers, the design solution will inhibit traffic to some extent. For example:

  A raised floor requires visitors to make a more conscious commitment to see the company's lines. Prospects must step up and in to see and learn.

  Inward-facing displays accomplish the same objective. You'll see the technique in a large-space booth rimmed with a back wall, with the exhibits inside, facing out against it. Small linear booth designs aimed at the same goal will place products on the aisle, but facing in.

  Some large exhibits are designed with a reception or sign-in area where booth visitors stop and register. Products or services may be visible but not accessible until after the visitor goes through the process. At a small linear booth, the products may be displayed along the back wall with a desk, half counter, or low fence restricting the free flow of people. See Figure 12.1.

- Most of us have to attract as many people as we can, thus accepting more curiosity seekers. Our booths will not include raised floors, inward-facing displays, or physical barriers. In addition, there are other design solutions aimed at building traffic:

  Carpet color and thickness can be subtle impression makers. A thick, inviting—perhaps expensive—carpet encourages booth traffic. It's even more effective if its color is in the same family as the aisle carpet. There is a psychological reluctance to cross the "carpet line" from aisle to booth.

  Outward-facing display, on the aisle or even at the center of an open booth space, invites visitors. Large exhibits will concentrate displays and demonstration stations around one or several island display stations, each easily accessible to an aisle. You'll see smaller linear booths with demonstrations or displays close to the aisle and facing out. Sometimes displays flow out from the back-of-the-booth wall to the aisle on a counter with a T at the end. See Figure 12.2.

  Colors and materials are often used by designers to solve problems. Some are warm, inviting. Mellow earth tones and softer tones of cool-side colors are most inviting, along with wood and carpet. Others are cold. Crisp blacks, silver, and strong blues fit into that group, along with harsh tones of warm-side colors. Metal and Plexiglas can be cold.

An exhibit makes its own statement. It can upstage the products it's helping to sell. One 25-year professional exhibit designer said, "We can create beautiful exhibits, so beautiful in fact they sometimes are better at selling themselves than selling products. After doing its job of attracting audience, an exhibit should almost disappear. Less is better. We've got to emphasize a combination of the products and salespeople who coexist in the space with customers. Evaluate design with product and people included, never alone."[3]

Product Influence on Design

There are four essential product situations.

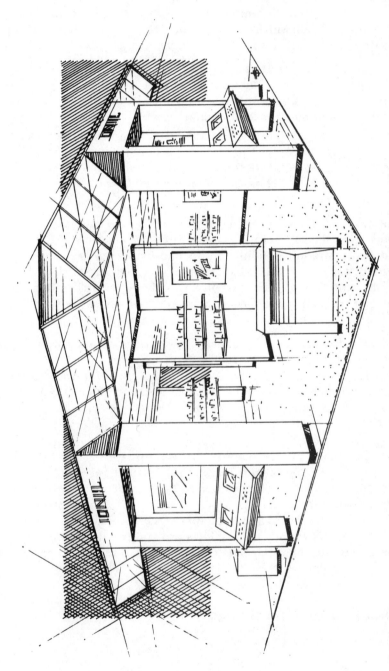

Figure 12.1. Designs with solid walls on the aisle edge discourage curiosity seekers. In this case, the displays facing out provide some information that allows visitors to make a decision: Visit inside or not. *(Design and sketch courtesy Lynch Industries, Pennsauken, New Jersey.)*

Figure 12.2. In contrast to designs that use more enclosed space, exhibits with display open to the aisle encourage more people to stop. However, these may increase the number of contacts with those who are not potential buyers. *(Design and sketch courtesy Exhibitree, Irvine, California.)*

Small Products to Be Displayed

If you are selling small things, either one or a number of different lines, vertical display is effective. Massing products on a wall, on a series of shelves, is a retail technique. Even if you sell to other businesses, the environment approaches that of retail selling.

The exhibit structure should be an attractive backdrop for products on a wall, perhaps from floor to the booth top. Counters and signs are less important. Highlight lighting can be very important.

Retailers, however, can't really duplicate concepts used in stores. For instance, glass-top counters don't travel well, take lots of space, and can force customers to stand away instead of moving in close. See Figure 12.3.

Small and Medium-Sized Products to be Demonstrated

The design emphasis lowers from the back wall to counters upon which demonstration units are placed. Or it is shifted to free-standing pedestals used for the same purpose. Just as with small product display, there is little space for large-sized graphic signs.

Demonstration Work Stations.   The industry is changing the height of counters and pedestals for product demonstrations. You've seen countertops that are 46 and 48 inches high; a few go up to 52 inches above the carpet. This puts the average small or medium-sized product at chest height. It accomplishes three goals:

- Salespeople and customers deal with the product without bending, a more comfortable posture for everyone.

- The demonstration experience becomes more intimate. Prospects get the feeling for operating the device as though they were sitting.

- Over-the-shoulder viewing is improved. Others can see what's going on without peering around backs. (There's a negative in this. A degree of prospect-salesperson privacy is sacrificed.)

IBM may not have pioneered the high-counter concept but uses it enough. One of its exhibits placed 48-inch-high pedestals on a 4-inch-high platform. The prospect experiencing the demonstration stood on the platform edge, 18 inches wide, gaining separation from others. But the crowd in back could still see what was going on.

When high counters and people are involved, there is less vertical space for signs. If booth height is 8 feet, an easy 6 are filled by people, product, and counter. See Figure 12.4.

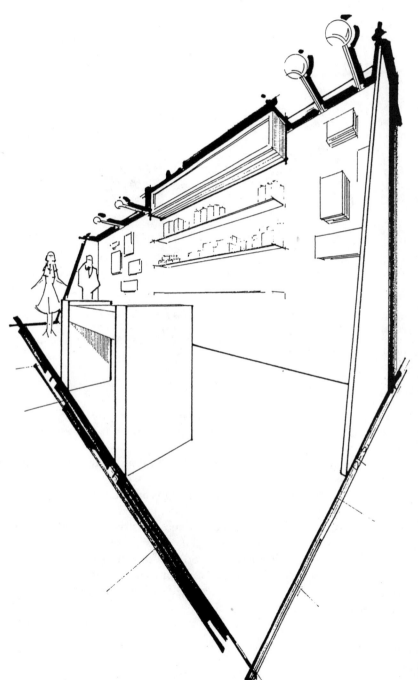

Figure 12.3. Exhibits designed to merchandise products for resale often serve a double role. In addition to presenting the products themselves, they hint at how retail sellers can display them in stores. *(Design and sketch courtesy Kitzing, Inc., Chicago.)*

Figure 12.4.   Lifting the height of a counter decreases space for graphics but makes product demonstration more "user friendly" and allows a second row of visitors to observe a demonstration while it is taking place.   *(Design and sketch courtesy of Bluepeter, San Francisco.)*

Services to Be Offered

If you sell a service, it can't be displayed or demonstrated like a product. You can't see it, touch it, or try it. You have to sell a concept, a promise.

Financial, moving, and consulting service companies are often faced with this problem.

Shelves and counters diminish. Graphic signs and the environment as a whole become more important. From a selling viewpoint, you have to be able to speak from graphics or audiovisual materials that summarize benefits or illustrate applications. The flat, vertical area for signs, video screens, and the like becomes vital. So do new techniques such as interactive videodisc-based "shows" involving the prospect, creative presentations, or other methods designed to inform and sway the thinking of visitors. See Figure 12.5.

Large Product Display

Helicopters, steamrollers, large machine tools, and rooftop air-conditioning units for commercial buildings can sometimes be displayed but cannot be demonstrated. The design problem is similar to selling services requiring greater emphasis on backdrop or presentation, less on shelves and counters. Even when you can demonstrate, product size becomes the focal point of design. You'll see very simple backdrops, perhaps with the supported of large photographs or artwork, often from floor to booth top. See Figure 12.6.

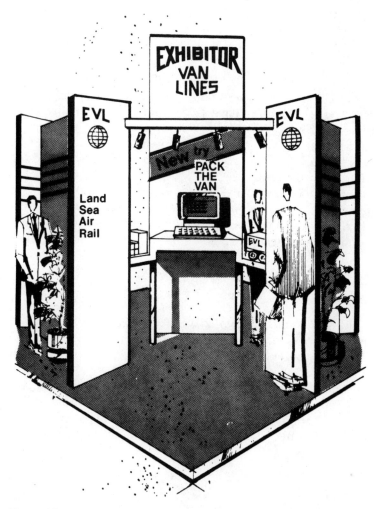

Figure 12.5.   If you offer services or products that cannot be demonstrated, graphics are important. Increasingly, interactive video "shows" that involve visitors are used to teach and sell in this situation.   *(Design and sketch courtesy Color and Design Exhibits, Seattle.)*

Show Environments, Schedules, and Exhibit Lighting

Can you tell your designer something about the places in which most of your shows are staged? Do you always find yourself in large convention-halls, or do many of your events take place in hotels or resorts? Do you participate in large national conventions that take several days to set up, or are you in smaller shows where you're given limited time for booth assembly? How often will your booth be used? Will it have to go on the road, show to show, before returning home for refurbishing? Answers to these questions will have an effect on design.

Snow Environments

If most of your shows take place in large civic arenas, your design will have flexibility. The buildings have large doors and generally good freight-handling facilities. Heavy crates will be used to protect materials. The designer will be able to concentrate on the potential for height extenders, either tower units rising above the 8-foot standard or elements hung from the ceiling.

Do lots of your shows take place in hotel facilities not built for trade shows? The exhibit will be designed so it can be packed in crates small enough to fit through smaller doors and on freight elevators. You won't worry very much about height extenders. Most of the rooms have low ceilings.

Schedules

If you will always be setting up in short time frames, the design will require many parts to be preassembled, requiring less time for setup on the floor. (You'll get larger and heavier crates, increasing transportation and drayage bills. Labor cost for setup will go down.)

How often will you use the exhibit? How often can it be brought into the shop for repair? This will influence the selection of materials, construction, and crating. If, for instance, your booth will be used locally 4 times a year, it does not have to be as ruggedly built as one going on the road for 6 months.

Exhibit Lighting

We mentioned carpet quality and color as a subtle yet important design factor. Lighting is not subtle. A high-quality lighting design is vital.

Figure 12.6. Large-scale backdrop graphics are used to create a setting for large products. In this case, a mirror surface is used. The graphic becomes the back and top of the machine itself. *(Design and sketch courtesy of Heritage Communications, Dallas.)*

Designers know that, but we don't. Their decisions combine our product display need with show environments.

High-ceilinged civic arenas, new or old, block or glass-walled, tend to be large, airy, and filled with relatively bright, flat light. Ceiling and wall colors are plain. Hotel ballrooms and meeting rooms are smaller anddarker. You'll often see brocade wallpaper and ornate carpet. Lighting is less intense. The show halls in some old hotels are converted garages. Lighting may be close, flat, and harsh.

Product display plays a part. For instance, a spotlight aimed down at a product highlights it. A fluorescent fixture above a sign provides "wash" light over the entire graphic. Hidden sidelights, as well as top-mounted spotlights, are effective in displaying products on shelves. Back-lighted transparency signs are a point of emphasis.

Our role, except for watching the budget, is to set priorities. What should be emphasized? The signs? The products? Which signs and which products? You can't ask the design to emphasize everything. Peaks and valleys of visual interest must be clear.

You'll know what you like when you see it. You'll know whether or not its overall look is appropriate for your company. But there's lots more to an exhibit design than that. We've focused on economic and product implications so that you can help your designer create a booth with the "look"; it must also be one that makes good economic sense.

Manager's Question List

Here's a summary of important questions to ask yourself before talking to your designer:

- How many shows a year will use the exhibit?

- Are they relatively close by, or is lots of shipping involved?

- Will the entire exhibit be used every time?

- Will there be lots of modification, show to show?

- Do all the shows take place in one part of the year, or is there time between shows for modifications or repair?

- Will display and demonstration products be shipped with the exhibit or provided from other locations?

- How important are exhibits to the company? Are we talking about one or two shows a year where buyers make big commitments, or are exhibit sales a secondary distribution method?

- What are the competitors doing? How do they exhibit?

Manufactured Exhibits

We touched on this in Part One, "The Quick Fix," but the development of these systems has been so influential in the exhibit medium that the subject demands more coverage.

Quite often, manufactured exhibits are selected by big companies for use by their local offices. In addition, some very large custom exhibits have been created using the connectors, extrusions, or panels manufactured for these systems. First-time exhibitors like manufactured exhibits for economic reasons and because they want to learn more about needs before investing in a custom design.

For those who did not read Chapter 3, let's get terms straight. Most often, manufactured exhibit systems are referred to as *portable* or *modular* by their makers. Some are lighter weight than most custom exhibits. Thus, portable. Other units can be used in multiples for spaces larger than the 10-foot standard. Thus, modular. Some of the latter are designed so that rooms and even ceilings can be erected.

The systems compete on the basis of price, portability, durability, lighting, ease of setup, flexibility, and the way in which you can apply graphics. Most are offered with counters or shelves related to a back-wall system. Increasingly, popular off-the-shelf systems are designed with connectors so you don't need tools to set them up. In virtually all cases, reusable containers are provided.

Costs and Sources of Manufactured Exhibit

As we said in Chapter 3, costs range from $1000 for a simple back wall up to as much as $5000 for a 10-foot booth with an extensive shelf or counter system. Some offer standard graphics as part of the package, but for the most part graphics are a separate purchase.

You probably have a custom exhibit builder with whom to talk. Most of them carry lines of manufactured exhibits or can aim you in the right direction. If not, take a look at the first section of Chapter 3, which tells you where to look in *Yellow Pages* and gives information about other directories and catalogs.

If you are serious about investing in one of these systems, perhaps for your local offices, you'll ask yourself many of the same questions you'd ask before talking with your designer about a custom booth. There are, however, some differences. Figure 12.7 is a guide to selecting the most appropriate manufactured exhibit system. When you start shopping, you should have a clear direction in mind. Otherwise, you'll be confused. Don't forget that manufactured system sales representatives don't know your business as well as your custom designer. They won't know the questions to ask you.

Graphic Signs

Chapter 3 contains graphic guidelines for first-time exhibitors. You may want to take a look, to refresh your thinking. Even those of us who have

Define thinking before shopping. You'll be able to balance the strengths and weaknesses of each brand by knowing what you need.

- Basic design considerations. Three situations:
  1. Small products display
  2. Small or medium-size product demonstration
  3. Services selling or floor-standing product backdrop

  Keep your situation — what you are selling — in mind. The booths offered will tend to emphasize one of these three capabilities.

- Ease of setup requirement. Two situations:
  1. Inexperienced people on an as-needed basis
  2. Experienced people consistently

  The relative ease with which people can learn to set up the unit is the issue. Some units easy to erect if you understand the "trick" in working with their connectors or panels. Can this be taught easily?

- Transportation considerations. Two situations:
  1. Commercial transport and handling
  2. Personal car or station wagon transport

  Booths and shipping cases trade weight for durability. Ease of handling is at issue. All are relatively lightweight. If commercial transport is used, more durability is required.

- The product display relationship. Two situations:
  1. Lightweight and not bulky products or services
  2. Bulky or heavy display products

  If your products are heavy or bulky, a portable exhibit can be heavier, more difficult to handle. Commercial services, transport, and setup will be needed anyway.

- Product line change. Two situations:
  1. Products will change by show
  2. Product remains consistent

  How easy is it to change graphics? If the graphics don't change, a unit allowing for easy art switching is not as important.

- Multiunit and alternate use considerations. Three situations:
  1. Exhibit always used as a stand-alone
  2. Two or more units used together at shows
  3. Exhibit has alternate uses — speaker support, lobby display as well

Figure 12.7. Manufactured exhibit system selection guide.

To what extent does the system have to be modular, building up from one? Closing area? Roof element? Speaker backdrop?

- Fundamental construction quality. Two situations:
  1. Used by few people on a consistent basis
  2. Used by a larger number infrequently

Basic construction quality must be better if lots of different people will be using the unit. If but a few are involved, they can be taught how to handle a more delicate or complex booth.

- Cost considerations. Four trade-offs:
  1. In freight and setup
  2. In graphics
  3. In flexibility
  4. In refurbishing

Prices, in themselves, are less important than the trade-offs.

Remember, custom designers automatically interpret these needs for you. Now you must do so yourself. Each system has strengths and weaknesses.

Figure 12.7. *(Continued.)*

been planning exhibits for years occasionally surrender to internalpressures to say more and more. Many people we work with don't understand that audiences will then register less and less.

Have you been to Las Vegas, Nevada? Casinos and hotels have made the Strip and downtown's Glitter Gulch into light shows, each a plethora of signs that flash and pop and seem to fight each other in an apparent attempt to attract our attention. The signs have become an attraction for the community as a whole. Individual messages don't register as much as a collective impression.

An arena floor can become a visual pollution center with its own plethora of signs that flash and pop and seem to fight each other. Our job is to register an individual message. For our own good, we should listen to our exhibit designers and keep things simple.

The graphic guidelines of Chapter 3 can be summarized. What we want to say must be turned into something our audience wants to see. You want to sell air conditioners? The buyer may want to save energy. You want to promote an ethical drug? The doctor wants to cure a patient. We have to think about our audience instead of ourselves.

Digital Equipment Corporation has followed a good practice. Large signs seen from a distance are quite simple, aimed at providing emphasis and attracting an audience. Small signs, with more text, are placed on counters next to equipment being demonstrated.

Height, Space, and Show Rules

If your exhibit will be used in a number of different situations, its concept will be based on standard space sizes and show rules. Its height will be limited to 8 feet along the back wall. The 8-foot-high part won't extend out more than 3 feet, with lower side walls from there on. See Figure 3.1.

If you are working on a large unit for an individual show, give your designer a copy of the show's rules. You may not be limited to 8 feet. There is probably a formula, however, for how much structure can be placed in different space areas. There will be a limit on altitude or on what can be hung from the rafters. Deviations from rules must be approved by show management in advance. A blueprint must be sent to the organizer.

There are other rules that affect exhibit design and fabrication, essentially for safety. Electrical codes must be understood, the same goes for fire prevention regulations. These both involve restrictions on materials, cables, and fixture selection.

Creating a Sense of Unity

An exhibit is a series of display or demonstration stations linked together. Writing stands, seating facilities, and stage areas can be involved. The design will provide space for people. In Chapter 6 we pointed out that, on the average, a designer allocates 65 square feet for each demonstration and selling area, including room for the exhibit and people.

Designers use a number of methods to create a sense of unity throughout the exhibit while at the same time creating natural paths for people to follow from one selling station to another.

- Colors, fabrics, carpet, and signs will provide a family feeling.
- Linear booths are often pulled together with a "header" running all the way across the front of the back wall.

Competition Impact on Design

We worry. We always seem to want to be higher, brighter, and more visible than our competitors. We want to be found. There is less to fear than we suppose. Attendees trace a pathway through the hall and walk by virtually every booth.[2] The larger the audience, the larger the number of booths, the greater is our inclination to spend more for tower units or other altitude extenders to make a competitive presence. How much we spend depends on the show.

- *Few exhibitors, small audience.*   No special attention-gaining effort is needed. Most visitors will see all the exhibits.

- *Large show and audience.*   Something special may be needed; however, what's done depends who needs to see you. If the *majority of the audience is your target,* it is probably cost-effective to erect a large booth with towers or hung signs. If the *minority of the audience is your target,* it may be more cost-effective to forego towers and the like, spending more direct mail or promotion dollars to tell your targets where you are.

Outside Source Choices

Most of us already know sources. In case you don't, here are some options to consider.

Full-Service Exhibit House

This term implies a business willing to provide a full creative and implementation services for exhibits. Most full-service houses are members of a trade group called the Exhibit Designers and Producers Association. The services they traditionally provide include:

- Exhibit and graphic sign design
- Physical production of exhibits and graphic signs
- Development of booth space layout and exhibit setup drawings
- Exhibit storage and freight management service
- Supervision of exhibit setup and tear-down at shows
- Crate design and manufacture
- Exhibit repair and refurbishing

Most often the term *full service* has been limited to involvement with physical presence. Experience and in-plant investment have aimed these firms toward work that keeps production facilities humming. Now, however, exhibit houses are increasingly starting to offer additional services to clients. These include:

- Exhibit marketing plan development
- Booth sales training
- Hospitality and special event management
- Live or audiovisual show production and management
- Show literature development and production
- Show-related direct mail or promotion management
- Research management
- Sales lead distribution and tracking

We obtain many of these services today from specialist firms. For the most part, full-service exhibit houses are not planning to compete; they simply package, using many of the same sources. The concept is based on advertising agency practice. The exhibit company will manage creative development and the overall process, enlisting outside sources as needed. Like ad agencies, their compensation is based on commissions and fees.

Independent Exhibit Designer

You can split the design function away from the rest and work through a design firm not related to a single production facility. This is often done because, right or wrong, there's a feeling that exhibit house designers unconsciously tailor thinking to the ideas that can be produced easily by the people and equipment in their shops. Supposedly, this vested interest restricts imagination. Conventional wisdom also has it that an independent designer doesn't understand reality, that his or her exhibits will be expensive to produce, and that there is no shop-designer relationship to produce effective "touches" or make subtle changes during construction.

There is probably some truth in both notions. Ask yourself, "What am I good at?" If you are strong on the practical side, you can afford to work with a designer who may not have a shop relationship. If you have a clear creative viewpoint, you can vote the other way. There's no perfect solution. Just find the right person to work with. Good communication and mutual trust are the most important factors.

Advertising Agency

Advertising agencies, especially those with clients selling to other businesses, are becoming more interested in exhibits. From a selfish viewpoint, they see potential for new billing. From a marketing communications viewpoint, they see a chance to improve clients' sales by blending media into a cohesive, related flow of communication.

Most agencies don't have in-depth experience with the medium, especially on the creative side. You might talk to your agency, however, about working more closely with your exhibit house, especially in context with show selection and promotion. An exhibit should not be wood, metal, and plastic standing alone on an arena floor. Instead, it should be the centerpiece of a marketing event.

Regardless of your design source, an exhibit will be more effective if you do personal homework first. Work really hard at developing crystal clear marketing direction. Don't generalize when you communicate it. Do not abdicate the responsibility of aiming designers at the target.

13

Promotional Activity Before and During the Show

Conventions bring attendees together to learn from each other, to renew old acquaintance and make new friends, to shop for jobs and have professional accomplishments recognized. In addition, conferees want to see what's new on the trade show floor. Many have specific buying missions. And though conventions are far more serious affairs than they used to be, people still want to have some fun too.

All the action takes place in just a few days, often away from home in unfamiliar territory. Time is squeezed in every way. Even learning how to do the ordinary things in life can take extra effort, from ordering a cup of coffee to finding the arena shuttle bus.

It isn't just attendees. Exhibitors have the same problems. And we face two kinds of competition. First, our competitors at the show. Second, less obvious, is competition for conferee time. They have more to do than can be done, even with candles burning briskly at both ends.

This is where promotion comes in. It helps both you and your prospects to allocate time. Attendees want to figure out where to focus their trade show hours. Many even make lists of exhibits to visit, along with seminars to attend before they leave home. And you don't want to waste time talking to the wrong people. Good promotions help the right buyers and sellers find each other.

Show Management and Exhibitor Roles

In Chapter 5 we talked about how to set goals for the number of people to reach. It's rarely the whole audience. This same is true for cost-effective audience-attracting promotions.

Role of the Show's Management

Show organizer responsibilities include promoting the event. Direct mail and advertising programs, covering both seminars and exhibits, are the focus of most of them. Sometimes ticket promotions are involved. The aim point is fairly broad. Organizers try to build total audience. See a crowded arena, and you'll find a happy show manager.

Role of the Exhibitor

Our own programs help to build that overall audience, but they are focused on the part of it we're looking for. We all say we're more interested in quality than quantity. The perspective is personal. Each company looks to build audience among those who are its best prospects.

Small-Show Promotions

Our listings in official show programs are a form of promotional activity. The programs are directional, like the *Yellow Pages*. Listings tell visitors who is showing what. There are some conventions where that is all you need.

At small shows, with few visitors and booths, there's time for everyone to see everything. Most conferees will visit the show floor and see most of the exhibits. A program listing and informative graphic signs at your booth should be enough.

There can be exceptions. If you are a dominant supplier in the meeting sponsor's industry, you may advertise simply because you feel it's expected. If your company is new to the business, you should promote *before* the event to develop greater awareness, regardless of the show's size.

Larger Shows

Promotional needs multiply as the events get larger, both in numbers of exhibitors and in audience size. The quality of a promotional effort is especially important for smaller and less well-known companies. If that's you, your promotion should be aimed at a target group and should be very well planned.

Literature and Premiums or Incentives

Lots of us automatically think about passing out literature at shows as part of our promotional program. Many of us like giving trinkets or prizes to visitors in hopes of creating a lingering memory.

Literature

Unread sales literature litters office credenzas, gathering dust until it finds its way into the "round file." Some show visitors justify trips by returning home with brochure-packed shopping bags.

How often have you heard, "We're not interested now, but I'll take your folder for future reference"? Have you heard your own salespeople say, "Take one of our brochures, and if you have any questions I'll be here for the week"? Both visitor and salesperson know the brochure won't be read. The exercise is an easy way out of an unproductive sales contact.

Sales literature is expensive. It's far more effective—cost-effective and otherwise—to take the name of someone interested and mail a copy after the meeting is over. If a visitor is serious enough to give you a name and address, there's greater potential for the folder or booklet to be read.

Do stock a small supply of literature at the booth. The quantity should be between 5 and 10 percent of the total exhibit contacts you estimate. See Chapter 5. Save it for serious customers, perhaps people who have given you a sales lead for follow-up after the show.

If the show is a large one, and awareness development is a major goal, you may want to distribute large quantities of literature even though readership may be low. If so, develop a special piece that is relatively inexpensive to produce.

Premiums or Incentives

Premiums, incentives, advertising specialties, or giveaways are sometimes called "trash and trinkets" by exhibit managers. We buy them nonetheless and we get them nonetheless. However, it's a good bet that most of the knickknacks you've garnered can be found in the upper right-hand drawer of your desk. Or perhaps in the pencil tray. Some people build collections of unused corporate coffee mugs.

There is great waste. It is not the fault of the broker or manufacturer. The fault is ours. We create our own trash-and-trinket problem. Often these items are purchased as afterthoughts. Clearly defined goals must be developed. If a memory is to be created, the item should reinforce your sales message.

Illustrations of Promotions Aimed at Different Goals

If goals are clear, you can organize a promotion to reach them.

Total Audience Promotion Ideas

Advertising in trade magazines. Industry magazines produce "show specials." They tend to be extra thick, with more ad clutter than normal. In addition to mailings, copies are distributed at the show. We don't think they are read until it's over. Think of conferee time squeeze. An ad in this issue alone is not the answer. A schedule of advertising, appearing in the months before, produces when it counts—at the convention. A major Trade Show Bureau study shows booth traffic is increased roughly 40 percent for each 4 pages of advertising run in the months before the show.[1]

Advertising in city show guides. A number of publishers prepare specialized visitor guides for distribution at large trade shows.[2] Readership probably depends on where the convention is taking place. A guide on where to go and what to do in Chicago or New York is likely to be read more than one on Las Vegas, Nevada. It's a small city and most Las Vegas visitors probably feel they have a pretty fair idea of where they're going in the evenings.

Mass media. Television and billboard advertising are often used to aim messages at the total audience. Major exhibitors at large shows purchase commercial time on VHF stations, especially during local breaks in network morning shows that prospective attendees watch at home. Outdoor billboard advertising along routes between hotels and convention center is often a choice.

On-location media.   Much more tactical promotion can be used to reach an entire audience at a smaller show. For instance:

If most visitors stay at one or two hotels, arrangements can be made to have hotel delivery of promotional materials to each room. One company made advance arrangements with the hotel and a newspaper distributor. Copies of *The Wall Street Journal*, with a letter from the exhibitor attached, were delivered to each room.

Another company arranged to have booth invitations placed in hotel mailboxes and message-waiting lamps turned on in all rooms.

A hotel's own TV channel, or one created especially to provide visitor information, may be a good advertising outlet. At some large conventions, special programming for convention attendees is produced on hotel channels.

Some exhibitors have used balloons flying above parking lots near the convention hall to remind visitors to visit their booths. Some companies hire professional hosts and hostesses to stand near the hall entrance or walk the aisles handing out maps to tell visitors where they are.

A number of organizers publish "Show Daily" newspapers that offer room for good, tactical advertising aimed at everyone.

Selected Audience Promotion Ideas

Most of us want to reach out just to part of the audience. Selective promotion is more cost-effective. It costs more per person reached, but the investment is less. Otherwise, you pay for waste circulation. In one way or another, direct mail is the common solution.

- Most associations or conference managers will make all or part of an attendee list available to exhibitors for this purpose. It's usually the list from the last year. In addition, exhibitors use commercially available lists. This is especially helpful if you want to reach a group the show's list doesn't break out.

- It's obvious that you should contact your own customers. What's surprising is that it's not done all the time, especially in large companies. Salespeople working at the show will contact their own customers, but others may not. The program should cover everyone.

- Invitations can include an incentive. A mailing can enclose one cuff link or one earring. Readers are told the other awaits them at the booth. The program can be used to reach other goals. For instance, customers can be encouraged to make advance appointments for times when the hall is not crowded. They can be invited to special briefings or hospitality suites.

- Lots of us ignore last year's leads from the show. Even if no sale was made, the prospect may be better than ever. There is another group that should be considered, depending on the situation. If you have a sales office in the city where the convention takes place, local promotion generates lots of interest.

Promotion Timing. Don't implement your program too soon; 2 to 3 weeks in front should suffice. Most people who have been considering attending an out-of-town show will have made up their minds by then. They are planning their time at the convention. (Your invitation may sway a fence sitter.) An in-town show requires less advance planning by visitors. Your invitations should role out even closer to the show date.

Secondary Market Promotions

Here is a special situation. You sell your products to several industries. One is holding its convention, and you are exhibiting. It is sometimes possible to arrange for VIP customers from the *other* industries to visit your exhibit out of hours, in the early evening or before the show opens in the morning. Show management may have to charge you extra to cover extra security or electrical expense. However, it can be worth it. The big investment has already been made. All you are doing is trying to make your exhibit work harder for you.

Often you can make the same kind of arrangement to hold a product introduction press conference right at your booth. You'll save dollars by avoiding duplicate setup, and the scene is unusual.

Audience Screening

Your company is new in the business. You don't have a large number of customer or prospect names from which to build. The content of your promotion can help prescreen those who should come to the booth. Aim at the total audience, but provide special incentive for potential prospects. Your invitation can include a drawing for an expensive prize with, however, a questionnaire to be filled in by the prospect as the drawing entry. You'll build an information base of potential customers.

Premium Planning

We've said advertising specialties or giveaways should be selected with care if memorability goals are to be reached. Two or even three levels of gifts can be used as a group. For instance, if your sales theme is the "cutting edge," a small pocket or purse knife can be a broadly distributed gift. A set of steak knives becomes the prize in a drawing, and VIP customers are given a set of quality kitchen knives. If your products are positioned as money savers, piggy banks and a money clip make the point.

Other devices serve in different roles. A shopping bag won't create a long-lived memory. It can, however, be a walking advertisement on the show floor. If traffic building is a goal, the bag makes sense.

If public relations is your goal, provide a seating area. Serve ice-cream cones. On a summer afternoon, the lines will be long.

Trade Show Artwork and Tickets

Large trade show organizers advertise their shows using themes and advertising "logos." Show management will provide reproduction quality prints of the logo or theme art for you to use in your own promotion.

A direct mail piece arriving 2 weeks before the event—with the show art on its envelope—will attract those planning to attend. It's more likely the envelope will be opened and the material read.

Promoters frequently provide us with complimentary show tickets. All too often companies distribute them to interested employees. We fail to take advantage of the opportunity to build traffic among our prospects. Either way, the show manager increases traffic. Our job is to make sure the traffic offers sales potential instead of simply creating employee clutter at our booths.

Live and Audiovisual Shows and Professional Demonstration

You can do a lot more than product display and demonstration at your booth. Professionally produced shows can help you educate large numbers of visitors, or attract smaller groups of potential buyers.

Show Goals and Staging

The way a show is staged depends on your goals.

- If your goal is finding prospects to talk to, stage it in a small area so it attracts small audiences for each presentation. Don't attract more people at once than you can talk to after it is over. The stage can be as small as 5 feet wide and 2 feet deep, elevated a few inches above the floor. As little as 40 square feet of viewing area is needed, a narrow patch near the aisle.

- If your goal is educating a large chunk of the audience, everything gets bigger, stage size, height, and viewing area. You'll attract more people, and most will drift away without meeting you after it is over. The viewing area should be near an aisle to allow easy movement in and out. Don't provide a seating area. Tired feet substitute for product interest.

- If you need to communicate a message in depth to serious prospects, another staging technique is used. The show is positioned away from the aisle in a larger booth space. Seating is provided. The show is longer.

Creative Development

The nature of the show itself should relate to both the audience and your own goals.

- A live show aimed at prospects can be a serious, professionally delivered talk supported by graphic symbols or signs placed on a Velcro-covered wall. Video or slide shows can also serve as visual aids. Many of us have scripted shows with magic, illusions tailored to sales points. Song and dance can be used, combining live entertainers with recorded music. Props of all types are employed. Often the most effective is the product itself.

- Professionally trained actors and actresses deliver excellent and entertaining presentations paving the way for salespeople. Don't use company employees in these roles. Professionals do the job better and more inexpensively. (The actor's fee may come from your budget, an employee's from another, but the *company's* cost will be higher if they are used and results will probably be less.)

- Be wary of pure audiovisual shows. The exhibit medium itself is "live." Halls are noisy and lighting is intense. Save sophisticated audiovisual productions for enclosed rooms in which lighting, sound, and the audience can be controlled.

Your exhibit house can put you in touch with companies that have experience in producing shows effective in the trade show environment. Or look in the where-to-buy-it guides mentioned in this book.

Trade Show Rules

As your show is produced, pay attention to show rules. They can impact on the creative process and production cost. For instance, sound amplification is often limited to what can be heard at the booth's edge. A show that is too loud interferes with exhibit neighbors and may be stopped. (The same concern emerges if noisy machinery is demonstrated.) Your booth and staging design may have to adjust because of these limitations.

Union work rules in the facility can impact on costs. For instance, there is often a limitation on the number of slide projectors that can be utilized before a local union projectionist must be hired.

Interactive Presentations

Audience involvement can play a part in any show. However, we're now starting to see audience-attracting, sales-education shows that involve visitors with computers instead of with other people.

Interactive videodisc technology is leading the way. Visitors touch buttons, or a video screen, and take themselves through a presentation. The approach has already "arrived" in some industries, including medical conventions. Properly produced, the shows can be quite involving and memorable. However, they can take longer to create and are sometimes difficult to adjust, convention to convention.

Secondary Uses of Audiovisual Materials

We've said audiovisual shows should be saved for enclosed rooms. However, a video tape of company TV commercials, or a simple series of slides cycling on a screen, can help attract attention from the aisle. Use the techniques as backdrop for other activity, not to deliver key sales messages by themselves. Be very careful with back-lighted slide shows. Images wash out in intense light; and the larger the screen, the greater the washout.

Figure 13.1. A marketing event can be created right at an exhibit. Visitors made repeated visits to check progress on building a sand castle that related to one of the products being offered by the company. *(Concept and photograph courtesy Giltspur Exhibits, Boston.)*

Professional Product Demonstration Team

Large or complex products can be demonstrated by a team. A professional actor or actress delivers an entertaining but formal presentation with the help of a technical person from the company. A salesperson is part of the team, answering questions and trying to close the sale after demonstration has been completed.

We place live or audiovisual shows in our chapter on promotional work because so many people think of an exhibit as static, a stage for products and salespeople. That stage can be much more.

For instance, McGraw-Hill Book Company used a new book about castles to create a marketing event at a recent American Booksellers Association meeting. At its exhibit, two professional sandcastle builders created one during the course of the trade show. Book dealers made repeated visits to the booth throughout the convention to check construction progress—and to be sold more McGraw-Hill books.

William Mee, president of the Trade Show Bureau, said, "Exhibits are not metal, plastic, wood, and carpet. They are marketing events, end to end." Promotions and presentations are among the elements that elevate an exhibit to the level of a marketing event.

14
Hospitality Management

Some of us are unconscious incompetents as event or hospitality managers. We don't know we don't know.

A second, higher stage of knowledge is that of being consciously incompetent. We know there is something to learn. A third level is being consciously competent. We know and can communicate knowledge. These two levels are where we fit in exhibit management. Exhibit mysteries are at least recognized as mysteries.[1]

There is a far greater chance for us to be unconscious incompetents in hospitality or events management. Everyone has given parties. That's what hospitality is all about, isn't it?

Not quite. The subject deserves a book of its own. If 20 people who earn $60,000 a year gather for any business reason, it is costing $1200 an hour just for them to be there. That's an expensive party. Even a superficial exploration will help us to improve our performance in the kind of hospitality activities that involve us most of the time.[2]

Exhibit Manager Involvements

For the most part, we get involved in one of the following ways:

- Providing VIP food and beverage services, transportation, and entertainment tickets

- Creating special events such as a private party or dinner for company dealers during a convention

• Furnishing the environment for news conferences, seminars, or sales
  meetings conducted in concert with a convention

Hospitality Goals and Measurement

Early in this book, we broke exhibit goals into four clusters. One covered
current customers or VIP operations, another related to enhancing
image. Hospitality activities are often used to help reach these goals.

Our underlying theme is that quantified goal setting and results
measurement improve planning and performance, helping us add the
extra special something that makes things work. Hospitality management is no exception. There are two ways in which goals can be set and
accomplishments measured with the help of numbers.

Cost Measurement

This is the cost-per-contact method—comparing the number of guests to
dollars spent. The range can be quite broad, depending on goals, the
number of guests, and the program. For instance, if you have to
entertain a large number of people, a cost of $15 or $20 per contact can
be a reasonable cost-management goal. If, on the other hand, the
underlying objective requires giving special treatment to a few key
customers, $100 or even $300 per contact can be appropriate.

Results Measurement

This is the cost-per-result method—comparing what was accomplished
to dollars spent. For instance, if the goal for a hospitality suite is closing
orders, how many orders and what dollar volume? You compare
revenue to cost in the same way we establish an expense-to-revenue ratio
for exhibits. See Chapter 10.

The kind of quality evaluation we hear now is little more than opinion:
"The food was terrific. . . . Everybody loved it. . . . The PR spin-off was
great!" It's rare to hear, "We signed 12 new dealers." Or, from a
customer, "I learned a lot." The kind of results measure we need makes
us identify how many orders were signed, asks us to specify what kind
and how much PR spin-off.

Our Need to Count

This is the hard part. At the same time as our jobs force us to move on
to the next project, we've got to find time to learn what happened as a

result of the last one. We have to build an information base to draw on. Bosses won't ask for it. They are happy as things stand. Do it anyway. There are two reasons:

- Setting number goals beforehand will change at least part of the program. The process stimulates thought. You may not save money, but you can amplify impact.

- With experience gained from event to event, you'll start comparing. If accomplishments for one don't match another, you'll ask yourself why. Future events will get better. You'll never find yourself in the position of claiming 10 years of experience but really having only 1, repeated 9 times.

Even if you are limited to cost-per-contact measurement, you can learn. Why did it cost $20 a head at one hospitality suite and $40 at another? What was different and was it worth it? The answers are not always obvious.9

Hospitality Suite–Special Event Difference

We need to define terms. We aim at making hospitality suite operations special, memorable. However, they are not "special events" by definition. A hospitality suite operation dovetails with an exhibit on the trade show floor. A special event has a life of its own. Although many of the same thoughts apply, we concentrate on hospitality activities related to exhibits at conventions.

Operations and Cost Factors

On one side of your mental planning grid should be the people to be entertained and the goals for those contacts. On the other side are costs and operations needed. They include:

Room or facility rent.   Most of the time you rent a suite or "function room" in a hotel or convention center. Think about *all* the ways you can use it, in addition to a base for hospitality.

Can it be a sales training room before the convention?

Could it become a day office headquarters during the show?

Is it suitable for a news conference?

Can the suite double as a "closing room" during the day?

Will the same room work for private group seminars or as a demonstration center?

If a special event is planned, such as a dinner for salespeople or dealers, it's likely you'll move it away from the hotel. Imagination and local contacts will help find a memorable setting.

Food and beverage. What you provide depends on when, how many, where, whom, and what you want to accomplish.

There are 5 times of day: breakfast, midmorning, lunch, midafternoon, and early evening. Each requires its own focus.

How many people will be at visiting you at different times? Why will they be there? Define this and it will affect what you order.

What kind of people are involved? Bankers require a different approach from retailers, government managers, or heavy machinery buyers.

How long guests will be at your suite is also a factor. How does your hospitality operation fit with competing events, other suites, or convention dinners? If everyone attends a dinner, you'll serve less.

Service personnel. Service is packaged with food from caterers. We should, however, know something about it.

One of the people assigned will be a supervisor. Know who.

Typically, one bartender will be assigned per 100 people. At large affairs there will be a "bar back," a person assigned to maintain inventory and help serve during busy periods. Ask about personality. Bartenders have to fit with your guests.

The type of food service dictates assignments. For instance, if guests select hors d'oeuvres from banquet tables, the service people clean, restock, and maintain presentation quality.

Decorations and display. To make hospitality memorable, something extra has to be presented.

Often it can be a specialized food party. A clam steam in Boston. A barbecue in Dallas. A smoked salmon tasting in Seattle. Add display materials or special lighting, and you have a theme party.

In other situations, room decor can be given special thought. Flowers that are not the standard provided by hotel flower shops can add the extra touch, with colors related to the color of tablecloth selected. (There are options in that area.) Food itself can become a most exciting display, and most caterers are very good at it.

A display of company products in a noncommercial setting can enhance sales goals. A simple two-projector slide show operating on a continuous basis can add sales punch and be an attention-getting device in your suite.

Entertainment. The extra touch can be entertainment of one kind or another. The room's size and adaptability will influence what you do.

A small suite can be transformed into a piano bar, or a strolling violinist can add a sense of grace.

A magician can entrance; a artist can sketch guests, providing something to take home.

In a larger room, a party can be developed around local arts and craftspeople creating handicrafts during the gathering.

If you're providing entertainment, make sure a contract is signed. There has to be a clear understanding of who is responsible for what. Entertainment costs can include fees, production expenses, and personal travel. If a group is involved, make sure you contract with the leader. Others should be employed by the leader instead of by you. Insurance coverage alone is reason enough to insist on this. Entertainment service is included in directories listed in this book.

Gifts. There is no substitute for imagination. The sketch idea works. If magic is presented as entertainment, a book on how to perform illusions, or an illusion itself, can be given away. A design company sold its services at a convention with a theme, "The Shape of Things to Come." A drawing was held, with the winner receiving a 10-speed bicycle, to help create a personal "shape of the future."

Host or hostess service. The controlling factor in a businesslike hospitality suite is supervising the flow of people. A host or hostess at the door provides control. Each visitor must be *signed in* and then introduced to a company representative stationed in the suite for that purpose. Visitors should be escorted by their salesperson, and salespeople cannot be allowed in without customers. (All too quickly, the suite can become a clubroom for employees with customers feeling unwelcome or outnumbered.)

Professional hosts or hostesses are more effective and less expensive than company employees. Employees are often intimidated by their seniors or don't take the job seriously. A professional solves problems without embarrassment. This can be especially helpful when the occasional tippler arrives. (Some of the most difficult problems emerge when salespeople forget they are hosts and become guests at their own party.) These situations require deft handling. Your exhibitor kit should include an order form from a local talent agency that provides host or hostess service.

Transportation and ticket services.   If you need to create a situation that links a salesperson with a customer for a long time, theater or sports tickets are a good idea. An extra touch can be providing limousine service for the evening. This will cost a bit more than a taxi, but the evening will be special. Catching a cab after the theater is an experience to be avoided. The goal is not simply to entertain, but to organize an experience that leads the customer to feel his or her business is highly valued.

Coat check and security.   When and where hospitality is to be conducted, the time of year, and the nature of the event will determine whether parking, coat check, and security services have to be part of the overall plan.

Invitation and response management.   To make hospitality special, try to develop a sense of exclusivity. Invitations should be sent in advance. (Some can be held back and given at the convention itself.) A mailed invitation should include an R.S.V.P. and specify a date by which response is expected. It should also include a telephone number, a person's name, and—if you want a mailed response—a stamped and self-addressed envelope. *Follow-up telephone calls* should be made to those who do not respond by the date specified. If your event is taking place in an unfamiliar locale, include directions on how to get there. If your hospitality location is in a hotel, you won't know the suite number until you check in. The invitation should tell guests to drop by the exhibit and find out where to go.

Sending invitations makes hospitality special, and the responses tell you how many people to "guarantee" to a caterer.

Figure 14.1 is a budget management form you can duplicate. See also Figure A.16, in the Appendix.

		Estimate	Actual
1. Room charge			
Room	_____		
Tax	_____ =	$_____	$_____
2. Food per person	$_____		
Times number of people	×_____		
Base cost	_____		
Times 15-percent gratuity	× .15		
Total before tax	_____		
Plus tax on base cost	+_____ =	_____	_____
3. Liquor, wine, beer, soft drinks			
Bottle cost	_____		
Mixers	_____		
Condiments	_____		
Supplies	_____ =	_____	_____
4. Personnel (host, hostess, bartender, etc.)			
Hourly cost	$_____		
Times hours open + 1½*			
and setup, cleanup	×_____		
Base personnel cost	_____		
Plus 15 percent gratuity	+_____ =	_____	_____
5. Leather-bound guest book and pens		_____	_____
6. Decorations—flowers, etc.		_____	_____
7. Entertainment			
Fees	_____		
Production (sound, lights)	_____		
Personal expense	_____ =	_____	_____
8. Audiovisual equipment			
Slide projector	_____		
Sound system	_____		
VCR	_____		
Easel	_____ =	_____	_____
9. Miscellaneous gifts, delivery service, etc.		_____	_____
10. Total		_____	
11. Plus contingency (10 percent)		+_____	_____
12. Total		$_____	$_____

*Presume suite will be open longer than anticipated.

Figure 14.1. Hospitality budget checklist.

Economizing on Hospitality Operations

Thought and good negotiating skills can help reduce costs. A professional events manager is a good idea for large-scale operations; but here we focus on ways to manage cost and quality in smaller, more frequently sponsored hospitality programs.

Catering Management

"Caterers are in the business of selling food. Most are willing to help clients save dollars, but only the best can anticipate what clients know and do not know about the variables."[3] We don't work with individual catering managers on a continuing basis. They don't know that we don't know. For instance, we might *say* we want to entertain 100 for 3 hours. We may *mean* 100 during a 3-hour period, with each guest staying under 1 hour. This changes requirements a lot.

Money-Saving Hints

To figure cost, catering managers ask us to guarantee the number of people who will attend. Even if fewer show up, the price remains the same. In a hotel, be conservative with the guarantee. Tell the caterer you're figuring low, however, so emergency backup can be provided if food runs out. Sometimes dry snacks, such as peanuts and potato chips, are acceptable when hot hors d'oeuvres are used up. In formal situations, most hotels can create more hors d'oeuvres quickly. If your event takes place someplace else, you'll have to guarantee more. There probably will be less backup available.

Food

- A rule of thumb is six snacks per guest at a reception. If 100 people are expected, plan 600 one- or two-bite snacks. But *know* your audience!

- One of the most expensive and special treats at a reception is a "raw bar" featuring clams, oysters, shrimp, and other shellfish. Oysters and shrimp are generally the most expensive items. To reduce cost while retaining elegance, reduce the ratio of oysters to clams. Crayfish or crab legs can be mixed with shrimp to produce the same effect. A service person should be stationed at the table. This reduces the tendency for some to take more than a fair share. If oysters are part of the raw bar, the service person can be a shucker—opening each as requested. This looks special and reduces consumption.

- Some of the food displayed on buffet tables is not eaten. For instance, a cheese round makes a nice appearance but is seldom touched. If you operate more than one evening, ask the catering manager to cut the round into pieces for the second evening.

- Fresh vegetables are becoming more and more popular as hors d'oeuvres. They are healthy and can be less expensive than more sophisticated hot snacks. You should also consider vegetable dips that are regional. For instance, avocados are locally grown in southern California. Combined with Mexican spices, an avocado-based guacamole dip could be both inexpensive and a special treat for people from other parts of the country.

Beverages

- You may face an option: pay for drinks by the bottle or by the drink. Most of the time you should buy by the bottle. After the event, return unopened bottles. There will be no charge. However, you own opened bottles. Keep them for a second evening. The same is true for mixers and juices.

- How much do people actually drink? On the average, 2 drinks are consumed in the first hour. The *maximum* is 6 drinks of one kind or another in 3 hours. If 100 are expected, a maximum of 600 drinks will be consumed. Most hard alcohol is dispensed in 4-ounce servings that include 1.25 ounces of liquor: 21 drinks a "fifth." Wine is generally served in 6-ounce glasses; soft drinks in 10-ounce glasses; and beer, 12 ounces each. Think about audience makeup and how long people will visit. You can estimate actual consumption.

- Buying bottles of liquor and wine through hotels and convention center caterers is expensive. There are times, however, when you can negotiate purchase of a partial supply, supplementing with additional bottles purchased at retail prices outside. It may be necessary to pay a "corkage fee," a labor charge for opening each bottle you bring in.

- Tastes are changing in what people want to drink. Soft drinks, juices, and especially mineral waters have emerged as social drinks. Wines, and especially the whites, are popular. People have less inclination to drink bourbon, gin, scotch whiskey, and the like. Vodka seems an exception. For a small affair, single bottles of each of the "hard" alcohols can be stocked, with a greater emphasis placed on wine, soft drinks, and beer. "Light" beer is appreciated by many at a convention at which too much food and drink is consumed over a few days. You can make your event a wine tasting. Dollars saved? No. The potential for a more memorable experience? Yes. A banana daiquiri or margarita party can serve as a focal point for food and decor, changing a cocktail gathering into a theme event.

• To control or reduce alcohol consumption, consider having waiters and waitresses provide tray service. However, they must be told that this is your goal. Otherwise, *more* is consumed. (Food consumption can be managed the same way.) Extra personnel cost can be more than offset, and an extra sense of grace added. In addition, visitors don't crowd around bars and buffets, improving the flow of people in the room.

• Don't think of bartenders as an extra cost. They actually reduce consumption and close the bar at a predetermined time without embarrassment to you. There may be no personnel charge if a minimum consumption per hour is involved. Typically, more than $150 of beverages per hour has to be consumed before caterers will agree to absorb bartender labor costs.

General

• How much people eat and drink changes with circumstance. For instance, if guests are attending a large dinner after your cocktail reception, you'll serve less. If nothing is planned, guests will stay longer.

• You can negotiate "extras" with catering managers. For instance, some hotels employ a full-time ice sculptor. You may be able to have a theme ice carving prepared at no added cost. And white tablecloths are not mandatory. Other items of decor such as candles may be added at no cost. Don't get into extras, though, until after you reach agreement on the basic package.

• Perhaps the single most important money saver—think about the audience itself. An informal theme party, based on the use of Mexican food, is less expensive than an elegant seafood buffet. Much of what you do depends on the audience, where the event is to take place, and what you want to accomplish.

Exhibit-Hospitality Tie-In

JanSport, the sportswear manufacturer, introduced a new line of outerwear at a ski industry convention. Several hundred dealers were invited to an informal private party celebrating introduction of the clothing. The tickets were specially produced T-shirts that guests picked up at the company exhibit. They saw the new clothing before attending the party. The T-shirt gift, exhibit, party, and new product line were tied together. JanSport did more than exhibit. It developed an overall program.

The same kind of thought and imagination can be used to make any hospitality program work better. It takes imagination and planning, but the results can be worth it.

15

Exhibit Transportation and Setup at the Show[1]

Uncertainties multiply as the days dwindle down. Before a show there comes a time at which most of us feel we start to lose control. Our responsibility remains, but the work falls to people we don't always know or trust. Until an exhibit starts moving to its show, the creative process is custom, a unique expression of our needs. After that, all our booths are rolling down highways and being trundled together across unloading docks. We've lost some of our treasured sense of individual treatment.

Exhibit Transportation Methods

In talking about the history of our medium, many of us point to the Bible or Marco Polo's silk route from the Mediterranean's edge across the top of Afghanistan to China. Today's concern with planes and trucks was yesterday's about the care and feeding of camels.

Impact of Deregulation

Three of our largest business segments—telecommunications, finance, and transportation—have been going through the agony of lowered government control of operations and pricing. In all three we're confused, not really knowing if what we're buying is best.

The impact of deregulation in transportation is clear to all of us who fly: airline financial problems, rate wars, shifting routes, and schedules. It may not be as apparent but is the same in freight management. Carriers, air and land, fight for market share in a very competitive atmosphere. We may benefit, but buying is confusing.

Types of Over-the-Road Freight Carriers

There are two over-the-road freight services we use. One is called *general (or common) carrier*, the other *van line carrier*. Costs for both are based on weight, distance, time, and labor; however, they operate in different ways.

General Carrier.   The companies providing this service move general freight around the nation. They use a depot system to keep trucks full and costs as low as possible. Freight is picked up and brought to a depot, where it's concentrated for long-haul movement. At a depot close to the point of delivery, the freight is shifted from the long-haul truck onto a local truck for delivery.

General carrier freight usually costs less than van line. There are, however, some things to consider:

- Somewhat more time must be allocated, though competition following deregulation has speeded things up. General carriers can provide nationwide service in a week or less.

- Many of the truck bodies used are not designed to carry delicate materials easily. Everything must be well packed or crated to absorb over-the-road shock and a good bit of handling.

- Delivery timing is less exact. For the most part, you'll have to ship goods to the show drayage contractor's warehouse to be held for the show. This increases drayage cost, though drayage contractors offer no-cost storage for 30 days.

Van Line.   We're more familiar with van lines. These companies move household goods, electronics, and other equipment. They are more expensive, though competition has forced prices down compared to general carriers. Most of us prefer the van lines.

• Large van line dealers operate special exhibit departments. The trucks are equipped with *air ride* suspension, instead of *spring leaf* suspension, to reduce shock. Truck interiors include lots of fixtures for tying down crates or pad-wrapped items as well as fittings for interior floors that reduce piling.

• You can time delivery easily, shipping directly to the unloading dock at arenas. This reduces handling and cuts drayage cost a bit.

• You can start shipment later, closer to when the exhibit has to arrive. If you cut it too close, however, cost will skyrocket.

• Sometimes heavy, expensive exhibit crates can be eliminated. Your materials can be pad-wrapped just like furniture. (Exhibits are exposed to handling risk at other times, and many of us think crates are required because of this. Experience has usually been good, however, especially when booths are large—those filling several trucks. Risks may be lower than we think.)

Air Freight

It's automatic. We think air freight when time is short. We don't think cost. There are times, however, when air can be the least-cost transportation service. If you ship a few small or medium-sized boxes, air freight may be less than van line. This is especially so if time *is* short and you'd have to pay for an expedited over-the-road service.

More handling is involved. Freight is picked up, transferred to the loading area at an airport, loaded on a plane, and put through the reverse process at the receiving end. Unless a higher cost straight-through service is ordered, the shipment is also subject to plane changes. Pack well.

Local Trucking

Lots of us exhibit locally. Scores of meetings take place in small, nonunion facilities. Your exhibit house's own truck and driver is the way to go—and the same person can set up the booth. This kind of service can also be provided by a local truck operator.

Van Line Pricing

When we talk transport, most of the time we refer to interstate van service. For most, that's where the big numbers are. And when we talk, we say we're confused. That's not surprising because just a few years ago we had no choice about what we'd pay. A maze of schedules called *tariffs* were developed collectively and approved by the Interstate Commerce Commission (ICC). No matter the carrier, price wasn't debatable.

Deregulation has come. The cost debate is on. Pricing complexity is alive and well, however, ingrained in the industry and blessed by its less powerful regulator. The ICC still approves tariffs, but haulers file exceptions, their own changes. We have to learn how tariffs, which are really just price schedules, are developed. Just as important, we have to understand how they are used. The terms are strange. We view the industry with suspicion because we don't understand terms and the carriers often don't take the time to explain.

Cost-Price Variables

Tariffs, now and before, reflect the impact of basic costs.

- *The amount of labor that will have to be provided.* For instance, schedules for moving household goods are higher than for other kinds of freight because of the time it takes to pack and load.

- *How far the shipment must be carried.* This is the most obvious variable, and most of us understand it.

- *How fast the freight must move.* Regulations prohibit driving more than 500 miles a day. If you've left it too late, a second driver must be added so the truck will keep moving. You pay more. Even small loads are priced at a minimum of 500 pounds by most van lines.

- *High-traffic routes.* There is heavy traffic between cities where lots of conventions take place. Loads are easy to find. Low-priced, point-to-point schedules are the result.

- *Taxes.* Various taxes for road use are paid by truckers and passed on in rates. For instance, vans 48 feet long are coming into vogue. An extra $250 is levied for rigs this big. Most van lines will avoid them except for situations in which the extra length saves adding another truck.

Exhibit-Hauling Tariffs

Cost variables are compressed into a series of schedules for hauling different types of goods. There are tariffs and tariff sections for household goods, general freight, electronics—the list seems endless.

Exhibit Tariff Sections. There are three basic price schedules in the exhibit tariff that reflect the cost variables:

Less than truckload (LTL). This schedule covers shipping a relatively small exhibit. Prices are shown in weight bands, ranging from 1000 pounds to 10,000 plus. (Van lines charge minimums: either 1050 or 2100 pounds.)[*]

Full truckload. You don't have to fill a trailer to use this tariff section. It comes into play when you have just over half a load. The schedule is based on a *presumed* full truckload, 24,000 pounds minimum; however, unit prices are much lower than LTL, resulting in a price break-point between the two schedules. We illustrate it later. The hauler has the option of finding another customer for the run, unless you actually do fill the vehicle.

Full-truck prices are expressed three ways. The least is for crated exhibits. A second, higher-priced schedule is applied for a mixed load of crates and uncrated materials. The highest is a schedule for uncrated materials alone. The terms used are *mixed* and *blanket* (or *pad*) *wrapped*. The higher schedules recognize that your shipment is large and they cover extra labor for packing and loading.[*]

Mileage schedule. These are the most expensive prices. They are used in three situations:

1. Mileage is charged for *exclusive use* or *expedited delivery*. These situations come up when you don't want to let shippers have the option to add another customer load, or time is so short that a second driver must be added to the run.

2. The mileage tariff section is used when you are moving between locations that aren't on the hauler's point-to-point schedule, even if your shipment goes through them. For instance, you may ship from New York to Madison, Wisconsin, with the truck going through Chicago—a "point." You pay mileage, however, for the full run.

3. Mileage pricing can be used when exhibits are not crated or there are a few crates and lots of uncrated material. This is a judgment call: 200 or more pads and the extra labor will probably force the carrier to charge mileage prices. (This is a negotiable item.)

---

[*] *Point-to-point.* Both the LTL and full-truckload schedules show prices on a point-to-point basis. The points cover high-traffic density routes beteen cities where most shows take place.

There are actually *two* mileage price schedules. One is used when an extraordinary amount of labor is required for packing on LTL and full-truckload shipments, the other for shipments between "nonpoints."[1]

Weight Basis and Dimensional-Weight Pricing

Prices on all the schedules are shown per hundred weight (cwt). We are charged for true weight *or* what is called *dimensional weight*, whichever is more. If you ship feathers or potato chips, you pay for space. If you ship a granite boulder, you pay for weight.

The dimensional-weight formula is *7 pounds per cubic foot*. For most exhibits, it produces pricing weight higher than true weight. For instance, you may have a crate that measures 7 feet deep, 4 feet wide, and 6 feet high: 168 cubic feet (7 × 4 × 6 = 168). Its true weight may be 650 pounds; however, its dimensional weight, at 7 pounds per cubic foot, is 1176 (168 × 7 = 1176).

You may think it possible to add the dimensional weights of all your crates and project the cost. This is not quite true. For pricing purposes, *cubic feet of empty space may be added*, using the formula. As the trailer is packed, space may have to be left—above or beside crates. You may even specify that nothing be placed on top of some. (The inside space of a standard trailer is 7 feet, 11 inches wide and 9 feet high—in back of the "step" at the front end, where it is connected to a tractor. On the 10-foot-long step, interior height is 8 feet, 3 inches.)

Let's go back to our illustration. Presume that our crate is placed upright in a trailer, in back of the step, with 3 feet above it to the roof. We'd have to add 84 cubic feet of air space (7′D 4′W × 3′H = 84). Air space would be added to the 168 cubic-foot crate, a total of 252 cubic feet. Shipping cost would be figured on 1764 pounds (252 × 7 = 1764). Van lines round the weight. This crate would be rounded up to 1800 pounds for pricing.

We save if the hauler can ship our crate on its *side* with the 7-foot dimension vertical. Only 2 feet remain to the rooftop, and less floor is needed. Air space would be 48 cubic feet instead of 84. Adding that to our crate produces 216 cubic feet and a pricing weight of 1512 pounds (216 × 7 = 1512). The line would probably round this down to 1500 pounds, saving 300 pounds of dimensional weight.

If you go to a lot of shows, your designer *should* worry about the size and shape of crates so they can be packed tightly. A good van line will take extra time and trouble to figure the least-waste packing plan. Graph paper is used. One van line agent uses Styrofoam crate models to see how they can be packed into less space.[2]

Break-Point Illustrations

Figures 15.1 through 15.3 are samplings of exhibit tariff schedules from one major van line. The illustrations that follow come from those price sheets, which are standard forms used by all the lines. Prices themselves, however, will differ to some extent.

Less than Full Truckload Illustration.   We are moving 4500 pounds of dimensional weight from Chicago to Las Vegas, on the point-to-point schedule. The weight band is 2100 to 4999 pounds. We have 45 hundred weights (cwt). The price is $29.90 per cwt; $29.90 × 45 = $1345.50.

The van line, however, uses a break-point comparison. The next weight band starts at 5000 pounds—very close to our 4500. So the load is priced at 5000 pounds, or 50 cwt. The price schedule shows $26 per cwt, $3.90 per cwt less; $26 × 50 = $1300. We pay $1300, saving $45.50 by shipping a weight of 4500 pounds as if it were 5000.

See Figure 15.1, marked "Section 5." This is the less than truckload tariff. Sheets like this are produced for each point-to-point route.

Full-Truckload Illustration.   We are moving 14,000 pounds between the same two cities. Because the load will fill only a bit over half a truck, the van line looks both at the LTL and the full-truckload schedules to see which is most economical for us. The LTL weight band is 10,000 and over. We are shipping 140 hundred weights, and the price is $25.15 cwt; $25.15 × 140 = $3521.

The van line turns to the full-truckload schedule, marked "Section 7" (Figure 15.2). Since our whole load is crated, Column A is used. (Column B is for mixed loads of crates and pad-wrapped materials. Column C is used for shipments entirely pad-wrapped.) The Column A cwt price is $13.65. The prices assume we are shipping a full load, 24,000 pounds, 240 cwt; $13.65 × 240 = $3276. We save $245 by shipping a weight of 14,000 pounds as though it were 24,000.

Mileage-Schedule Illustration.   Assume our 14,000 pound shipment from Chicago to Las Vegas is *not at all crated*, that it requires an extraordinary amount of packing, more than would be covered by using Column C on the full-truckload price sheet. As a result, the mileage price schedule is used.

ICC NOAM 414-B	NORTH AMERICAN VAN LINES, INC. (a Delaware Corporation)	1st REVISED PAGE 74

SECTION 5 - TRANSPORTATION RATES

		TRANSPORTATION RATES				ITEM
		1,050 to 2,099 lbs.	2,100 to 4,999 lbs.	5,000 to 9,999 lbs.	10,000 lbs. and over	
BETWEEN:	Chicago, IL and a 50 mile radius					
AND:	Cincinnati/Dayton, OH	$26.75	$18.50	$14.25	$12.45	
	Cleveland, OH and a 75 mile radius	28.10	19.35	15.00	13.20	
	Columbus, OH	25.85	17.85	15.65	15.05	
	Des Moines/Marshalltown, IA	25.45	17.60	13.65	12.05	
	Detroit, MI and a 75 mile radius	26.10	18.00	13.90	12.25	
	Ft. Wayne/Wabash, IN	21.60	15.10	11.70	10.05	
	Harrisburg/Lancaster/ York, PA	31.55	21.60	16.90	15.95	
	Houston, TX	37.85	25.70	20.05	18.75	
	Indianapolis, IN	19.00	13.40	10.60	9.05	
	Lansing, MI	23.85	16.60	13.05	11.30	
	Las Vegas, NV	44.25	29.90	26.00	25.15	
	Louisville, KY	26.75	18.50	14.25	12.45	
	Milwaukee, WI	15.95	11.40	9.40	7.95	502
	Nashville, TN	25.85	17.85	14.50	13.10	
	New Orleans, LA	33.35	22.80	16.95	15.80	
	⬇ Oklahoma City, OK	33.00	22.30	17.95	16.10	
	Phoenix, AZ	41.80	28.35	25.50	23.85	
	Pittsburgh, PA	26.85	18.50	14.30	14.00	
	Reno, NV	48.00	32.40	28.10	27.25	
	Rochester, NY	27.50	18.95	14.70	14.40	
	Salt Lake City, UT	47.85	32.30	27.35	23.90	
	San Antonio, TX	42.25	29.25	24.70	21.65	
	St. Louis, MO	26.45	18.25	14.10	12.30	
	⬇ Syracuse/Auburn, NY	31.20	21.05	16.80	14.95	
	Los Angeles, CA area	50.85	34.25	29.65	28.80	
	Sacramento, CA area	61.65	41.30	34.40	31.85	
	San Francisco, CA area	53.80	36.20	31.40	30.35	
	Denver, CO area	36.80	25.05	19.65	18.95	
	N. Florida area	41.05	27.80	21.80	21.30	
	S. Florida area	46.60	31.45	26.60	23.35	
	Kansas City, KS/MO area	27.00	18.65	14.40	14.15	
	Boston, MA area	33.30	22.75	17.65	16.85	
	Minneapolis, MN area	32.70	20.80	16.50	14.75	
	Atlantic City, NJ area	30.60	21.00	16.30	15.50	
	New York City, NY area	30.10	20.65	16.10	15.40	
	Philadelphia, PA area	29.90	20.55	16.10	15.40	
	Portland, OR area	49.05	33.05	28.50	27.70	
	Dallas, TX area	34.15	23.30	18.60	17.95	
	Seattle, WA area	48.75	32.85	28.35	27.55	
	Washington, DC area	28.15	19.40	15.65	14.95	
	State of Connecticut	33.30	22.75	17.65	16.85	

ISSUED: March 24, 1986	Issued By Robert W. Seelfrank Assistant Traffic Manager P.O. Box 988, Fort Wayne, Indiana 46801	EFFECTIVE: April 7, 1986

The Provisions Published Hereon Have No Environmental Impact. Abbreviations and Reference Marks Explained in Item 10,000.

Figure 15.1. This is a sample less-than-full truckload (LTL) exhibit tariff section. Published on a point-to-point basis, prices are expressed in cost per 100 pounds dimensional or actual weight, whichever is more. Break points are used to calculate cost. For instance, it's less expensive to ship 4900 pounds as 5000 because cost per 100 is lower. *(Reproduction courtesy of North American Van Lines.)*

The distance is 1744 miles, in a mileage band that extends from 1701 to 1750 miles on the schedule. There's also a weight band, just as in the LTL price sheet. We fit between 12,000 and 15,999 pounds, 14,000 pounds or 140 cwt. The price is $37.65 per cwt; $37.65 × 140 = $5271.

Since our weight is close to the next weight band, 16,000 pounds plus, the van line compares. The cwt price is lower, $37.10; $37.10 × 160 = $5936. This time we don't save. There's not quite enough to make the break. It would cost $665 more to ship our 14,000 pounds at the 16,000 pound rate. This mileage chart, Figure 15.3, is identified as "Section 3."

ICC NOAM 414-B	NORTH AMERICAN VAN LINES, INC. (a Delaware Corporation)	1st REVISED PAGE 120

SECTION 7 - TRANSPORTATION RATES

		TRANSPORTATION RATES			ITEM
		COLUMN A	COLUMN B	COLUMN C	
BETWEEN:	Chicago, IL and a 50 mile radius				
AND:	Cincinnati/Dayton, OH	$ 4.75	$ 5.90	$ 6.80	
	Cleveland, OH and a 75 mile radius	5.00	6.25	7.10	
	Columbus, OH	5.25	6.30	7.70	
	Des Moines/Marshalltown, IA	5.85	7.10	8.75	
	Detroit, MI and a 75 mile radius	4.60	5.75	6.65	
	Ft. Wayne, Wabash, IN	4.45	5.55	6.75	
	Harrisburg/Lancaster/ York, PA	7.70	9.30	10.90	
	Houston, TX	9.45	10.95	12.60	
	Indianapolis, IN	4.60	5.70	6.90	
	Lansing, MI	4.80	5.95	7.20	
	Las Vegas, NV	13.65	15.80	18.40	702
	Louisville, KY	4.70	5.90	6.75	
	Milwaukee, WI	3.55	4.45	5.35	
	Nashville, TN	6.35	7.70	9.15	
	New Orleans, LA	8.85	10.40	12.25	
	⬇Oklahoma City, OK	8.30	10.00	11.70	
	Phoenix, AZ	14.65	17.15	20.25	
	Pittsburgh, PA	6.15	7.30	8.80	
	Reno, NV	15.10	17.90	20.45	
	Rochester, NY	7.10	8.65	10.20	
	Salt Lake City, UT	12.10	14.45	16.65	
	San Antoino, TX	10.80	12.95	14.95	
	St. Louis, MO	4.50	5.50	6.50	
	⬇Syracuse/Auburn, NY	7.60	8.35	9.75	
	Los Angeles, CA area	15.00	17.25	19.45	
	Sacramento, CA area	16.05	18.45	20.75	
	San Francisco, CA area	15.40	17.75	20.00	
	Denver, Co area	10.20	12.05	14.40	
	N. Florida area	10.90	12.85	15.35	
	S. Florida area	11.25	13.10	16.05	
	Kansas City, KS/MO area	6.15	7.25	8.55	
	Boston, MA area	8.45	9.95	11.40	
	Minneapolis, MN area	5.65	6.70	7.90	
	Atlantic City, NJ area	8.20	9.60	11.40	
	New York City, NY area	7.20	8.65	9.90	
	Philadelphia, PA area	7.80	9.20	10.95	
	Portland, OR area	16.15	19.10	21.80	
	Dallas, TX area	9.25	11.15	12.95	
	Seattle, WA area	15.25	17.65	20.45	
	Washington, DC area	7.45	8.80	10.50	
	State of Connecticut	8.00	9.45	10.85	

ISSUED: March 24, 1986	Issued By Robert W. Saalfrank Assistant Traffic Manager P.O. Box 988, Fort Wayne, Indiana 46801	EFFECTIVE: April 7, 1986

The Provisions Published Hereon Have No Environmental Impact. Abbreviations and Reference Marks Explained in Item 10,000.

Figure 15.2. This is a sample full-truckload exhibit tariff section. You do not need a full truck to use this price sheet. If you are shipping well over half a load, the van line compares LTL and full-truck sections to see where you pay less. The three prices for each point depend on packing time. Column A is for crated exhibits, column B for a mix of crated and uncrated materials, column C for pad-wrapped exhibits. *(Reproduction courtesy of North American Van Lines.)*

Creating and Managing an Exhibit

ICC NOAM 414-B	NORTH AMERICAN VAN LINES, INC. (a Delaware Corporation)	ORIGINAL PAGE 66

SECTION 3 - TRANSPORTATION RATES

WEIGHT CATEGORIES

MILES	500 to 999 lbs.	1000 to 1999 lbs.	2000 to 3999 lbs.	4000 to 7999 lbs.	8000 to 11999 lbs.	12000 to 15999 lbs.	16000 lbs. and over
1751 - 1800	$77.45	$59.00	$53.00	$46.55	$40.75	$38.30	$37.65
1801 - 1850	78.10	59.55	53.65	47.45	41.85	39.65	38.75
1851 - 1900	78.65	60.40	54.40	48.55	42.75	40.75	39.95
1901 - 1950	79.30	61.10	55.20	49.55	43.80	42.85	41.00
1951 - 2000	80.05	61.75	55.75	50.30	44.85	43.00	42.20
2001 - 2050	80.65	62.40	56.55	50.95	45.90	44.10	43.30
2051 - 2100	81.20	62.90	57.10	51.85	46.90	45.10	44.40
2101 - 2150	81.85	63.75	57.85	52.40	47.45	45.85	44.95
2151 - 2200	82.40	64.40	58.50	53.10	48.10	46.40	45.75
2201 - 2250	83.10	65.10	59.10	53.65	48.75	47.00	46.30
2251 - 2300	83.95	65.65	59.95	54.40	49.45	47.45	46.90
2301 - 2350	84.50	66.40	60.45	55.10	50.00	48.10	47.45
2351 - 2400	85.05	67.00	61.20	55.65	50.55	48.65	48.00
2401 - 2450	85.55	67.65	61.75	56.30	51.10	49.30	48.65
2451 - 2500	86.10	68.40	62.40	56.85	51.75	49.75	49.20
2501 - 2550	86.65	68.95	62.85	57.40	52.20	50.40	49.75
2551 - 2600	87.15	69.65	63.50	57.90	52.75	50.85	50.30
2601 - 2650	87.60	70.30	64.00	58.50	53.10	51.65	50.75
2651 - 2700	87.95	70.95	64.50	59.00	53.55	52.00	51.20
2701 - 2750	88.30	71.30	65.00	59.50	54.10	52.55	51.85
2751 - 2800	88.60	71.55	65.50	60.00	54.65	52.90	52.30
2801 - 2850	89.10	72.00	65.95	60.45	55.20	53.35	52.85
2851 - 2900	89.40	72.20	66.20	61.00	55.55	53.65	53.10
2901 - 2950	89.65	72.60	66.65	61.45	56.00	54.20	53.55
2951 - 3000	90.10	72.90	67.20	61.85	56.40	54.65	54.00
3001 - 3050	90.55	73.55	67.65	62.40	56.85	55.20	54.50
3051 - 3100	91.05	74.05	68.10	62.85	57.40	55.65	55.10
3101 - 3150	91.55	74.55	68.75	63.50	57.90	56.20	55.45
3151 - 3200	92.15	74.95	69.20	64.00	58.35	56.65	55.85
3201 - 3250	92.65	75.50	69.75	64.50	58.85	56.90	56.30
3251 - 3300	93.10	75.95	70.30	65.00	59.30	57.45	56.75
3301 - 3350	93.60	76.50	70.85	65.50	59.65	58.05	57.20
3351 - 3400	93.95	77.00	71.10	66.00	60.20	58.35	57.65
3401 - 3450	94.30	77.40	71.55	66.45	60.65	58.95	58.20
3451 - 3500	94.60	77.65	72.10	67.00	61.20	59.30	58.50

	Issued By Robert W. Seelfrank Assistant Traffic Manager P.O. Box 988, Fort Wayne, Indiana 46801	
ISSUED: August 8, 1985		EFFECTIVE: September 8, 1985

The Provisions Published Hereon Have No Environmental Impact. Abbreviations and Reference Marks Explained in Item 10,000.

Figure 15.3. This sample is a mileage price sheet used for loads of loose materials. Another is used for crated exhibits. They come into play when you are not shipping to high-traffic points or when expedited or exclusive-use delivery is needed. The industry standard is 500 miles of driving a day. If you ship between points but time is tight, it can cost less to pay a second driver (.15 cents a mile). Use the LTL or full-truck sections for price. *(Reproduction courtesy of North American Van Lines.)*

How to Reduce Costs

There are lots of things you can do to keep costs low:

▪ Project what your average load is—the average dimensional weight you move. See if, most of the time, you should be shipping with an

LTL schedule or a full-truck price sheet.

- If you are in a large number of shows, avoid pad-wrapped materials. Try and avoid late shipping—exclusive use or expedited delivery.

- If your schedule is not extensive, and your exhibit fills several vans, it can be more economical to avoid crating. Crates themselves increase shipment size substantially. The mileage schedule is more, but you may need fewer trucks. You and your designer should work with a van line before making the crate or no-crate decision.

- Check the "points" on competing tariffs, especially if your own headquarters is in a smaller city. Most points are the same, but there are differences. For instance, if you are in Fort Wayne, Indiana, one of the major van lines has its corporate headquarters there. So, Fort Wayne is on its point list.

- If you are in a number of shows a year, negotiate a discount with one van line. Typically, discounts start after a predetermined amount of weight is carried in a year.

- If you are building a brand-new exhibit, alert the van line early. Be aware that a first-time shipment can run high. It's almost part of our culture that new exhibit construction goes down to the wire and there is confusion in packing.

- If you go back to the same cities constantly, compare the price sheets of a number of van lines. Prices are close to each other, but there are some differences.

- Makes sure the actual weight of your exhibit shows on its papers (bill of lading and highway weight station tickets) even if your shipment is priced on the basis of dimensional weight. These same papers are used to bill drayage service in convention halls—priced on the basis of actual weight. If the higher dimensional weight is all that's shown, that's what you'll pay for in drayage.

Services at the Show Site

Your first experience as part of a major exhibit hall setup can be one of life's adventures. At the start it's clear that your booth will never be erected in time; just as clear that nobody else's exhibit will be ready either. The hall is a mess. Yet everything comes together just in time.When the first visitors arrive, you'd never think that chaos existed a few short hours before. Looking back, we see the "grand plan."

Grand Plan

The show's manager is the planner. Among other responsibilities, the organizer provides a contractor to administer the flow of materials into the hall and contractors to arrange for setup labor and other services. (Labor unions, and in some cases contractors, have contracts with the facility. Others are hired by the show manager.)

We have coordinate activities—from drayage to carpenter, from decorator and electrician to rug installer. Many of us hire professional setup management to do the job. Exhibit houses offer freight and field service management, and there are independent companies specializing in setup management.

The exhibitor kit provided by show management includes contracts and order forms from its contractors. They are listed in Chapter 2. Our goal here is to outline the interrelationships involved and suggest ways manage the process economically.

Drayage Contractors

It's really impossible to say one role is more important than another, but think about the drayage function. It's vital. The contractor controls the flow of materials into exhibit halls. Visualize 50 or 100 of us showing up at unloading docks simultaneously, each with our own crew. Real chaos. At large trade shows, several *million* pounds of freight are moved in a matter of hours. The drayage contractor performs four services for us:

- Local warehouse storage is provided, tied in with hall delivery.
- Work teams are provided on the loading docks to move exhibits and equipment to each booth space.
- Empty crates are removed and stored for the duration of the show.
- At the convention's conclusion, the process is reversed.

Costs for drayage are based on weight: a price per 100 pounds. There are two choices. One includes use of the contractor's warehouse facility. The other, priced somewhat lower, is for freight delivered directly to the arena unloading dock.

Prices can range up to $30 and more for each hundred weight (cwt), so drayage can get expensive. And don't automatically presume dollars can be saved by delivering direct to the hall. Lower drayage cost can be offset by higher over-the-road transportation costs. Don't forget that when you are going directly from one show to another, moving to drayage saves because of no-cost storage.

Contracts must be read and understood. The companies use standard forms that don't necessarily make sense in individual situations. When you spot something, don't hesitate to talk to the contractor. If your point is a fair one, you should get cooperation.

A case in point. The show took place in the Las Vegas Convention Center. The drayage contract included a surcharge for delivery direct to the hall in a van with a nonstandard bed height above the street (48 inches), or one that had to be unloaded from the side. This surcharge covers extra labor cost when forklift trucks and dollies cannot roll into and out of truck interiors from a loading platform—perfectly acceptable and understandable in many situations.

Docks are not used, however, for exhibit loading at the Las Vegas Convention Center! Everything is lowered to the floor. There is no labor cost difference, regardless of truck bed height, back or side loading.[3]

We and our exhibit houses point to these situations as evidence that show managers protect the interests of vendors they appoint instead of the interests of those who pay the bills. Often this is not the case. The failure is more likely one of omission, a simple failure to think. The show management industry is going though a reexamination of practices, and greater attention is being paid to looking closely at each situation.

Official Freight Contractors

Large-scale exhibitors use a van line on a contract basis or bid individual shipments among a group of them. Most of us, however, don't exhibit that often. A show's appointed freight carrier is a viable best choice for over-the-road hauling. You maintain one point of contact, and coordination becomes the responsibility of the contractor.

Official Labor Contractor

This company creates a labor pool to install exhibits. It assigns craftspeople; it bills us and pays them.

Unions. Job functions are split among specific crafts, depending on the union contracts in force in the facility. Titles and responsibilities differ somewhat, city to city. The unions themselves differ, too, depending on which bargained for what jurisdiction in each arena. In Chicago, New York, and Philadelphia, for instance, the carpenters' union performs much of the work. The teamsters have most of it in Las Vegas, and the decorators dominate in Miami, Dallas, and along the west coast.

But that doesn't mean one union does everything. For instance, in Chicago carpenters erect exhibits but don't hang graphic signs unless tools are required. Decorators place the signs. In most places, "riggers" hang materials from arena ceilings and operate forklift trucks in the hall. But this is not always the case. For instance, again in Chicago's McCormick Place, a rigger opens equipment crates as well, lifting items out and placing them. You'll find different situations everywhere. For instance, if your shows require extensive heavy machinery installation, you may find a union craft involved. In some cases, the members serve as carpenters or decorators at shows that do not feature heavy equipment installation.

New York's outspoken Mayor Edward Koch wrote what amounted to an open letter on union work rules and practices while negotiations were underway for jurisdiction in that city's Jacob Javits Convention Center. He accused unions of "featherbedding" and their members of demanding "kickbacks" or "gratuities" and of "theft."[4] He echoed sentiments expressed by exhibitors, not just about New York but about other cities as well. Even when rules make sense, however, we often try to subvert: we either don't know the rules or we try to avoid them.

The show's exhibitor kit contains forms for ordering labor. They can be completed in advance or on the show floor at the contractors' desks during setup. It is wise to contact the vendors ahead of time for advice on exactly what will be needed.

Independent Labor Contractors

Some exhibitors like to employ an independent contractor to hire and supervise setup. A prescreened group from the overall labor pool will be used in an attempt to ensure higher quality performance. In addition, independents provide a supervisor with whom you can work over time. You have to give the show organizer written notification that you plan to use an independent labor source. The show's official contractor has to plan the size of its pool. And the unions that supply labor to both must estimate needs, making plans for more people if the calls will strip local membership rolls.

Electrical and Telephone Service

Electrical.   The roles of the electrical contractor and union differ, depending on the arena. The function can stop with delivery of electrical service to the booth. At most, however, an electrician must actually plug in all lights and appliances. There are some halls where jurisdiction bargaining was intense and the resulting job rules add to cost. (For instance, if an electrical fixture is attached to a panel, both a carpenter and an electrician must install it.)

Telephone.   An order for telephone lines should be in the exhibitor kit, but telephone sets may not be included. You may have to bring your own phone or get one from another source.

Decorating

The decorating function includes things done for show management as well as for ourselves. A decorating company will help show management lay out the trade show floor itself. It will provide "decoration" for the convention and dress the hall, providing the pipe, drape backdrops for exhibit booths, and aisle carpet. Most of these companies maintain inventories of furniture and decorative props, everything from hay wagons to smoking stands. Many decorators stock rental exhibit structures and provide a sign-making service.

General Contractor

We get confused as to which company provides what. Some with "exposition service" in their names rent furniture. Others have the "decorating" name but provide labor. Don't worry. As the companies providing show services grew, they took on additional management functions. From our perspective, it doesn't matter.

The general contractors are packagers for both the show organizer and ourselves. They compete for shows. In addition to demonstrating ability to do the job, they bid on the basis of show manager cost. In return for an opportunity to sell to us, the general contractor will offer low prices to show management for what is provided to the organizer. At some large events, goods and services are donated to the promoter. When we complain about prices, we have to remember that in most cases we're not only paying for ourselves but also subsidizing the cost of serving the show as a whole.

Are you asking, "If the general contractor does all this, what does the show manager do?" Don't forget that show management is also responsible for selecting and working with the facility itself, perhaps gathering hotel rooms, developing an educational seminar program, and promoting the show to potential attendees and exhibitors.

Other Services and Rentals

In Chapter 2, you saw an extensive list of specific services and rentals you may need—from security and photography to plant rental, from audiovisual support to booth cleaning and host or hostess service. The exhibitor kits include forms for ordering them.

Union Influence

We've said that local work rules can affect both cost and supervision needs. Exhibitors often discuss differences between "right-to-work" states and those where there is less flexibility. Either way, when all is said and done, it costs money and takes time to erect an exhibit.

A lot of it boils down to frustration with union officials and overall contracts. It *is* less confusing, and less costly, to install an exhibit in a place like New Orleans, where workers in one union are allowed to perform more functions, compared to New York or Chicago, where a half-dozen or more crafts can get involved.

The frustrations emerge on both sides. All of us have seen exhibitors who don't know the rules, or want to subvert them, trying to save a few dollars by doing work that belongs to one of the craftspeople. However, Mayor Koch's outspoken comments cannot be ignored. They were influenced by exhibitor and show manager perceptions communicated to him, but his most important motivation was a desire to see New York compete effectively for more shows.

Top-level union leaders are starting to recognize that they play a major role in a very competitive game. The unions *are* taking some steps to improve quality and price performance.

- Unions are starting to sponsor worker training programs in some cities, including San Francisco and Houston, seeking to provide more highly skilled workers on the show floors.

- One of the problems faced by union locals has been finding people when their rolls are depleted by a big show. Increasingly, they are working with each other when this happens, instead of searching for workers with no professional background to fill in.

- One recent suggestion has been that union members wear magnetic stripe plastic identification badges at shows. They would distinguish professional workers from fill-in labor. It is thought that many theft and poor attitude problems can be laid to fill-ins. (The magnetic stripe would also be used for logging in and out, reducing clerical work and the potential for payment errors.)

- There even has been discussion about moving toward a flextime kind of compensation system. Overtime would start after a given number of hours were worked, instead of being paid automatically after a certain time of day and always on weekends.

Responsible show and exhibit managers don't fight fair pay for professional work. Increasingly, there's too much at stake at the shows to put up with less than first-class labor. They *are* concerned about poor attitudes and unreasonable practices. Since it is a two-way street, however, we have to be responsible and reasonable too.[5]

Show Management Influence

We said show managers have lots of responsibilities, from dealing with the facility and picking contractors to seminar production and show promotion. Exhibitors say organizers don't treat them like customers— even though they seem to pay most of the bills. In a way they are right. The reality is that *attendees* are the customers of both the exhibitor and the show's management.

It's true that after appointing a group of contractors, many promoters seem to walk away, not accepting any responsibility for helping to supervise them; but some good things are starting to happen:

- The National Association of Exposition Managers has sponsored a nationwide series of "Labor Forums" to help educate us and to act as a sounding board for problems.

- An effort is underway in the show management industry to review and improve the way information is presented in exhibitor kits, a key source of our confusion. It's not enough to say, "It was in the contract." We have to *understand* or we may break rules without knowing it.

Facilities Influence

A major civic arena in Boston has just expanded, but no attention was paid to the loading docks. The new hall in New York does not provide parking space. Chicago politics always seems to find a way to make things difficult in its hall. We mention three large cities, but it seems that few of the arena developers have taken the time to evaluate what's happening around them. For instance, did any of them talk to the trucking industry and learn that the future would bring 48-foot vans? There are three areas of concern:

- Building design influences how the structure can be used. Is it a convention facility, complete with meeting rooms and quality food potential? Or is it a facility aimed at housing public events such as concerts or sports events?

- Basic labor contracts are negotiated with the hall. To what extent do facility managers understand show and exhibitor needs when they appear at the bargaining table?

- How much public support is provided? Increasingly, convention centers are asked to pay their own way instead of gaining some form of subsidy (such as a hotel room tax) that allows them to rent the space for less. More cost burden is absorbed by exhibitors.[6]

Hints for Avoiding Last-Minute Shock

There are a number of things we can do to avoid problems. Facility, freight, service, and show managers correctly point out that some of the problems can be traced right back to exhibit managers. Here are some "hints" on how to avoid them.

Read the exhibitor kit.   Read it with care, both the show's rules and the exhibitor services contracts included in it. Discuss questions with show management or its vendors in advance.

Carry all paperwork.   When you leave for the show, don't forget your papers: booth freight handling and service contacts. Show setup becomes a paper blizzard. Help others to help you, and things will get done much more easily.

Bring cash.   You have to pay for some things before the event or as you go. Too many of us, even with big companies, forget about bills after the shows are over. Check your order forms. You can estimate what you'll need. Add a little extra because *some* gratuities may be appropriate.

Use new shipping labels.   Make sure your crates and cartons are clearly labeled. Remove old labels. They can create confusion. Include the show name and your booth space number. And be clear. Do not use a standard typewriter face. Handwrite, large and clear, or type with an "orator" typewriter font at the minimum. Think about what faces a worker inside an unlighted moving van at night.

After exhibits are set up, empty crates and boxes are stored. Cardboard cartons must be placed inside larger crates. (Ask an exhibit neighbor if you don't have crates.) Empty-crate stickers are provided. Fill them out with a broad-point, waterproof marking pen in a dark color. Place them on two sides of each crate. Some exhibitors spray-paint their crates to ease the identification process.

Make arrangements for postshow freight. Do it before the show starts. Drayage and official freight contractors are constantly faced with exhibitors who simply leave after an event with no arrangements made for what to do with their exhibits!

Know your exhibit weight. We pointed out that drayage bills are calculated on the true weight of your exhibit and that you should make sure this weight shows on shipping papers. Spot the problem later and you can argue later, but often with no luck.

Understand damage and liability responsibility. One of our nagging problems is assigning responsibility when exhibit materials are damaged or someone is hurt. Know where you stand.

1. Understand your own insurance coverages.
2. Make sure external damage notes are made as freight changes hands. Many van line operators place representatives on the unloading docks at shows to check for damage.
3. Talk with freight companies about the insurance coverage they provide and, in the case of van lines, what the driver's responsibilities include. (Most operate with "owner operators," and they may be partially responsible for over-the-road quality control.)
4. Check your space contract to see what liability coverage is provided by show management and what you are responsible for. Insurance costs have increased substantially and it can be expensive for show managers to obtain full coverage. The result is a legal pass-along. Be alert for it and talk to your own attorney or insurance vendor.
5. Prevent damage during the show. There are lots of ways to break exhibits. Good supervision is the best answer. There are, however, some things that don't pop to mind. Sometimes our empty crates are not empty. We store things in them not being used at a show. Alert the handler. Have you ever seen handlers play

"pitch the penny" with empty exhibit crates? Young, fill-in handlers stop short with a forklift truck, letting empties slide off the end. The game? To see how close crates stop to a line or wall. Sometimes they miss.

Don't rely on "fragile" marking.   We like to mark crates fragile, hoping they'll get extra care. The word has lost meaning. At least one exhibitor ships large electronics devices in crates with plastic windows, providing a dramatic picture of what's inside.[7]

Pull it all together.   The fewer the pieces, the less confusion you'll have. Combine as much as you can in as few different shipments as possible. (Send lots of small boxes separately and you'll start paying minimums, including one charged by drayage.) In addition, things won't get lost and you'll be able to order setup labor when you need it.

We began by saying that as days dwindle down to show opening we feel confusion and lack of trust in the others who start to control our ability to produce results. We can point fingers at others, but we have to point fingers at ourselves too. We must help others to help us, managing the process instead of allowing the process to manage us.

16

Exhibit Sales Staff Selection, Training, and Management

Page skimmers have noticed that in several places in the book we ask everyone to read the *next* chapter, 17. It covers exhibit selling technique. Even the smallest, newest companies can compete effectively with the "big boys" at a show if they know how to perform like champions at the booth. If you are doing your own exhibit and will be selling by yourself, or with only one or two others, you can move ahead to Chapter 17 if you wish.

But please turn pages slowly. There may be something here even for you. This chapter talks about what surrounds floor performance. Picking, training, and managing a sales staff is often afterthought—work given less attention than graphics, structure, and product. This is a fundamental error that is many times masked by success. The medium, per se, can be so effective that results look good no matter what. Because of this, many companies don't probe the upper limits.

Selecting a Sales Staff

A convention and trade show is a stage filled with people who want to share with each other. But there are two different groups. Our prospects are one group, an extended family. We are the second, not as tightly knit but an extended family nonetheless. This stage, and the little appreciated intensity we need to sell effectively at a show, must drive both recruiting and training staffs.

Staff-Selection Factors

There are four things to consider:

- Audience interests: The staff should match.
- Where the show takes place: Audiences tend to be regional.
- Personality and prospecting skills: Salespeople must be quick.
- Need for technical support or expert backup.

Who Should Be Part of the Staff

Likes attract. Evaluate the characteristics of those who make up your target audience at the show and match it. Your prospect profile becomes your staff profile.

In case you didn't read Part Two, the show's manager should be able to tell you a lot about its audience profile. Even if audits or registration data from past events are not adequate, the organizer should be able to provide insight. In addition, take a long look at the convention's educational sessions. Visitors decide to attend as much, or more, for the program as for the exhibits. Last, check the *content* of show advertising. It'll tell you whom they are shooting for.

Geographic matching. Even "national" meetings tend to draw more heavily from the region in which the conference takes place.[1] On the average, 20 percent of the audience travels less than 50 miles to the show. Slightly over half travel less than 400 miles to attend. Check this with your show manager. The organizers should be able to estimate how their show compares with the average. Your sales team should mirror the geographic profile of the audience.

Types of prospects. Break a business-to-business show into segments by functions and by job title.

There may be top-level generalists: presidents, general managers, treasurers, and the like.

You may find "end users," such as department heads, plant managers, and accounting vice presidents.

Some prospects may be senior staff specialists: purchasing agents or engineers who specify or recommend purchases.

Each of these groups will look at your products from their own perspective. Your team should include a mixture of skills to match. The audience seems "heavy" with technical staff? Put more people on your team with similar expertise.

In addition to audience matching, there are other factors:

- *Personality blending.* Evaluate personalities. It is not necessary for everyone to be a glib, hail-fellow-well-met type, but each team should include at least one salesperson with an outgoing personality. He or she can encourage others not to be shy about introducing themselves.

- *Female-male balance.* Increasingly, women are moving into influential management and buying positions. Most women have had to work very hard to get ahead. This includes selling. Lots of times they are better at the booth than their male counterparts.

Team Concept

You may have an on-duty team of four or five at a 20-foot booth. In that team there should be a mixture of ages, sexes, races, ethnic, and technical backgrounds—and personalities.

Recruiting a Sales Staff

Knowing the ingredients to blend is less than half the battle. The tough part can be recruiting those ingredients. Selfish motivation inspires all of us to one degree or another. It is especially powerful to salespeople who earn on commission. If going to a show translates to dealing with their own accounts and prospecting within their own territories, you'll find them eager.

Selling to other people's accounts is never as attractive. We have to make sure that longer range benefits are clear and that nondollar rewards are enough to overcome reluctance.

Recruiting Package

Packaging is important. A casual request to help will be treated casually. On the other hand, if you prepare a written plan and recruiting package which proves that thought and sound business judgment are involved, you'll get a professional response.

The package can be based on the written exhibit plans we talk about in both Parts One and Two. Essentially, everyone has to be convinced that care has been exercised in making the decision on participating, that there is a solid rationale for selecting people to work at the show. Altogether, the package elevates the decision-making process.

Package Elements. The items in the package should include:

- Basic information about the show—what, where, and when
- Goals established for the company at the convention, quantified to the degree possible
- Analysis of the audience expected, complete with anticipated geographic and market makeup and composition by job title
- Outline of staff requirements based on the audience analysis
- Outline of activities including preshow promotions, special events at the show, and VIP hospitality
- Copy of the prior year's convention program with emphasis given to the seminar program and competitors at the show

Put your package in a folder and cover it with a memorandum asking for specific help. The memo should point up immediate values to the company or individual.

In addition to providing a plan that shows short- and long-term benefits for the company as a whole, a recruiting effort can point out personal benefits for those who sell at the show. These can include:

- Attending seminars, enhancing knowledge of the industry
- Gaining prestige by attending national or regional meetings, rubbing elbows with sponsoring industry leaders
- Making appointments in advance to meet their own accounts who will be at the convention
- Learning exactly what competitors are trying to sell

- Being in contact with in-company VIPs who attend the show

One top-level salesperson said, "I'd pay my way to the national convention myself if I had to. For the whole year afterward, I start conversations with, 'Did you happen to catch the seminar on XYZ at the convention?' I gain instant credibility."

Out-of-Pocket Expense Coverage

Budgets are always a problem. Occasionally, people willing to give time to be part of an exhibit staff can't afford the expense for travel, hotels, and so on. Try to create and manage and budget that covers this. The advantages are:

- Your boss and the company become aware of exhibit costs that are often hidden.

- Salespeople may be providing sales leads to others. They are giving enough in terms of time.

- If you hold expense account purse strings, a new level of discipline can be exercised. (One Fortune 1000 company follows this practice and sends people home when their performance is poor.)

A *warning*: If you pay out-of-pocket expense for others, set limits. Pay only the basics. If a team member wants to entertain a customer from home, his or her own budget should cover that.

The travel cost of last-minute substitutions should be absorbed by the office from which you recruited in the first place. Late plane reservations cost a lot more than those made in advance.

Local Exhibit Recruiting

Most of us prepare packages of one sort or another for out-of-town shows. They seem more serious, and the travel part requires something on paper anyway. We fall down when the show is in our own back yard. You've got to put the same level of effort into preparing for local shows as you would for one 3000 miles away. Some of the information may be known, but you must still communicate serious purpose.

Preshow Training at the Site

A sales team was going to exhibit at the Consumer Electronics Show in Las Vegas during the first week in January. It conducted preshow training back at home during December, the day after the office Christmas party. Half the staff arrived in Las Vegas a day late.

Other companies conduct "briefing" at the booth 15 minutes before the show opens. Half the people don't show up until well after the opening bell. Either way, it's no wonder the sales teams don't take the shows seriously.

Even if you sell at three or four shows a year, the experience is infrequent and all of it represents less than one-tenth of a year's work. Exhibit selling will forever remain a venture into unfamiliar territory. Staff people will focus on what *is* familiar, current customers. The great opportunity offered at trade shows, exploring for new customers, will take a back seat.

Proper training is a must. Everyone is reminded of product specifics. They are refreshed on floor-selling techniques. Most of all, people are made aware that the company takes exhibit selling seriously. To be effective, the training class must take place just before the show so the material is fresh. The booth is not the spot.

Training Rooms

Rent a "function" room at the convention center or at a hotel close to the arena. Even if your show is at a local convention center, it is well worth the added cost to rent a room there. (Often, meeting rooms have been taken over by the show's sponsor and won't be used until after the show opens. Rental cost may be negligible.)

A meeting room in a hotel out of town may cost you nothing if you serve a meal to the group as part of the deal. If your company pays employee expenses anyway, the added overall cost to the company may be close to zero.

Even if you do spend a few dollars, it's worth it. The underlying goal is to convey a sense of importance to the exhibit. Use the term *training* instead of *briefing* and make sure it takes place in a formal setting. Be professional and the staff will be professional.

Room Layout.   Professional educators know the importance of room layout. The setting must give authority to the leader and reduce the potential for distraction.

Small Groups. The team is small, eight or nine at the most. A standard, rectangular conference table is likely to be the choice. Capture a table end as the place from which to teach. Papers, binders, handouts, and such should be spread out so that the first chair on either side of you will not be filled. Don't let anyone sit at the other end, either. Put a coffeepot there. Center attention on yourself and avoid any kind of attention-getting distraction.

Larger Groups. Sales teams for big companies at key shows can be large: 20, 30, and even 200 people are not uncommon. Seating should be arranged theater style, with an aisle down the middle. If there is room enough, worktables with seats behind should be provided. A podium is required. Use both the podium and the aisle as places from which to teach. Public-speaking lessons may help you.

Use handouts and audiovisuals. Even simple-view graph slides—on an overhead projector—give emphasis and symbolize serious purpose.

Meeting Agenda

No matter how small or large the group, break the meeting into modules.

Introductions. Start by introducing yourself and asking everyone else to do the same. Touch on personal, professional strengths and exhibit experience. It's really important, even if everyone knows each other already. People must "learn" each other in the unfamiliar environment. Team members will start to figure out whom to depend on in different situations. And, if you *don't* know everyone, what you learn may lead·to team shifts to get the right blend.

Show summary. Summarize why the company is exhibiting. Hold specific quantified goals until later in the meeting. However, point out overall goals and results from past exhibits. Outline the overall program, including hospitality suites, press conferences, and seminar programs. Include an overview of the audience as a whole and your target groups within it.

Company VIP remarks. You should invite a company leader, either your boss or someone else "up the line," to make a few remarks. The remarks can be limited to an overview of overall company direction and how the exhibit ties in with it.

Floor performance. At this point, introduce the exhibit-selling-techniquemodule itself. Information you can include is in Chapter 17, and a handout is available for you to copy. *At the conclusion of this module, you should take a break.*

Product or service outline. Each item at the show must be covered, even those familiar to all. You, or another speaker, should emphasize the basics. Salespeople familiar with a product often get embroiled in details and forget the main benefits—the focal point of the short presentations that must be made.

If a new or enhanced offering is to be introduced, the need for product information is clear. You'll probably have a company expert explain it. What may be less clear to the company expert is that there isn't time to make *everybody* an expert. Just the basics are covered.

Exhibit layout. Show a sketch of the booth layout, explaining how products are positioned and pointing out where you expect traffic flows to come from.

Supporting activities. Expand on the summary explanation of how hospitality activities, news conferences, and seminars will fit in.

Administrative requirements. This module includes:

Shift assignments, daily work schedules, postday or postshift meeting schedules.

Paperwork required (such as sales lead and order processing), expense account management, and assignments to attend seminar sessions.

Key account list sharing: These lists should be placed in the booth and referenced by *all* at the start of the day. A copy of the work schedule should be placed there as well, so that inquiring customers can be told when their salesperson will be at the booth.

Specific goals. This "classroom" section of the program should end by citing specific, *quantified* goals to be reached both for the show as a whole and on each day. Translate them into daily performance objectives for each team member. We pointed out earlier that some of us are reluctant to establish specific goals. What happens if the goals are too low, reached too soon? What happens when they are set too high and can't be reached at all? Either way, the show will be more successful than it would have been otherwise. People on unfamiliar ground need guideposts, and goals are guideposts most of us understand. If you are looking for sales leads, set one single qualifier: *Take a lead if it's the kind you'd like to follow up yourself.*

A contest can help stimulate professional activity. It is at this point in the meeting that an incentive program can be introduced. Dollars are not important. Recognition is. A trophy or even a bottle of wine can symbolize that recognition.

Exhibit visit. Save this until last. The closer to the show opening, the better. However, allow enough time to become comfortable in the environment, to learn how to deal with products at the booth, to rehearse sales presentations there before the show.

Social experience. Before or after training, but always before the opening bell, sponsor a group social activity. It can be a staff luncheon or dinner—even a breakfast before training. We pointed out that people have to sort themselves out with their peers at an exhibit. Let this happen before the show starts. Otherwise, it will happen at the exhibit while customers are ignored—like it or not.

This kind of program works, even if only three or four people are involved.

Management During and After the Show

To get top results, the team has to work with very high energy. Members have to be on their feet, alive and alert. Don't ask anyone to work this way for more than 4-hours a day. If the exhibit is in a hotel where everyone is staying, break things up—two on and two off. If a convention hall is the scene and you can't get back and forth to the hotel easily, a single 4-hour stint is all right.

Booth duty is only part of what takes place. You have to take time to walk the floor and note what competitors are offering. Convention seminars must be evaluated and audited. Staff members must meet with their own customers when they are not on duty.

Staff Schedule

It's easy to set up a booth work schedule. All you have to do is blend the skills, personalities, and experience of the team. Even when doing this chore, however, you have to be flexible. There are slack hours when seminars are on, when you can make do with fewer at the booth, freeing up others to attend a session. There are other times when it's "all hands." If you know the convention, you can anticipate a slow last-half-day and let part of the crew go home a night early.

It becomes more difficult to adjust things as the show runs on. After each day you may want to make adjustments, either to improve booth operations or—more frequently—to help individual staff members make their own commitments. Figure 16.1 is a staff schedule illustration.

Postday Critique

At the end of each day, or shift, hold a critique meeting at which you accomplish the following:

- Clean up paperwork. Review sales leads and orders and write them clearly. (Memories play tricks later.)
- Tabulate results from the day. Tell sales stories that might help others.
- Bring up problems with prospects or products. Discuss and solve them if possible.
- Make adjustments to correct team problems.

Keep the meeting tight, well organized, and short. Everyone will have plans to meet their customers or to attend other events shortly, but the meeting is important. Without continuing dialogue and results checking, an exhibit staff can start running off course.

Last-Day Operations

It's especially important to make sure the last day's orders and leads are completed before people depart. There is always extra pressure that day—packing, checking out, and meeting plane schedules.

Paper is our primary exhibit product. Misplaced orders or sales leads do no good. Unless people follow up their own leads, with commissions hanging in the balance, the exhibit job seems complete when they walk off the floor! Not true. Good, accurate pass-along information can be worth its weight in gold. (By the way, anticipate complaints about lead

Overall Exhibit Schedule

Exhibits open	From–to	Hours	Deduct	Active hours
Day 1: Sunday	2 p.m.–6 p.m.	4	2	2
Day 2: Monday	9 a.m.–6 p.m.	9	2	7
Day 3: Tuesday	9 a.m.–6 p.m.	9	2	7
Day 4: Wednesday	9 a.m.–3 p.m.	6	2	4
Total		28	8	20

Team Assignments

Teams identified by color: blue and gold.

Sales Team Schedule

Saturday: All check into hotel in time for 6:00 p.m. staff dinner.

Day 1: Sunday	8:30 a.m.–1 p.m. training session
Day 1: Sunday	2 p.m.–6 p.m. Blue team
Day 1: Sunday	4 p.m.–6 p.m. gold team (all hands for reception)
Day 2: Monday	9 a.m.–1 p.m. gold team (p.m.—seminars/appointments)
Day 2: Monday	1 p.m.–6 p.m. blue team (a.m.—seminars/appointments)
Day 3: Tuesday	9 a.m.–1 p.m. blue team (p.m.—seminars/appointments)
Day 3: Tuesday	1 p.m.–6 p.m. gold team (a.m.—seminars/appointments)
Day 4: Wednesday	9 a.m.–noon blue team (early checkout—flights)
Day 4: Wednesday	Noon–3 p.m. gold team (a.m.—seminars/appointments—later flights)

Note: Teams will meet at the exhibit 15 minutes before team start time each day. Each meets again after each tour is over for a 20-minute critique. Customer appointments and seminar participations should reflect this. Any *gold* team members desiring an early-p.m. flight on Wednesday please advise. Early release a potential.

Figure 16.1. Sample work schedule. In Part Two we developed hypothetical exhibit marketing plans. This estimate of when floor traffic will be light or heavy comes from them.

quality. Make sure the people who take the leads write their names on them. You can refer complaints to the source.)

Your Role on the Show Floor

Try to avoid selling. Your job should be to support and to supervise. Duties should include:

- Observing and coaching sales team members.

- Handling unusual or difficult visitors. These can include press representatives, complaining customers, students who want to take valuable sales time, and VIPs from within the company. (They should be asked to leave the booth during heavy traffic times.)

- Making adjustments in teams as the show progresses, and acting as a central information or complaint bureau for staff members.

- Gathering information about competitors, directly or through staff members. The same is true with information gleaned from seminar sessions or private research programs.

- Making arrangements for exhibit tear-down and transportation after the show.

- Reserving space for your exhibit at the following year's show.

- Ensuring that leads and orders are properly written, and keeping track of all the activities that lead to postshow evaluation—including statistical results reports.

- Conveying a continuing impression that the show is a serious business activity—on the show floor, in the hospitality suite, or at the news conference.

Nondollar Performance Rewards

Earlier we mentioned that competition can stimulate performance but that expensive awards are not necessary. As much as all of us in the selling business are interested in financial reward, we are also attracted by psychic reward. Our competitive nature makes us interested in virtually anything we can earn as a result of our work.

You can have individual and team awards, but keep things in perspective. Sales lead quality is the issue, not the number of leads taken. The quality of an order is the issue. It does little good to take an order if the customer has a history of slow payment.

A special dinner can be given after the show to honor the teams. Presentation of a cup or desk plaque is another possibility. A picture in a company periodical can be important. People will always say that a dollar in the pocket is all they look for, but that's not at all true. A dollar in the pocket, yes, but recognition and respect from peers counts too.

Your Jobs After the Show

We cover part of it in other chapters. Here we concentrate on what you have to do in context with the sales team and its product:

- Both sales orders and leads must be processed. This is no small chore, and you have to gather everything *yourself* to make sure nothing gets lost.

- The exhibit medium is people, both sales team members and outside suppliers who have helped you. The extra touch, symbolizing a professional, can be a series of congratulatory or thank-you notes to those who deserve them. Recognize people and you'll improve show cooperation in the future.

As you know, the next chapter is all about selling technique. Teach it well and you'll gain, establishing yourself as a leader. It's the key to success for everyone—your company, your customers, and yourself.

17

Exhibit Floor Selling

Like a scene from a film, it was 11 in the evening and country rock star Jerry Lee Lewis was moving onstage at Mickey Gilley's western-style nightclub in Pasadena. The house band had finished its music; the "Colorado Kool-Aid" and Lone Star "long necks" were working magic among the hundreds of urban cowboys and cowgirls gathered.

Another scene went on 15 miles west of Gilley's, in a place where the food was less funky and more flambé, where Colorado Kool-Aid was replaced by Courvoisier. Instead of the flying fingers of Jerry Lee Lewis on his piano, diners watched the glossy nails of a honey-haired harpist at the Brownstone, an antique-decorated restaurant in back of a garden on Virginia Avenue just off Westheimer.

Two scenes. Two shows. Some of the players were from yet another taking place at the same time—one that centered on the city's huge Astrodome, its Astrohall, and the parking lots all around. This show had spread to the bars at Gilley's and across the candlelighted tables at the Brownstone.

It was the Offshore Technology Conference, a meeting for the oil industry and those who sell to the people who deliver "black gold." Houston, Texas, was hosting an industry that helped build the city.

At Gilley's clusters of sales cowboys and cowgirls from Cleveland and Kenosha, with newly bought boots and hats, were watching the action and trading stories about who was doing what to whom back in the office. Meanwhile, over at the Brownstone the silver-haired sales vice presidents were doing their best to ensure that last year's big customers were not seduced away by a competitor.

The Offshore Technology Conference illustrates the action, the social and business intercourse that takes place at any convention, large or small, in town or out. We have to understand what happens and, more important, why.

Psychological Implications

How many times have you caught yourself at your booth engaged in pleasant conversation with someone else from your own company? How often have you found yourself leaning against the exhibit back wall or counter, far away from the aisle, waiting for visitors to come to you? Or sitting behind a table with your head bent over some writing?

We don't know what we *should* be doing? Most of us ought to know. We've been exposed to one or more sales training aids, ranging from a booklet distributed by the Trade Show Bureau to expensive custom programs presented by well-qualified consultants.[1] Little emphasis is given in any of them, however, to the natural, acceptable, behavioral barriers that emerge at trade shows. These barriers are why the silver-haired vice presidents give exclusive attention to key customers. They are why we spend more time with each other than in meeting new people, at night around a bar and on the show floor too.

We cluster together or pay attention to the customers we already have because it's comfortable. It's natural. What is *not* natural is aggressively reaching out to a new "suspect," especially if you are looking for leads that others can follow up and sell.[2]

Barriers

If we understand the symptoms and can spot them, in ourselves and in our teammates, we can work together to overcome them.

Fear of Rejection. Prospecting is never easy, but at least the office cold call, letter, or telephone call is preplanned. "Suspects" are thought about one at a time. Although we're rejected more often than not, rejection is palatable and impersonal in what we feel is a pure business environment.

At trade shows, we must single out visitors to say hello to instantly, often based only on the color of a badge. We don't even know their names until after we start the dialogues. In addition, the environment at a convention is both business and social. Somehow rejection can seem more personal, especially when the event takes place at a resort and attendees are casually dressed.

Defining Roles.   It's fairly easy to spot fear in ourselves. What's not so easy to spot, and more universal, is a need to define roles with our peers. Even if everyone knows each other well, we have to get reacquainted in the unfamiliar environment. Unconsciously, we're trying to sort out who is going to do what at the show. That is why office "war stories" are told, personal futures compared, and company policies complained about.

If you read Chapter 16, you'll remember two steps you can take to help solve this problem. First, at the start of a training meeting make sure people introduce themselves and include their business and personal backgrounds. Second, the team should gather for a social get-together before the show starts.

Training meeting and social hour or not, you have to try and get this need taken care of before the exhibit opens. Otherwise, you'll do it right at the booth, ignoring potential customers as they walk past. That's a guarantee! The behavior is natural and if you don't take the barrier down before the opening bell, you'll do it during the show—missing business in the process.

Know the symptoms, and kid each other when they emerge at the exhibit. "Whoops, we're telling company war stories. . . . You guys went over the demonstration three times already! . . . Who's that hiding behind the potted palm?"

Self-Fulfilling Prophecy.   The next barrier to overcome is embodied in our internal attitude toward success or failure. This one is really buried inside and rarely surfaces.

If you arrive at the show excited and have a true desire to succeed, you will. If you don't, you won't—and, as the hours move along, you will unconsciously create any number of quite sensible reasons for self-justifying failure!

You can spot symptoms in yourself and work on them. Here is a sampler of things we say when we don't have a positive outlook:

- "Prospecting isn't that critical. Our most important customers are those we've already got."

- "It's too bad we forgot the spec sheets—makes it tough to make a coherent presentation to a prospect."

- "I can't ask my customers to come to the booth at a special time."

- "I'll have to run over to registration and get another program."

- "When the demonstration unit broke down, it killed the day."

- "I had to spend a lot of time with that one, but it helped to solidify the lead."

Paperwork Completion. The best of us are terrible when it comes to paperwork. The best salespeople seem to be bright, quick thinkers who are not too interested in detail. Handwriting may be sloppy, and the more formal education, it seems, the worse it can get. A group of MBAs at an exhibit can produce practically indecipherable follow-up information.

There's tongue in cheek in this. MBA or not, however, the problem is serious. An exhibit's product is paper—very valuable paper. It does little good to write an order or lead that can't be read by someone else. It's tough to shift gears at the end of a successful sales contact, methodically writing down details in the middle of show floor hubbub. You have to make yourself do it, or at least make rough notes you can clean up later. Even if your memory is terrific, you can forget nuance, details. And there will be other pressures at the end of the show day, just at that moment when you promised yourself you'd clean things up. Get over the paperwork barrier quickly.

Retail Influence

The way we have to operate owes much to retail expectations. In some respects, a trade show floor is a retail environment. Without realizing it, even industrial product buyers expect to be treated in much the same fashion as we are treated in a quality retail store.

Do you often see salespeople smoking in a quality store? No. Do you often see them sitting down? No. Do they carry containers of coffee around the store? No. Do you see them huddled together talking after you enter? No. Do you see merchandise spread about in a confusing, unattractive manner? Dirty fixtures or windows? Hardly. Do salespeople in quality stores dress casually? Not often.

Lots of what we have to do is based on retailing reality, modified to fit the circumstance. For instance:

- Wear your name badge on your right side, so it can be seen when you shake hands. It's courtesy. It is easier for a visitor to catch your name if it can be seen while you are saying it. Make sure the type is large, easy to read. (Some companies bring their own nameplates, using show badges only to get into the hall.)

- Here is another. Speak clearly. Ambient sound in arenas and hotel ballrooms is loud. One in ten people suffers a degree of hearing impairment. Most don't even know it. And when they don't hear you, they don't say, "What was that?"

Before the Show

Getting set for selling is half the battle. You have to prepare yourself in two ways, one obvious and the other not so obvious. The obvious includes all those specific things about products and orders, the technical elements in selling. The not so obvious is making sure you are comfortable so you can concentrate, right from the start.

- Make sure your travel and hotel arrangements are confirmed. If the show is in town, know where you'll park your car.

- Write letters of invitation to all your customers. Try to make appointments for when the traffic on the show floor is light or you are not on booth duty. You'll be able to spend more time with them.

- Make sure you arrive 15 minutes early, and plan other activities so you can stay 20 minutes after the show day is over to clean up that paperwork.

- Wear standard business dress for your industry and region, even if the convention takes place at a resort and visitors will be dressed informally. This can mean doubling your wardrobe. You may need casual clothes after hours, "dressing down" for the occasion.

   Business dress conveys business purpose. For the shy, it is also insulation against feeling that show floor rejection is personal. More important, it is an underlying courtesy. (Remember our retail expectations.) We represent our companies and must look that way.

- Wear comfortable shoes. Standing 3 or 4 hours on hard concrete, though carpet covered, is wearing. Podiatrists say that when feet get tired the rest of the body and the mind soon follow. Older, comfortable shoes are a must; for women, low heels.

Show Floor Selling Hints

Sales Conversation

An exhibit sales conversation is broken into three parts: introduction, presentation, and "close." We have to control all three, sensing when to move from one to another. The first is introduction.

Introduction. This is when you screen your prospect, finding out whether or not there will be mutual benefit in conducting a sales conversation.

- *Search and reaction.* Stand at the edge of the booth, facing oncoming traffic. Check the eyes of visitors and look at the badges they are wearing. At most conventions, color codes differentiate exhibitors, press, speakers, and spouses. Attendees, potential prospects, can be identified. Know which is which.

    You see inquisitive eyes and the right color badge. Now evaluate "body language." It offers clues to personality and attitude. A bit rushed, businesslike? Or relaxed, on a stroll? Try to match or mirror this visual message in the way you introduce yourself.

- *Greeting.* Clearly, words and techniques will differ, depending on the situation and your personality, but here are some pointers:

    Say hello and stop the visitor. Call the person by name and set up a learning situation for yourself. Ask about interest or responsibility. It's an open-ended question, one that can't be answered "yes" or "no." You have to *listen to and evaluate* the response.

    Develop two or three ideas on how you can do this, and practice them. Don't memorize but have a conversational flow in mind, such as, "Mr. Jones—Bob Smith. We have exciting things to show you, but what are you looking for at the show?"

    Never start a conversation with, "Can I help you?" What can you say after people respond, "No, I'm just looking"?

- *Response.* Listen and decide. If there's potential, lead your prospect to the part of your display that's of interest. If not, be honest but offer the visitor the option of looking around alone.

Your greeting, response, and decision should take under a minute.

Presentation. Your basic presentation should be a summary, taking only a couple of minutes after the greeting, response, and decision.

- Construct it the way a newspaper article is written. All the essentials should be touched upon in a very short time. Each can then be expanded upon as necessary.

- As you touch on points, ask questions to keep your prospect in the conversation. The prospect will provide clues on how you are doing and how you should adjust the presentation. For example, "How does this feature compare with what you've got?" Stay in control of the dialogue, but be flexible and shift directions to reflect prospect interests.

- Often visitors arrive in pairs, or a second person joins during a presentation. Be sure to include everyone in what you are saying.

Rehearse in advance, but don't memorize. Do have a firm grasp of key features and applications so you'll know how to adjust.

Close. The clues will lead you to the close, an initial expression of interest. Closing questions should be asked within 5 minutes, including the minute of greeting.

- At this point, a "yes" or "no" question is best. "Are you interested in ordering at the show?. . . Do you think we should set up an appointment in your office after the convention?"
- Don't press too hard if there is objection. Probe for an honest response. Don't force a sales lead for its own sake. Listen and sense the ultimate value of what's offered to your prospect. Ask yourself, "Would I like to get this lead to follow up?"
- If you take a lead, ask for a business card or write down full information. Don't depend on the credit-card-type name registration machines used at many shows. The facts are not always complete, and visitors often don't bother to have clerical errors corrected.

In addition to writing down what your prospect is interested in, note why. What is the particular reason that the product appeals? Is there any competitive information to remember? We said before that you may not be able to get it all down at the moment. But be sure to clean up notes before day's end.

Contact Conclusion. Most times you *don't* make a sale or take a lead! After a simple thanks, both of you go on to other things. When you do have success, there is a tendency to linger longer than necessary. Both of you are happy at the outcome. In addition, your reward is moving back out to that booth edge, starting all over again.

Write out some closing lines in advance. As with the other parts of the presentation, don't memorize but keep a flow in mind. By the way, don't end contacts by handing out sales literature. There is little likelihood that the pieces will be read, and brochures are expensive. It's far more economical to spend a few minutes creating a conversational goodby. If brochures are requested, mail them later. It's another contact opportunity.

Voice and Body Language

Throughout your presentation be conscious not only of what is said but also how it is said. And understand body language, how to read it and how to use it.

Voice

The way you use words, and your voice, can have an impact on what's communicated.

- Your words and tone of voice should attempt to mirror the prospect. If she or he seems formal, quiet and businesslike, follow that approach. If your visitor projects a relaxed, friendly image don't be fooled by it, but assume a more casual demeanor.

- You have to project, just like an actor on a stage. We said that one in ten people suffers a degree of hearing loss, and the sound level is high in exhibit halls. Speak clearly. Make your lips round, almost pursed, instead of flat or wide. *Think of your mouth as an inverted megaphone with the wide end at the back.* Even if you talk softly, you project more. Try it. Now.[3]

- Present an image of relaxed competence, not one that makes you appear to be superficially extroverted, hail-fellow-well-met.

Body Language

You can observe it and use it. We've mentioned one example, watching the pace of a prospect walking down an exhibit hall aisle.

- When you are at the edge of the booth looking for prospects, stand erect with your hands at your sides or with your fingers laced together in front, in a cup below your waist. The appearance you convey is one of alertness, a readiness and willingness to serve. If there's little traffic, keep moving slowly back and forth to avoid giving an appearance of guarding the booth.
    Think of the alternatives. Parade rest, with hands behind the back, makes you into a military guard. Arms folded across the chest? Even

more defensive. Hands in pockets? You don't care. Sitting behind a table? Might do a favor by answering a question or two.

- Don't get so tied up in your presentation that you miss signals being sent by your prospect. For instance, if your visitor glances at a watch it means things may be running too long, that the prospect may be running late for something. Ask about it. Another is when your visitor glances back to a product after you've moved to another in the presentation. Stop. There's a question to answer.

- You can signal the end of a demonstration with body language. You're standing side by side, bending over slightly looking at the product. Simply straighten up and turn to face your prospect.

Team Signals

Private signals can be worked out to smooth the flow of work. Team selling and problem solving can be a help. Here are examples:

- A visitor simply does not want to leave. The contact may have been pleasant, but the attendee does not understand you have more work to do and does not take a hint to leave.

  Have a body language signal that means help—something subtle, such as pulling on an earlobe. It tells your teammate to enter the conversation and remind you of an appointment or phone call. You thank your teammate, allowing that person to leave, and then conclude the contact.

- Every so often a visitor may launch into a complaint or negative comments about a product. You want to move that person out into the aisle, away from other prospects, to solve the problem. In addition, there are times when it is effective to introduce an "authority figure" to help reassure the prospect.

  Establish a verbal signal to alert a teammate that he or she is being introduced as that authority figure, a manager or product specialist. For instance, it could be the use of formal address in introduction, "Mr. Green, I'd like you to meet Ms. Jones."

  The authority figure leads the prospect out of the booth and continues the contact.

Working with Outside Entertainers

Do you work with professional talent at your booth: demonstrators, greeters, or live show narrators who help to draw visitors? Don't treat the show as something apart, but instead integrate the entertainment people into the team.

For instance, at the start of a live presentation, you should become "audience," standing close to the performers. People like to join in with others already watching a performance. As the show attracts visitors, edge back through the crowd reading badges. At its conclusion, introduce yourself to one of the visitors.

When professional shows finish, visitors often introduce themselves to the entertainers. Don't expect performers to have enough product knowledge to complete a selling contact. Work out a method in advance that allows you to enter the conversation and take over the contact. Sometimes a good performer can hold a prospect in social conversation while you take care of the first contact you made at the end of the show. You'll have to work quickly, however, and step in as soon as possible.

Professionalism

We know we can't smoke, drink, eat, or make a mess at an exhibit. There are other ground rules that improve our effectiveness.

- You need good sleep. Even if you have to entertain clients in the evenings, try to end them early. You have to be alert. Working at an exhibit after only 3 or 4 hours of rest is tough. You'll be dull, mind and body. Your performance will suffer.

- Don't let down when the aisles are not crowded. We're bored, we lose sight of objectives and get into conversations with each other. It is during these times that some of the most serious exhibit shoppers come to the show floor. They know it's going to be quiet. They feel they'll learn more. The ground rule: Stay on the alert.

- Try to attend educational seminars when you are not serving at the booth or meeting with your own customers. You'll learn things to use in sales presentations, gain credentials, and even spot potential customers among those who attend.

Exhibit selling is not easy. We don't do it very often, and the techniques are different from those we use day to day. You need to refresh yourself. Read this chapter before every show and make a copy of Figure 3.6, *the dos and don'ts of exhibit selling*. Put it in your briefcase.

You'll be able to entertain key customers, share some "Colorado Kool-Aid" with friends and associates, and be a sales prospecting champion at the same time.

18
Postshow Operations

When the public address announcement closes the show, there isn't a moment before the first of the forklift trucks appears. Empty crates are moving to spaces, to be packed. Aisle carpet is being rolled up. The craft teams are busily taking apart what was assembled only a few short days before. The chaos of setup returns.

We've touched on what has to be done at different points after a show. All too many of us think our jobs are complete at the closing bell. Sales leads and even orders have been left on countertops, or packed in crates, never to be seen again! The sales team sometimes walks out without a backward glance.

Dismantle and Shipping

The obvious sometimes eludes us. Show service personnel tell stories about finding exhibits standing alone, with not a single company representative in evidence, during moveout. One can almost visualize a complete exhibit—graphics, structure, counters, display products, and half-filled ashtrays—standing alone on a carpet island in a quiet sea of concrete, halfway across an empty and dimly lighted arena.

During the show, you have to order labor to take down and pack your exhibit. The same is true for products. Arrangements for shipping must be made and labels written.

As units are dismantled, panels, parts, and display products must be checked for damage. A list of damaged or marred elements must be prepared. This is especially true for exhibits that move from show to show without exhibit house intervention. At many companies, the booth will be used next by another group. If so, you have to accept responsibility for the company's appearance at the next show even though you won't be there.

Give special care to little things—literally. Exhibits are sent out with spare fittings, built-in boxes for bolts, basic setup materials such as tapes, wire, touch-up paint, brushes, and even special tools. (See Figure 3.4.) Display products are sent to shows with connection cables, spare parts, and instruction manuals. All these things must be found and packed. And everything must be accomplished very quickly. In most cases, the time allocated before the hall must be vacated is less than half the time allowed for installation.

Make travel plans with the removal process in mind. Some of the show service industry disasters result from the exhibit manager's failure to make a plan. Sketchy verbal directions left behind for service personnel are not enough.

Paper Products

We've emphasized that any exhibit's most important product is paper. Sales leads. Orders. It's all very nice to talk about establishing presence, reaching public relations goals, but the value of an exhibit is measured by the paper it produces.

- Sales orders and leads

- Requests for literature or information of a general nature

- Information about what competitors exhibited at the show

- New information about the industry and its problems, frequently backed up by papers presented in seminars or technical sessions

- Data for research—questionnaires filled in at the show

- Copies of trade periodicals distributed at the show, as well as pickup of press releases appearing during the show

- Final lists of personnel at the show, along with notes on individual productivity

- Copies of preliminary contracts or agreements with show management regarding space for the following year's show

- Exhibit transportation documents, bills and receipts for expenses that were incurred at the show, and copies of work tickets or removal orders that will result in bills mailed to the office later.

- Exhibit and product crate lists, with a complete inventory of what is in each, along with damage or replacement notes on any items needing attention before the next show.

We've pointed out the need to process sales leads and orders every day during the show to avoid getaway-day crunch. At that point your time is going to be crowded with other demands that can't be avoided.

Back in the Office

For most of us, managing an exhibit is an infrequent chore, probably representing as little as 10 percent of our jobs. Work from the other 90 percent piles up while we're away. Meetings are scheduled. Customers call. Bosses demand reports. The in-box fills. Even if you've called in every day, there hasn't been time to cover the demands.

In spite of them, it is essential that your first day back be considered another show day. Sales leads and orders must be sent on, reports written, and damage advisories given to the exhibit house.

One Fortune 500 company exhibit manager found a pile of leads marked "hot" on top of a sales office desk 6 weeks after his show. By then, the leads had turned to ice. At the same time, top management was questioning the validity of exhibiting. The problem was not the medium. It was the company's use of exhibiting's paper product.

Fast follow-up is essential. Prospects should be contacted within a week after the show, even if only to set up an appointment. Don't forget that show visitors comparison shop and may have given a lead to a competitor as well as yourself. (An exhibit manager *attended* a show to shop for portable exhibits for his company. Four leads were given to exhibit manufacturers. The local dealer for one made contact 6 months later, 3 months after units were purchased from a competitor.)

Postshow Reports

Here is a list of the reports you may need to generate:

- Exhibit damage report
- Product or demonstration damage report
- Competition analysis report

- Preliminary results report for management
- Preliminary budget report

When you send leads on to be followed up, attach a short form that can be filled out and sent back evaluating the quality of each. Don't make it complicated. Ask for simple things.

- Potential to close: high, medium, low, or No
- Potential dollar value within 1 year
- If sold, value of initial order

Request response in 30 days. For those that don't come in, ask again.

If several people have been part of the sales team, you should write each a thank-you letter. As part of that letter, you should attach a blank form upon which each can make comments and suggestions for future shows.

Sometimes we sponsor postshow outside research to help evaluate our exhibits. We have to provide final information about the products displayed, along with products offered by competitors, so that the questionnaire can be written. If you've done some research of your own at the show, perhaps on how people like a product feature, completed questionnaires have to be organized so that they can be evaluated.

Unless your show is purely for order writing, you'll have to wait for a while before making a final evaluation as to how well you did. A second and final report can be delayed for as much as 6 months. For it to be of value at that time, however, you have to keep track of order and lead activity, research results, and press pickup. That report can also include both recommendations for change and a sense of what sales team members, responding to thank-you letter questionnaires, recommend.

Chapter 10 makes the point that you have to evaluate exhibits against each other and that we've got to remember their essential supporting role. Make sure everyone you talk to understands that focus. You're trying to make something good into something better. That process starts the day you get home from the show.

19
International Exhibits

People from overseas who want to exhibit here will learn more from this book than the reverse. This one small chapter just scratches the surface for those of us who want to market overseas. Nevertheless, the book's focus on the techniques used for audience analysis, goal setting, and matching products to interests are valid regardless of where in the world we exhibit.

Decision Process

A number of factors will influence your decision to exhibit and influence the goals you set. Here are some questions to ask and answer:

- Has product distribution been established? Do you have a sales team in-country, or distributor partners in place? Or, is your goal to further the process of finding potential in-country partners?

- Do you need immediate sales, or is your goal one of longer-term trust building? Is it market research?

- How much do you know about your product's suitability in the country being considered? For instance, if you manufacture window screening and want to sell in Europe, you'll find it little needed in Holland and a good part of the rest of northern Europe.

- Who are your potential customers? How many and where?

- What is the show like? Who is the organizer or sponsor? What is its past history? What can the sponsor tell you about audience breakdown? Even in Europe, a most sophisticated exhibiting market, there may be less information available than you'd like. Many countries have stringent privacy protection laws that, to a degree, inhibit show organizers gathering audience demographics.

Information Sources

There are a number of sources that can provide insight:

- The United States Department of Commerce in Washington is a key source; however, you can also contact that department's commercial officers at embassies in countries being considered. The Commerce or State Departments in Washington can provide addresses and names. (Or check the district offices of the Department of Commerce in major cities here.) The commercial sections in our embassies will help individual firms or, more often, groups of companies to participate in foreign trade shows. Leave lots of lead time![1]

- Your own trade association may be packaging information about international opportunities for members. The U.S.-based International Exhibitors Association has information packages to help firms in overseas exhibiting. In addition, it has "hub city" chapters in some important overseas exhibit markets.

- If you have an in-country sales team or partnership of one type or another, the people there should be able to provide the best information of all, both about shows and potential.

- Most of the countries in which we might consider exhibiting maintain consulates in our major cities. They represent the interests of their nationals here and try to help improve trade. They, too, can be an excellent source of information and advice. In addition, many of our national trading partners operate trade bureau and chamber of commerce offices in our large cities. (Lots of them are located in New York City, listed in the Manhattan *Yellow Pages* under "Business and Trade Organizations.")

Until quite recently most of us did not have to think much about the international selling. The domestic market was enough. Even now there is a certain insular quality in our outlook. We presume too much and know too little. We cannot presume. Much of the progress made here by business people from overseas is a direct result of learning before selling. European, African, South and Central American, Middle Eastern, and Asian businesses take this approach. Think of the Japanese and, increasingly, the Chinese. They learn about us before they sell to us.

Exhibiting Differences

The differences between exhibiting here and in other countries fall into three areas. First are the broad cultural, religious, and historical differences affecting all levels of communication. Second are specific differences in the ways in which exhibit marketing operations are implemented. Third are pricing, product packaging, and product knowledge differences.

Cultural Differences

We are faster paced than other cultures. A slower pace, more patience, and trust building are required overseas. In many countries personal values are more intertwined with business than is the case here. In addition, a greater degree of formality is traditional.

People from most other countries are more adaptable to different cultures than we are. An international focus has been part of their lives for a long time. There is an instinctive understanding that one does not try to impose one's own values or traditions on others—especially when trying to sell. We don't sense that, much to our distress.

English is an international language, but that does not lessen the customer's national traditions and values. Your prospect may speak English and still not buy even if your products are better and cheaper than the competition. The quality of your communication and your sensitivity can count as much as the product itself.

Here are some illustrations of communications differences:

- *Names.* They are important everywhere and they can be confusing. If you meet an American woman named Kim Kresge-Reilly, you assume she is married and that her husband's name is Reilly. She could be addressed as Ms. Reilly.

  In parts of Europe it is the same but names are reversed. The husband's name would be in the middle. In Holland, for instance, Mrs. Lytsman-Piernbaum would be addressed by her husband's last name: She would be Mrs. Lytsman.

  In Latin America a full name includes the last names of both parents. The short form, most often used, is the father's. Its placement depends on where you are. In Spanish-speaking Argentina the father's is the middle name: Raul Mendoza Miller would be called Mr. Mendoza. In Portuguese-speaking Brazil it's last: Raul Mendoza Miller would be addressed as Mr. Miller.

Asian, Middle Eastern, and African name traditions differ too. It is critical to learn proper form. In addition to knowing how names are used, we must wait to be asked before using first names.

- *Role of women.* They are starting to emerge in business around the world, but many of the cultures in the Middle East and South America are conservative, slower to change. The same is true in Japan. It can be difficult for an American woman to work alone in some areas. Very much can depend on the individual. A woman may be quite effective, but she must be sensitive to the problems. The goal is selling, not changing another culture.

- *Language and gesture.* Words and even gestures take on different meanings in different cultures. Political, religious, and sexual overtones can create different meanings. Coca-Cola had to be renamed in China because the spoken words implied something akin to an animal fluid. One of Sikorsky's helicopters is named the Spirit in the United States. The company found that the word is used in a strict religious context in certain countries. We use a gesture to indicate that everything is okay, making a circle by touching the end of the thumb to the end of the first finger. In some other cultures the gesture is an obscenity. In Japan it signifies money.

  We must use formal English. Even if we're talking with people from other countries who seem to know English very well, they are unlikely to understand our jargon: on the same wavelength, shotgun approach, or buzzword.[2]

- *Product design and packaging.* A greater emphasis is given to the appearance of even the most mundane industrial product's package, and to the product itself, especially in Europe. Germany's Hanover Trade Fair administers a major design competition for the products exhibited. Utility, cost, and service are not enough to gain sales.

Exhibit Development

From graphics to take-down, there are differences that must be understood. For instance:

- *Copy length.* Vocabulary and grammar are more specific, more precise in many languages than in English. It takes more time or space to say the same thing. Sikorsky uses the rule of thumb that 20 percent more time is needed for translations of audiovisual materials, 20 percent more space is required for printed brochures and graphic signs.

- *Colors and flowers.* In many countries, colors and flowers are used to convey specific messages with which Americans are not familiar—most of them related to mourning, death, or special events. For instance, in Japan the 16-petal chrysanthemum is reserved for the imperial family's crest.

- *Exhibit spaces.* Show organizers may provide more than we are used to. Small exhibit spaces may be rented in 3-by-3 or 3-by-4 meter units, but special floors under which utilities run are provided at many shows. The spaces may be delineated by full walls on three sides, with the open side facing the aisle. The height of the wall may be 4 meters, allowing construction of a second deck. A special ceiling may cover the entire exhibit area.

  Exhibit designers will focus more on what they can do *within* the space, called a *shell* than on designs here that of necessity include construction of standing back walls.

- *Exhibit construction.* In Europe—and in many other parts of the world—exhibit builders set up shops at the site of the show, instead of following our prefabrication and on-site assembly process. Although fully prefabricated, reusable exhibits are starting to be seen, most are built from the ground up and few are saved after a show.

- *Show length and type.* Our conventions and trade shows last 3 or 4 days. In other countries, 5 and more. We have a great proliferation of relatively narrow interest, industry-specific shows. In other countries, more shows seem to be "horizontal," larger and longer lasting fairs that attract audiences and exhibitors representing broader interests. You'll have to work harder at attracting those who should be especially interested in your specific products.

  You'll also have to work harder at providing more prepurchase information. There will be greater emphasis on learning, in advance, more of the things we teach customers here after they buy. How does a product work? How is it installed and serviced? Who will be available to help if problems emerge?

  Good advance promotion among current customers and prospects may be more important. Many American firms may be going througha time of trust building, learning.

- *Buyer behavior.* Two United States and United Kingdom exhibit research firms have compared findings. There are surprisingly similar attitudes among visitors at American and English trade shows. While both firms shy away from making specific judgments about other European trade show audiences, they feel there are more similarities than differences. If a company can sell effectively at a trade show in the United States, it should be able to sell effectively at overseas shows, at least in Europe.[3]

Pricing

United States companies just starting out in international markets must be prepared to talk price at exhibits, even if the goal is simply to create awareness or gage product potential. Import duties, freight cost, and especially the potential impact of changes in the relative value of the dollar are subjects of considerable interest. Are prices fixed or do they shift with the dollar's exchange rate? This kind of question will be asked.

Need for Overseas Advice and Help

English language copy must be translated, and not just literally. The translation should be done by a person brought up in the country where the show is taking place, then retranslated back to English to confirm meaning. The work can be done "in-country" or by a person from the country living in the United States. The nation's consulate or trade mission here may be able to provide a list of qualified people.

When you visit a country, it is best to have a translator alongside, not only to perform language services but also to warn when you might be making social or business communications mistakes. Visit the show site in advance to meet the organizers and show service people. Local traditions and conditions must be explored in advance. It's well worth the extra time and money for the trip.

A complete information package must be prepared for all who will attend the show. Perhaps our biggest problem is remembering that we are the visitors, the foreigners. Our hosts may fully understand American traditions and outlooks, but will they buy from us if we do not try to understand their traditions, outlooks, and special needs? The evidence says no, even if we have a better product or service.

An overseas exhibit contractor should be employed. The show's organizer can recommend one. An in-country sales team can explore the market. An international trade association may be able to help, or a competitor who has been in the country before can be asked for advice. And, as we indicated before, the International Exhibitors Association can be asked for information. There are international exhibit service firms, many based in the United Kingdom or Hong Kong, that can organize exhibit operations worldwide.

Transportation

Cargo moves on paper. This is especially so with any sort of international freight movement. No matter how small the exhibit or product, no matter how light in weight or small in size, shipping can plunge an exhibit manager into a wonderworld of paper. An incomplete list of forms to be filled out includes such things as:

1. Shipper's export declaration

2. Commercial invoice

3. Certificate of registration

4. Certificate of origin

5. Bill of lading

6. Carnet

7. Export license

8. Master airway bill

9. Shipper's letter of instructions

We can't complete the transactions. But we do have to know that international shipping takes *time*—not only for the cargo movement but also for the processing of paper. We have to deal with an international freight forwarder or custom house broker and remember that at least two governments, and more than one department in each of them, may be involved.

There are some ground rules and terms you may have to understand:

- *Bond.* A bond representing 40 percent of the shipment's value may have to be paid. The money is held to pay import fees in other countries in case you sell the products instead of bringing them back home.

- *Export license.* It can take up to 6 months to clear an export license. You must describe what you are shipping in full detail.

- *Carnet.* This is like a passport for goods. It is often required when salespeople carry samples through several countries.

- *Export declaration.* A relatively simple form, it must be filled out to help the government keep track of the dollar values of exports and imports.

- *Literature.* You may have to pay an import fee on anything that will be left in the country where the show takes place. Most often, sales brochures fall into this category. They should be marked "Printed in U.S.A." A printer's invoice can establish value.

- *Shipper's letter of instruction.* An SLI is required to set value for insurance and customs purposes.

We said many exhibits are built on site at overseas shows. This reduces transit cost and paperwork. You are left with little more than display products, literature, and giveaways or gifts to ship.

Transportation Costs

It's impossible for us to cover specific expense, but there are some differences between domestic and overseas shipping to keep in mind. They affect what you have to spend.

Each shipment is broken into three parts:

- Part 1 is from your location to the point at which the freight moves out of the country.

- Second is the movement across international waters.

- Third is movement in the country where the show is taking place.

An overseas shipment can be handled as a single job. The in-country portions at either end should be part of an overall package. If the bill of lading shows an overseas destination, the van line carrying the freight to your port of embarkation does not have to use its U.S. tariffs to figure prices.

Shipping back and forth between the United States and Canada is easier. Presuming all the paperwork and clearances have been obtained, you can load an exhibit and display products on a van in the United States and never off-load until the trailer reaches the show hall in Canada. This helps reduce cost and the potential for damage.

Exhibit Construction

We mentioned on-site exhibit construction. There are advantages, but quality is uneven, depending on how much experience local craftspeople have with exhibits. In Europe, for instance, quality is high. It is less so in Latin America, parts of Asia, and in other developing countries. European exhibit firms often send their own people to supervise building, sometimes working themselves alongside local labor teams.[4]

United States Department of Commerce

The United States is interested in fostering export and operates exhibit programs that involve bringing companies together for a collective presence at overseas shows. Some are good opportunities. Others may not be as meaningful from a sales viewpoint.

First, serious show visitors have specific product and product application interests. They will not necessarily visit a pavilion sponsored by the United States (or any other country) simply because it is nationally sponsored. If you participate, focus attention on your own promotional program to attract your own target audience.

Second, keep in mind that the educational seminars presented by the fair organizer must cover subjects that will attract your audience. Prepurchase education is a must for buyers everywhere. The sessions are every bit as important an attraction as having the chance to see competing products, side by side, on a trade show floor.

This chapter is little more than a primer on international exhibiting. It raises more questions than it answers. Getting started won't be easy, but the rewards—in both sales and personal development—can be great. We just have to remember to bring more than our products to market. We must bring understanding for others, both personal and professional. We must bring a product plus: knowledge.

20

Exhibit Marketing in Real Life: A Case History

If you read Part Two, you followed two hypothetical exhibit-marketing programs we used to help explain planning procedure. Now we tell the story of how both Parts Two and Three were applied in real life: a real exhibitor, designer, builder, trade show, and product with real goals and costs and results—a gut rattler of a marketing program centered on an 8-by-10-foot booth space at a single trade show.

Exhibitor

Mitchell A. Fink Associates (MFA) is a little company based in New York. Not even 10 people work there. For over a decade it has created expensive, custom computer software for Wall Street financial institutions. Along the way, MFA developed special expertise in writing programs for investment advisors, firms managing other people's money.

Then, encouraged by a trade association, the Fink group wrote an off-the-shelf program for small firms that can't afford and don't need big computers and custom software.

June: the Situation

The software product was being fine-tuned. The MFA team had been working for a year. Two programmers were devoting full time to it. An outside company had been hired to write its user manual.

Company owner Mitchell Fink knew his product had to be introduced in the fall. He had never done that before. There was no advertising agency to call on, and Fink had never sponsored an exhibit. Nonetheless, he decided to unveil his product at a show. The event's organizer, a trade magazine, had provided a list of 1500 people it claimed as visitors at the prior year's show. Fink found 250 prospects among them.

The Microcomputerized Investing Conference/Exhibition was scheduled for October 29th and 30th in New York City.[1] The hours the exhibit hall would be open had not been published when Fink made his decision, but he figured 16 hours selling time in 2 days.

Most of the 8-by-10-foot booth spaces were offered at $800 each. A few, in places that seemed to offer potential for more traffic, were priced at $1200. Fink decided to plunk down the extra 400, renting 80 square feet across the main aisle from a cocktail bar. His logic: Wall Street people like a spot of something after work.

Mitchell Fink used a draft of this book to help plan his program.

MFA Objectives

Fink set goals in three areas: sales, awareness, and image. In addition to booth space, he decided on a suite at the hotel for private demonstrations and customer entertainment. MFA also decided to organize a seminar for the educational conference tied in with the exhibition.

Sales Goals

- *Selling contacts at the booth: 320.* There would be 2 people at the booth for 16 hours, each making 10 contacts an hour. Using our waste-factor calculation, Chapter 5, Fink felt he'd reach all 250 identified as his target. (Normally, you'd subtract potentially slow times and be left with total active hours. Multiply this lower number by 10 contacts per person to develop the contact objective for the show as a whole.) Fink decided to ignore slack-hour analysis for goal-setting purposes.

- *Qualified sales leads: 32.* Fink, now more conservative, said no to the book's advice that he could convert 20 percent of their contacts into leads. The 32-lead goal was 10 percent of 320.

- *Private demonstrations in the suite: 15.* Of the 32 leads, Fink felt a half-dozen would want an in-depth demonstration in the suite. The balance of demonstrations would be given to people he termed "friends of the court," big current customers and trade press representatives.

- *Sales conversions.* He was conservative again, rejecting the 50-percent conversion ratio we suggest. He opted for one sale in eight, four sales from 32 leads. The product was to be priced at just under $8000. The resulting revenue goal: $32,000.

- *Sales of major custom software projects.* Fink felt his new product would renew interest among traditional, large customers. So he set a sales goal for major custom software projects: Two sales within 14 months after the show. Revenue potential: $120,000.

Image and Awareness Goals

- *Advertising and direct mail.*   MFA felt it had to advertise both the firm and the product before the show to build booth traffic. The preshow promotion goal was 10 advance appointments.

- *Current customers to be entertained: 20.*   Fink knew current customers would be curious. He wanted to respond. Although they were not potential buyers for the new product, the firm's reputation would be enhanced. One or two might think about new major projects that could involve MFA.

- *One postshow article in a trade magazine.*   There are a large number of small investment advisory firms, too many to contact in a short time. A responsibly written, positive "review" in a trade magazine could stimulate interest and build trust.

- *Seminar leadership.*   Fink's seminar program would be purely educational; however, it would enhance the MFA reputation.

Sales Operations at the Show

Four people would split booth duties, and each pair would work 2-hour shifts. Fink would supplement during high-traffic hours. Upstairs, in the suite, the firm's senior software designer would give private demonstrations. Fink himself would be there when not at the booth. Three other employees would drop by at times to help and gain experience. The whole company would be involved in one way or another.

Exhibit Marketing Program

The marketing program was to involve advertising, direct mail, current customer advisories, publicity, booth selling, private show demonstrations, and hospitality.

Mitchell Fink did not want to buy an exhibit. He didn't feel comfortable making the investment. But he sensed the table and drape provided by show management would not project the image he needed. He said, "There's a big difference between inexpensive and cheap." His decision—rent an exhibit and buy custom graphic signs for it.

The preshow promotion program would include the following:

- The firm mails a monthly newsletter to about 100 customers. The plan called for 3 articles about the product and exhibition starting in August, 3 months before the show.

- A direct mail piece was to be prepared and mailed to a list of approximately 400, including the last show's visitor list. Two waves would be sent, the first 2 weeks before the event. The second was to be a duplicate mailing 1 week in advance.

- lp;&2qSince the show sponsor was a trade magazine, a quarter-page ad was to run in its "show issue," distributed before the conference.

Plans were set by the end of July. There were 3 months to go.

Exhibit House Operation

Mitchell Fink called a New York City-based exhibit company. It had a branch office in North Carolina operating a rental service.[2] In addition to custom building, it owns and rents lightweight manufactured booths. In addition to the booth, the exhibit company offered Fink creative design, graphics production, freight, and setup services—typical "full service" for exhibit designers and producers, nationwide.

But MFA needed more. It had no advertising agency. There was *no name* for its product and no graphic logo. One was required, not only for promotional use but also for copyright registration.

The exhibit designer performed the following services for Mitchell Fink. Starting in July, the exhibit designer

- Consulted on what to name the product.
- Designed the graphic presentation of the name.
- Designed the graphic approach of the booth as a whole, including back wall, rug, counter, and signs citing benefits and features. See Figure 20.1.
- *Changed* the product name and logo in September, when the MFA attorney found a similar name registered by another company.
- Developed additional signs for the MFA suite and signs to go around a post at the outside corner of the firm's booth space.
- Designed both the direct mail and magazine ads.
- Produced the cover art for the users' manual binder supplied when computer programs are purchased. (Just before the show, the binder maker reported that delivery would not be in time. The exhibit company silk-screened two sample binders for the show.)
- Designed the sticker affixed to the computer program disks.
- Shot a black-and-white photograph of the binder for software catalogs and press releases.
- Arranged for shipping and setup of the booth. (At the end of the show, it taught MFA people how to erect the booth themselves.)

The only production chore not managed by the exhibit company was printing the direct mail piece and disk sticker. Fink wanted a local company to do that work.[3] In addition, Fink took care of renting the hospitality suite.

Most exhibit programs don't include developing product packaging. Many companies have agencies to help with direct mail and advertising. Some exhibit designers and producers are redefining roles, however, expanding what they consider full service to include a broad spectrum. Fink was working with one of these "new wave" organizations.

October

The National Horse Show takes place in New York's Madison Square Garden each October. The trade show was taking place at the same time in the Penta Hotel, just across the street from the Garden. All the suites

Figure 20.1. The exhibit was rented to Fink Associates by the exhibit company. The back wall was manufactured by Exponents of San Diego. The exhibit company also provided custom graphics, carpet, and counter. *(Sketch courtesy Cindy Spuria, Alan Sitzer Assoc., New York City and Carrboro, North Carolina.)*

had been booked by the horse show organizers. Since the show was a local event, the promoter had booked meeting rooms and the exhibition hall but no rooms for visitors.

Fink knew that and was prepared. He spent an hour in the hotel lobby on the day before the show negotiating, changing the room reserved to a suite. It wasn't easy, but Fink won.

In addition to private product demonstrations, the suite was to be used as a place for employee training and as a resting spot between shifts on the show floor. The Fink team had brought three different personal computers, two for the suite and one for the booth.

Sales training was conducted the night before the show, using material from Chapter 17. In addition, everyone practiced giving hands-on product demonstrations. After the first show day, a critique session was held. (A problem emerged. Employees, including Fink himself, were not writing thoughtful notes about the interests expressed by prospects.)

Costs and Results

Costs

Over all, MFA spent $17,000 on the marketing program. The largest single investment was the dollar value of the *time* spent by Fink and his team. They estimated this at $3000. The dollars didn't come from an exhibit budget, but the hours could have been spent doing other things for the company. Out-of-pocket cost, including the $1200 for space, was $13,862. What follows is a summary.

Exhibit House Costs

- The rental fee for the 10-foot booth structure, an appropriate counter, a rug and rug pad was $1815.[4]

- The exhibit company charged $1800 for *design* of the product name logo for the booth and for printed items, including design of the direct mail piece.

- Booth graphics *production* cost $3435. This included a two-panel "header" at the top of the booth, four overlay graphic panels, easel signs, a special overlay "introducing" panel, and product name logo panels to place on the column at the booth space corner.

- The charge for design and printer's "mechanicals" for two magazine advertisements, one for preshow use and one for use after the show, was $400.

- The artwork for printing the instructional manual cover and the computer disk sticker, and for silk-screen printing the art on sample binders when the binder order did not arrive, was $225.

Altogether, development work cost MFA $7675.

Transportation and Show Service

- Shipping the booth to and from the show drayage contractor's warehouse, before and after the show, was $400.
- The cost of drayage itself, bringing the booth to the space from the contractor's warehouse and taking it back after the show: $250.
- The total paid for union setup people was $324. Four hours were paid for moving in, at $42.25 an hour: $169. The move out only required 2 hours; but since the show closed at the end of a day, the move out was on overtime, at $77.65 per hour: $155.30. Exhibits of this type can be assembled without professional help; however, we have to understand many shows take place in facilities that employ union labor throughout. Know the rules before the show.
- The cost for 1 electrical line with a 4-way box was $18.[5]
- Flowers for the booth were $56.25.

The total was $1048.

Printing and Mailing Cost

- The direct mail piece was designed in two parts, a card surrounded by a vellum wrapper. The printing company prepared 1000 cards and 2000 wrappers. The extra wrappers were saved for a future mailing with a new card. Printing cost $750.
- Postage was $176.
- The other cost was for 800 of the company's no. 10 envelopes. No special order was placed, but we estimate $20.

Total: $946 including allocation of envelopes. (The time for addressing, inserting, closing, and mailing was included in the employee time cost estimated by Fink.)

Advertising. A quarter-page ad in the preshow edition of the trade magazine cost $250. The periodical had promised Fink a "good position" in the book. The ad appeared in an obscure place. The journal gave Fink a quarter-page space in its next issue at no cost.

Hotel Cost Incidentals.   MFA's hotel bill was $553. It included over $40 in room service and some phone charges. Hotel room service is costly, and one order for coffee took 45 minutes for delivery. The hotel's 10-cup pot was not insulated. Customers drank cold coffee. For future shows, MFA plans to buy a coffeepot. Even if left after the show, MFA says it will save money and serve better coffee. The team supplemented hotel food and beverages by shopping outside. About $150 was spent. Altogether: $703.

Since the show was local, employee travel costs were limited to $100 for extra cab and parking expenses. Grand total: $803.

Results

If you can, quantify your results and related them to cost. The ultimate is preparing an "expense-to-revenue" ratio comparing one exhibit to another. Mitchell Fink was not able to create a viable ratio. It would be several months before all returns could be counted.

MFA considered the experience a success, however, and has now purchased the booth rented and plans to exhibit at four shows a year. The identified show results were as follows:

- The preshow program resulted in 6 prospects making contact before the convention. The first wave of direct mail resulted in 1 response. The second wave generated 5. (The goal was 10.)
- Approximately 200 selling contacts were made at the booth, over a third less than the goal. (There were slack hours not anticipated when setting the goal. In addition, the show audience was closer to 500 than the 1500 promised.)
- A total of 48 leads were generated, 16 more than the goal. About 24 percent of the selling contacts at the booth resulted in a lead of one kind or another! They broke down as follows:

    Solid sales leads for the new product: 14. Fink said, "I may be a bit generous with this figure, but it's pretty good."

    "Suspect" leads that might not be productive immediately: 18.

    Trade magazine representative leads: 5.

    Mailing-list-only suspect leads: 9.

    Special-situation leads, one for a possible product improvement and the other for a potential new business outlet: 2.

- The suite operation produced 10 private demonstrations and entertained a dozen old customers and friends. (The goal was 15 demonstrations and 20 customers to be entertained.) This breaks down to:

    Demonstrations to solid leads and suspects: 5.

Demonstrations to media representatives: 3. An article on the product was promised.

Demonstrations to old clients or "friends of the court": 2.

MFA had prepared two product demonstrations for the show. One was a short form used at the booth. A full demonstration of all features was provided in the suite. The team reported visitor resistance to the term *suite*. (They will change this to *demonstration room*.) During the preshow program, an effort was made to make private appointments for times when Fink felt traffic would be light at the show. However, visitors did not wish to commit themselves to specific times.

One sale was made at the show. The revenue was $4500. Just before opening, Fink announced an introductory price would be in effect to get more programs in use quickly, stimulating word-of-mouth promotion. Within 3 months after the show, 5 programs had been sold and installed. A number of proposals were being reviewed by potential clients.

Analysis

The audience was smaller than the organizer had projected. The show management group is not professional. In addition to what appeared to be lackluster show advertising, the staff had problems in the hotel. The floor plan was changed without exhibitors being notified. The prime, extra-cost booth spot rented by Fink was shifted to a back aisle. The cocktail party promised by show management was poorly run and was executed off the show floor instead of in the exhibit area itself. Specific comments on the overall program were:

- New product introduction increased cost substantially.

- Immediate dollar return was not as high as anticipated; but all returns are not counted.

- Staff gained selling skills, not only for exhibits but in general sales and product demonstration as well.

- Image and awareness of the firm in its industry was improved. Presentation quality was important in this respect. The MFA group feels that major custom software writing projects will emerge from enhanced awareness and reputation.

- One major trade magazine article appeared after the show.

Mitchell Fink used the information in this book as intended. He used its planning section as a guide, without adhering to every specific. He knew his goal was much more than a booth.

As an exhibit manager, Fink displayed two characteristics that help make events successful. First, he delegated. He did not insist that his personal taste be represented in each detail. Fink built a team. Second, he planned far enough in advance so that work could be done thoughtfully and at the lowest reasonable cost. A 12-to-16-week planning and implementation cycle is ideal for many exhibits, even without new product introduction. Emergencies, such as the product name change, were taken care of without fuss. In fact, there were no costly last-minute changes.

During the final days before the show, the MFA team was able to concentrate on personal performance instead of an exhibit. Personal performance is the key to exhibit marketing success.

PART 4

The Industry and Corporate Management

21
Exhibit Industry: Who Does What

This chapter is both an overview of how our industry is moving and the place where we list sources of information. Readers of Chapter 15 will see that we touch on some of the issues presented there.

The industry is a hand with five fingers and a thumb. Exhibit managers are the thumb. Show organizers are the first finger. The thumb pays most of the bills. Show managers gather the audience. The other fingers of this hand serve both of us and, collectively, we reach out to serve the show visitor.

- Exhibitors
- Show managers
- Exhibit designers and producers
- Show service contractors
- Transportation companies
- Facility managers

There are natural alliances. On a daily basis exhibitors work most of the time with exhibit designers and producers. They know each other better and understand each other's problems better. Show managers work consistently with the service industry and facilities managers. Again, they know each other better and there is more mutual understanding. Transportation people work with all of us and may have better feeling for all parts of the industry than anyone else!

Until very recently, exhibitors and their exhibit-builder allies seemed to be carrying on in an adversarial relationship with show management and show service organizations. In some cases, the real argument has been with facilities management and show labor. The show manager and decorator were bad news messengers.

Exhibitors

Exhibitors, and to a lesser extent show visitors, finance the event. Exhibitors rent space, purchase an exhibit, have it transported and set up, all in return for an opportunity to sell and are ultimately responsible for making a decision to participate at any show. What exhibitors do, or should do, is what this book is all about.

Exhibit Designers and Producers

Primarily, these firms create and produce physical presence. As full-service agents, they also provide storage, repair, and other management services. They will arrange for transportation and work with show management and its contractors to set up and administer the operation of an exhibit at a show.

The exhibit production industry was rooted in furniture making and industrial design. As a result, the capital investments in plant and machinery drove it toward providing services that kept shops humming. For instance, many have provided "free" design service so they could capture construction contracts.

The exhibit design and construction business is growing, but our needs and technology are changing. As both costs and potentials become better understood in exhibiting companies, roles and skills are changing. We spend more time inside our companies planning, less time implementing. We ask our exhibit companies, more and more, to operate as general contractors, like advertising agencies.

Increasingly, exhibit companies will take charge of the design and production of show literature or brochures, preshow direct mail and advertising. They will manage development and production of audiovisual or "live" shows. Some will offer special events and hospitality management, exhibit sales training, research management, sales lead distribution, and literature request fulfillment—even show selection consulting.

Many of these services have been provided directly to us by specialist firms. However, increasing internal pressure translates to less time to act as our own general contractors, coordinating an exhibit house with others. We focus more on show selection, evaluating how to use the medium most effectively from an internal viewpoint. As with company advertising people, our jobs have started to shift toward providing direction.

The exhibit companies can't provide services for free. Many are drifting away from the practice of providing no-cost exhibit design. Some operate more like advertising agencies. Basic creative and management services are provided internally, with external sources called on as needed. Charges are based on time fees and markups of services provided by outside sources.

Consultants and Advertising Agencies

In a Chapter 17 note, we mention a listing of exhibit management consultants. Individually, they don't offer all the services we need. However, the emergence of specialist exhibit management firms is yet another indication of the medium's increasing impact, along with a greater understanding of how money can be wasted without integrated planning. Advertising agencies, as well, are taking increasing interest— especially those that have learned how to handle "trade" advertising clients at a profit.

Transportation Companies

Transportation companies, essentially van line truck operators, work in the industry in two ways. First, they work directly with exhibitors or exhibit houses in transporting exhibits to and from shows. Second, they work for show managers to provide freight services from a local warehouse to the hall and back. A show's official freight company provides over-the-road freight service for exhibitors along with service to the show manager. In addition to truck transport, air freight companies are provided by show managers as official contractors, though exhibitors can employ their own sources.

Facility Managers

For the most part, we are not directly involved with the managers of the exhibition halls in which we exhibit. Instead, we deal with show managers who have rented the facilities.

Over 40 of the 240 major hall facilities in the United States are privately operated, most of them by large hotels. The balance, however, were built and are operated by local government authorities. They are sponsored to attract visitors to their communities.

Many of them attempt to serve in three different capacities. First, they provide meeting rooms for conventions. Second, they include open, flat rooms in which trade shows can be mounted. Last, they often include auditorium-type seating arenas for major public events, sports and other forms of entertainment.

Arena managers not only operate the halls but, along with others in their communities, are responsible for attracting trade shows and conventions into their facilities. Working with local visitor and convention bureaus, and hotels, they create package proposals with which they tempt show managers. Most medium-sized and large shows are scheduled years in advance. The sales packages have to include blocks of hotel rooms set aside in advance and other necessary support, such as reservations for private bus services.

Facilities provide the essential. Electrical connections, high-pressure air, telephone, food, and plumbing are included. The actual services are provided by local companies who have won contracts with the hall. Unions are also involved. They compete, in their contract negotiations, for show hall work. An electrical contractor and its union have a joint interest in securing exclusive contracts to work in an exhibit hall. Some exhibit hall contracts are bid on the basis of franchise fees. When you complain about the price of a hot dog or a cup of beer, don't forget that it includes something for the authority running the hall. (The contracts are rigid. In one case, a major convention center lost a food show because its contract food vendor would not let exhibitors serve their samples in booths.)

Local politics can play a role in who manages a facility and how it is administered. Most halls do not operate at a profit. Sponsoring governments have been willing to operate them at a loss, making "profit" in the jobs created and the business generated for hotels, restaurants, and related enterprises.

Facilities management is going through change. There is a proliferation of new or expanded halls. From New York and Chicago to Jacksonville, Florida, and Casper, Wyoming, the competition to attract shows is intense. And local governments are reacting to increasing public pressure to reduce taxes. They no longer feel they can justify as much taxpayer support for their arenas.

There are two implications. First, more publicly owned facilities are being asked to act as their own profit centers. For instance, some are going into the food and telephone service business themselves, instead of contracting out. More professionally trained managers who understand the needs of show managers and exhibitors are being employed by halls nationwide, from Anaheim to Indianapolis, from Denver to Seattle. In addition, some are being allowed to hire staff without traditional civil service strictures. Funding, other than through hall rentals, is being managed more creatively. The Washington State Convention Center and others are partially supported by taxes levied on hotel rooms.

The second implication? Contractors and unions are adjusting prices and work rules to keep halls competitive. There is more progress to be made, and competition is leading the way to improvement.

Show Managers

For the most part, show organizers operate under the aegis of industry groups. In some cases, associations employ in-house managers. Others employee professional event management organizations on a contract basis. There are, as well, entrepreneurial organizers who create trade shows and seminar programs without association ties.

Looking broadly at the field, show managers who have enjoyed success in the past have been excellent individual salespeople who knew how to package short-term real estate rentals. As the stakes have risen, however, many are starting to see that they are managing a marketing communications medium, just like the publisher of a newspaper or the radio station manager.

What does show management do? For those who did not read Chapter 15, here is a list:

- Obtains a hall and meeting facilities, and packages hotel rooms and other basic services required by those who travel. Much of this work is done through facility and convention bureau managers.
- Organizes services for exhibitors. These can included decorating companies, drayage, setup labor, and related services and rentals.
- Develops (show management or its sponsoring association) an educational seminar series attractive to the audience.
- Prepares and executes promotional programs to inform and attract both audience and exhibitors.
- Acts as the overall manager of operations during the event.
- Sells exhibit space to us.

The ultimate responsibility is this last one. Show managers are real estate people who rent an exhibition hall—sometimes for as little as $1 per square foot for the period of a show—and resell the space to us for more. Earlier we indicated that the average among the top 200 shows is in the $10-per-square-foot range. Some rent for up to $20 per square foot and more.

Show managers or their associations also gain revenue from attendees. Visitors often pay several hundred dollars to register at a convention and trade show, or a smaller fee to visit the exhibit floor if they do not opt to take part in the seminar program. Public shows aimed at consumers sell tickets.

Often, the quoted prices are not an indication of revenue reality. At many business trade shows, exhibitors are given tickets to distribute to their customers. One high-technology trade show organizing group "preregisters" potential visitors who subscribe to industry trade magazines at no cost. Public show organizers frequently distribute complimentary or low-cost tickets to exhibitors and civic groups.

Conflicts in intent often arise between exhibitors and show managers. From our vantage point, charging fees for visitor tickets, except for those we give to our own customers, helps to create a more serious audience. Show managers feel they'll rent more exhibit space if the total audience is higher. Find a full hall, and you'll meet a happy show manager. The more sophisticated are increasingly concerned with audience quality, however, understanding that we want much more than quantity.

Show Service Contractors

Exhibit managers are more familiar with the services required in an exhibit hall than with how they are provided. If you are not, see Chapter 15. What becomes confusing is who provides the services. Who is the decorator? Who is the drayage contractor? What does the term *labor contractor* mean in context with the drayage contractor or decorator?

Show service companies, like others in the industry, have grown up over the years. Functions have been combined as one business organization profits and expands its operation. One might assume that decorating companies provide decoration. True enough, but many of them also act as official contractors for in-hall labor. A freight-transfer van line provide drayage labor as well as off-site exhibit storage and shipment. It all boils down to who manages the process.

Official contractors are hired by the show manager. They serve both the show management team and the exhibitors. It is here that conflicts can arise between exhibitors and the show. We tend to think of some shows as mini-monopolies.

Industry Associations

The exhibit industry is maturing. As the number of meetings, facilities, and exhibitors expand, there is a growing sense of the overall enterprise's seriousness. One result of this emergence is the creation of associations within the industry aimed at solving problems and setting standards—as well as providing continuing education for members. Since the exhibit industry serves associations aimed at the same goals, it is no surprise that it has created its own. Figure 21.1 is a useful address list.

Our major association is the International Exhibitors Association. IEA has grown steadily over the years and has recently become large enoughto have its own association management team in place on a full-time basis. The association changed its name in 1984 to reflect international membership. It operates with a series of "hub-city" chap-

---

Trade Show Bureau
P.O. Box 797, 8 Beach Road
East Orleans, Massachusetts 02643
Telephone: (617) 240-0177

International Exhibitors Association (IEA)
5103-B Backlick Road
Annandale, Virginia 22003
Telephone: (703) 941-3725
Telex: 628605 IEA HEADQUARTERS

Health Care Exhibitors Association (HCEA)
5775 Peachtree-Dunwoody Road, Suite 500-D
Atlanta, Georgia 30342
Telephone: (404) 252-3663

National Association of Exposition Managers (NAEM)
334 East Garfield Road
Post Office Box 377
Aurora, Ohio 44202
Telephone: (216) 562-8255

Exhibit Designers and Producers Association (ED&PA)
1411 K Street, NW, Suite 801
Washington, D.C. 20005
Telephone: (202) 393-2001

Exposition Service Contractors Association (ESCA)
1516 South Pontius Avenue
Los Angeles, California 90025
Telephone: (213) 478-0215
Telex: 181149 WEST LSA

Figure 21.1. A listing of selected exhibit industry associations, publications, and reference sources.

International Association of Convention and Visitors Bureaus (IACVB)
Post Office Box 758
Champaign, Illinois 61820
Telephone: (217) 359-8881

Convention Liaison Council (CLC)
1575 Eye Street, NW
Washington, D.C. 20005
Telephone: (202) 626-2723

Tradeshow Week Publications
12233 West Olympic Blvd., Suite 236
Los Angeles, California 90064
Telephone: (213) 826-5696
Telex: 194351 SHOWCOINT

Exhibitor Magazine Publications
745 Marquette Bank Building
Rochester, Minnesota 55903
Telephone: (507) 289-6556

Exhibit Builder Magazine
Sound Publishing Company
Post Office Box 920
Great Neck, New York 11022
Telephone: (516) 466-5750

Successful Meetings Exhibit Schedule
1518 Walnut Street
Philadelphia, Pennsylvania 19102
Telephone: (215) 546-3295

Tradeshow and Convention Guide
Billboard Publications: Amusement Business
Post Office Box 24970
Nashville, Tennessee 37202
Telephone: (615) 748-8120

World Convention Dates
79 Washington Street
Hempstead, New York 11550
Telephone: (516) 483-6881

Figure 21.1. *(Continued)*

ters in the United States and overseas. It also provides members with an
ongoing publications service.

Another influential exhibit management association, smaller than
IEA, was created specifically by exhibit managers in the health care
industry. The Health Care Exhibitors Association (HCEA) provides an
annual educational seminar program and tailors its activities to the
special needs of the group.

The primary association for exhibit builders is the Exhibit Designers and Producers Association. As with IEA, ED&PA has recently grown to the point of employing a full-time association management team.

The National Association of Exposition Managers (NAEM) is the primary association created by the show management part of the industry. In addition to focusing on the problems experienced within the membership, NAEM serves as a networking forum and a vehicle through which facility and show service managers can concentrate their selling efforts. It sponsors industrywide seminars on special issues.

The Exposition Service Contractors Association (ESCA) is another association that was grown to the stage of requiring full-time professional management. Its members are companies that focus on providing the official services to show managers. Another association in the same field, with members who act as independent contractors for exhibitors, is the Trade Show Services Association (TSSA).

The "old" association for facilities managers is the International Association of Auditorium Managers. However, some of the issues and problems faced by auditorium managers differ from those faced by people who operate convention and trade show facilities. As a result, many exhibit facility managers are allied with the International Association of Convention and Visitors Bureaus.

There are other associations. The Professional Convention Management Association, for instance, is an alliance among those who produce medical conventions. In addition, there are associations such as Meeting Planners International and others indirectly allied to exhibit management. The industry is an alphabet soup of association initials.

A degree of official cooperation has emerged in the industry as well. For instance, the Convention Liaison Council is funded by several of the associations. It attempts to solve problems among them and publishes educational information. The Trade Show Bureau, often cited as a source for research information in this book, is perhaps the most well-regarded nonprofit organization in the industry. It is also funded by the associations, as well as by individual members. The Trade Show Bureau specializes in research and providing information to members, advertising agencies, and educational institutions. It is focusing increasing attention on encouraging exhibit and show management subjects as part of college-level marketing and marketing communications programs.

Publications and Reference Material

There is an increasing body of periodical literature providing information about the exhibit medium. Both *Marketing Communications* and

Business Marketing magazines carry articles, and aspects of the industry are touched upon in *Successful Meetings* magazine. *Meetings and Conventions* and *Meetings* magazines cover exhibit management as well.

There are specialist publications entirely devoted to the exhibit industry. The oldest and most highly regarded news source is *Tradeshow Week*, a 12-page weekly newsletter styled somewhat like *The Kipplinger Letter*. It provides spot news and short features and includes show lists 6 and 8 months in advance for domestic and international trade shows. Another, more scholarly approach is taken by the monthly slick, *Exhibitor* magazine—a journal that publishes in-depth articles, including case histories, about various aspects of the exhibit marketing management. The International Exhibit Association publishes a monthly magazine, *IdEAs*,which focuses on emerging trends. Another high-quality publication, created specifically to cover design and construction subjects, is *Exhibit Builder* magazine. Additional journals are emerging. Among them is *Exhibit and Trade Show Manager*.

In addition to periodical literature, there are a number of reference books. *Successful Meetings* publishes an annual hardback, *Exhibits Schedules*, which lists the names of shows. *Tradeshow Week*, with encouragement from the Trade Show Bureau and the International Exhibitors Association, now publishes *The Tradeshow Week Data Book*. It is well-regarded because detailed information is provided about each show. The goal is to become a compendium much like the *Standard Rate and Data* book used in advertising. There are other lists, including *World Convention Dates* and the Health Care Exhibitors Association's *Convention Schedule*, which covers medical meetings. Another hardbound, released first in 1985, is the *Trade Shows and Professional Exhibits Directory*, published by Gale Research. Yet another, published by Billboard Publications, is the *Trade Show and Convention Guide*. It also contains entertainment-booking sources.

Reference material is not limited to lists. As we said, at several points in this book we have used Trade Show Bureau information. There are other reference sources. *Exhibitor* magazine publishes an *Illustrated Buyers Guide to Exhibits*, a fulsome compendium of modular exhibit systems. That company also produces *The Handbook of Trade Show Marketing*. The most prolific information publisher is *Tradeshow Week*. In addition to the weekly newsletter and annual show list book, it publishes an annual *Major Exhibit Hall Directory*, providing show managers with detailed information about facilities, and *The Tradeshow Week 200*, a detailed analysis of the 200 largest shows held each year.

The addresses for key publications and reference sources appear as part of Figure 21.1.

22

Exhibit Medium: An Emerging Giant

Did you see the movie *Stripper*, or perhaps an earlier eighties epic named *Health*? Perhaps not. Neither was Academy Awards material, and we suspect that neither will find itself a place in anyone's retrospective film festival in the 1990s.

Why point them out? Robert Altman's *Health* was filmed at a convention and trade show for health afficionados staged for the movie at the Florida-Spanish pink-stucco Don Cesar Hotel in St. Petersburg, Florida. *Stripper*'s backdrop was a convention of the Canadian and International Burlesque Artists' Associations at the Sahara Hotel in Las Vegas.

Novels, plays, and movies often dramatize or present a caricature of "life as it is," with players acting their roles against backdrops familiar to us. Although it seems doubtful that conventions and trade shows will supplant police stations, hospital emergency rooms, neighborhood bars, and old wars as settings for theatrical production, the exhibit medium has started to become much more a part of our lives—enough a part for theatrical producers to use the shows occasionally as structures upon which to build their offerings.

Historical Perspective

Of course, trade shows and fairs have been part of the world's commercial culture for a long time. Biblical reference tells us that the trading of information and goods among like-minded people at temporary facilities—the essence of the medium—was taking place at the time when Christ walked the earth.

For over 1500 years, trade fairs were our primary mechanism for converting goods into money and money into goods. The fairs were the world's banking system and it was very efficient.

Knowledge was traded as well as goods and money. For instance, Marco Polo opened the great silk route across the middle of Asia in the early fourteenth century. Among the results: Some of the oriental rug designs woven today in China were actually created in the great rug factories of Persia and Moghul India in the fifteenth century. Knowledge traveled east and west along the route. China responded to design demand.[1]

Some point to the emergence of trade fairs in the heartland of Germanic Europe 3 centuries ago as the start of the industry as we know it, while many point to the first World's Fair. It took place at the Crystal Palace, a temporary glass building erected for a 7-month fair in London in 1851. It was followed by the great Paris Exposition with its far more permanent reminder, the Eiffel Tower.

Some maintain that the history of here-today-gone-tommorrow commercial and educational gatherings in America started with the medicine shows that traveled our land in the nineteenth century, giving advice and selling. (We understand that one still exists.) And most state and county fairs include "commerce and industry" exhibit halls. Many of the exhibitors are professionals on the circuit, traveling from one to another year-round.

The business trade show concept grew in the United States during the early part of the twentieth century. The author's grandfather sold bedsprings he manufactured to the furniture industry at its trade shows in the 1920s and 1930s. Where? In Chicago, which for decades has served as our unofficial convention capital.

Medium Today

For practical purposes, the consumer fairs, business conventions, and trade shows we experience are a phenomenon of the last 2½ decades. And this emergence owes much more to the increasing complexity of business life, the specialization of commercial enterprise, and technological development than to Middle Eastern or European tradition.

Alvin Toffler, in his book *The Third Wave*, outlines the framework for a bright and new worldwide social order based on the productive uses of the technologies we've created since World War II.[2] Our once monolithic industrial society has splintered because of technology.

Specialized knowledge and our need for continuing education have exploded. In addition, our enhanced ability to travel and communicate has made our interests less local or regional. At one time, friends and associates were close to us geographically. Now, networks of like-minded people gather to trade information and goods around the globe. At one time, products were take-it-or-leave-it. Now, most of what we buy is semicustom, including the cars we order.

Meeting and Trade Show Explosion

These increasing needs for specialized knowledge and specialized purchasing, plus the increasing ease of travel, are creating a massive convention and trade show infrastructure. As late as 1977 there were less than 5000 conventions and trade shows held annually in the United States. There are almost twice as many today.

People in the industry think first about the large-scale exhibit showcases that attract scores of thousands of visitors and fill huge arena floors with hundreds of exhibits. The last International Machine Tool Show featured over 1100 exhibits and attracted an audience of over 75,000. A recent Summer Consumer Electronics Show presented almost 1400 exhibitors to just under 100,000 wholesale buyers. In spite of declines in oil industry activity, Canada's National Petroleum Show attracts well over 900 exhibitors and a professional audience of over 34,000.

In addition, conventions and trade shows have emerged where there were none years ago, fulfilling new needs for information and trade. For instance, in some industries subgroup associations have been formed, complete with their own conventions and trade shows. The banking industry has its own meetings for communications and computer specialists. The same is true in the department store industry. The National Retail Merchants Association meeting does not stand alone. There's the NMRA Electronic Data-Processing conference as well, and discount retailers have their own show. The computer industry itself, first supported by large general-interest computer technology conferences, is subdividing. A proliferation of new, special-interest trade shows is emerging as the influence of the older large shows, such as the National Computer Conference, seems to decline. The biggest food industry show is for chain management, the Food Marketing Institute, but wholesalers have their own special convention. There are two major conferences and trade shows for booksellers. The American Booksellers Association attracts over 800 exhibitors and almost 8000 buyers. The Christian Booksellers Association attracts over 300 exhibitors and about

4000 visitors. And over 250 booths and almost 6000 people are brought together at the Golf Course Superintendents Association of America meeting.[3]

Much of the increase, however, appears in the number of special interest conventions and shows that are promoted on local, state, or regional levels. Wholesale gift and hardware purchasing shows seem to take place everywhere. The information-intensive industries—including medical, insurance, and other financial service fields—sponsor more and more regional and local meetings.

Exhibition Hall Explosion

Most of us are aware only of the shows aimed at our own needs and the consumer fairs that attract thousands to look at boats, antiques, cars, and home and garden supplies. These shows are but the tip of an increasingly large iceberg.

City and state governments, however, are very much aware of the trend. We pointed out in Chapter 21 that there are hundreds of government authority or agency owned and operated convention centers in the United States. Everyone thinks of Chicago's McCormick Place, the Las Vegas Convention Center, or the Jacob K. Javits Convention Center in New York City. Not so widely known by the public at large may be the huge facilities in Anaheim, San Diego, Indianapolis, Dallas, Denver, Miami, Seattle, Atlanta, Kansas City, St. Louis, and virtually every other big-league city in the nation. And little known at all on a national level are the scores of newer halls in smaller cities such as Newport News, Virginia.

There is even less general knowledge about the exhibition halls developed in the private sector, mostly by hotel owners. Most are smaller than publicly operated arenas, but some are sizable. For instance, Chicago's Hyatt Regency Hotel, on Wacker Drive, was built as a high-rise cap on top of a 160,000-square-foot exhibition hall buried 3 floors beneath the hotel's front desk. The Las Vegas Hilton offers over 100,000 square feet of exhibition space in the hotel, just across the parking lot from the Las Vegas Convention Center. Gone are the days when a hotel could place the occasional small trade show in its grand ballroom or in a parking garage under the building. Almost all new or remodeled hotels catering to commercial travelers feature formal exhibition halls as well as meeting facilities, and hotels are starting to reorganize in response to convention business. Historically, meeting planners had to deal with a number of different departments individually to obtain the services they required. Now, hotels are starting to provide convention service managers to help major buyers.[4] Hotels have now captured over one-third of our trade show business.[5]

Impact on Exhibitors

There was a time when we thought about exhibiting only as a way to meet our current customers—to entertain them and write their orders. This remains a goal, but times are changing.

Toffler's changing technological society has meant an increase in business volatility. Industries, products, and companies are changing and will continue to change at an accelerating rate. Yesterday's information is old and may not be useful. Yesterday's customers may be gone. There is an increasing need, for old and new companies, to find new customers—for either new applications of current products or for products that did not exist a few short years or months ago. (It almost seems that the road to business failure is paved with companies which have attempted to continue selling the same old product to the same old customer. Product or customer must change.)

As a result, the essential value of the exhibit medium as a low-cost prospecting tool—finding new customers—is being understood more and more. The issue is actually larger than one of dollars. The figures cited early in this book, from the Trade Show Bureau, compare the cost of an exhibit contact with substantially higher cost of an office call. Finding that office at all is an even more important issue for many! Simply locating interested prospects in our volatile and specialized business world, regardless of cost, can be reason enough to exhibit at the right show.

Impact on Show Managers

Some shows seem like institutions, and their managers reflect this status. For instance, the managers of the National Computer Conference, or the National Association of Broadcasters convention, have had every right to feel that there is a great stability in the shows they have created. But there is increasing competition brought on by essential change in the industries they serve. We've mentioned the emerging proliferation of specialized computer shows. And the broadcasting industry is segmenting, with cable TV gaining strength. Several cable TV conventions are now on the scene. Many companies serving over-the-air broadcasters have products for their cable cousins as well, or sell the same thing to both. They exhibit before both parts of the industry. As cable increases in importance, some companies may shift more exhibit dollars there. And there's an even newer show in the broadcasting industry, built around an annual conference of broadcasting company financial managers. No show organizer can be comfortable.

Research Information

We suggested in Chapter 21 that many of the old-line show managers are excellent personal salespeople. They sold their space with little marketing backup. Now, however, exhibiting costs have risen dramatically and the need to measure exhibit results has never been higher. Exhibit managers have become increasingly concerned with audience analysis—not just the total attendance but how that audience breaks down by interest. Shows are starting to recognize that failure to provide this information can lead us to reduce investments. When we experience low results, we blame the shows instead of what might be our own poor performance. We don't know our audience and presume it was not there. By providing sophisticated audience data, the show manager blunts complaints, helps us plan, and prevents problems.

Educational or Technical Sessions

Show attendees are as much interested in educational programs as in the trade shows at the conventions they elect to visit.[6] Those who make decisions on whether or not to attend base judgments on what they feel they'll get from the seminar program. The essential question is, "Can I learn at least part of what I *have* to learn over the next 24 months?" Progressive show managers focus more attention on these continuing and practical education programs than in the past.

Promotional Programs

Increasingly sophisticated corporate exhibit managers are asking penetrating questions about the promotional program mounted by a show's organizer. More are advertising trained. They know the impact of a media plan aimed at a specific audience. Better equipped show managers are providing detailed information, facts on both content and media direction. This allows a company's exhibit manager to target his or her own promotional program.

Show Selection

Early in this book we defined four different types of shows, which depend on the interests of both exhibitors and conference attendees. A *vertical-vertical* show is one at which both the members of the attending association and the exhibitors have narrow interests. At the other end of the spectrum are *horizontal-horizontal* shows at which one can find exhibitors and attendees alike with broad interests in various markets and products. (The others: *vertical-horizontal* and *horizontal-vertical*.)

Our approach as exhibitors is less academic. For each of us there are only two kinds of shows. One provides an audience most of which is interested in what we have to sell. The other, far more common, is one that provides an audience only part of which is interested in our offerings.

The first is likely to be smaller than the second, gathering a small audience that's narrow in its interest. The Association of Operating Room Nurses comes to mind. The larger, more horizontal show, may actually be a forest in which more prospect "trees" can be found than in the small show. But we must work harder both before and during the event to find them. Regardless of type, we have to know far more than the size of the total anticipated audience to do our jobs well.

First-Year Shows

They have to be analyzed with care before you agree to participate. The nature of the show, the apparent support it is getting from its target industry, the nature of the seminar program, the size and sophistication of the show's advertising and promotion package, the experience and financial backing of the show organizer—all have an impact on the potential for success.

This last issue is all-important as the industry continues to segment. There will be new shows created each year to meet emerging needs, and some of the older showcases will decline. Look at what the show proposes to deliver and how it plans to get there; most important, look at who is developing the property.

Keep in mind that trade shows are not created for us. We think of them as selling opportunities on neutral ground, but that's not why they are created or why they succeed. Instead, they come into being to serve the needs of buyers. Attendees are trying to learn in the seminar program, to compare notes with peers, and to decrease investments of time and money in the purchasing process. They want to see what's new in products or services and the companies offering them. They want to narrow down the number of potential vendors to talk with after the show. So, ultimately, think about what is being delivered to the buyer attendee. If that's good, the show will probably prosper and so will you.

It is our increasing customization and specialization within business life that has made trade shows enough a part of our culture to find themselves cast as backdrops for movies. It's sometimes foolish to predict the future with a projection from the past, but one thing is sure: business life is not going to become less complex. This means more trade show selling.

23
Exhibit Manager

You may call this oversimplification, but there are only two kinds of businesses: little and big. First, a look at "little"—where leaders are entrepreneurs and wear many hats.

Smaller Companies

The Fritz & LaRue Company is not well known to most of us. Neither is Mitchell A. Fink Associates. Fritz & LaRue is a major importer of oriental rugs, however, and readers of Chapter 20 know that MFA has been developing computer software for financial institutions on Wall Street for over a decade. By IBM, TRW, or General Foods standards, both companies are small. Just about 10 people are employed at MFA and not many more at Fritz.

During his time as president of Fritz, Leslie Stroh, now a publisher of specialized business magazines, faced the need for a new marketing approach for his company. He had to open showrooms at furniture industry buying centers in North Carolina, Illinois, Texas, and California. These centers are used for quarterly trade shows at which the retail industry buys inventory. Chapter 20 tells the story of how Mitchell Fink used the exhibit medium to introduce his firm's first off-the-shelf computer software.

Stroh and Fink are typical small business leaders. They wear many hats, including that of exhibit manager. The problems they face are those of complexity and, necessarily, gaps in knowledge. As exhibit managers both were completely responsible for their use of the medium, including the bottom-line results achieved.

Larger Companies

At the other end of the spectrum is "big": IBM, TRW, General Foods, Kodak, and all the Fortune 1000. They have exhibit managers. The responsibility and authority vested in these managers is vastly different from when Leslie Stroh or Mitchell Fink or any small business person acts in the role.

The function in larger companies depends on the industry, the size of the company, and the way in which it is organized. You may or may not have a job title that includes the word "exhibit." In most larger companies, two kinds of people are involved with exhibit management.

Sales Manager

A degree of autonomy is given to local or division sales managers. The sales manager, or that person's assistant, faces many of the same problems that affect the small business president, wearing too many hats. The problems of complexity and lack of knowledge emerge.

Corporate Exhibit Manager

Most professional exhibit managers at the corporate level know the complexities and potentials of the medium, but their roles and responsibilities are usually limited.

They may be responsible for large national convention exhibits, exhibitions at annual shareowner meetings, and the like. They may be responsible for providing standard exhibit booths and graphics for the use of the field sales managers.

Still, most wear but half a hat. They don't always select shows and are not held ultimately responsible for results. They act as coordinators, advising but not deciding. For the most part, they deal with implementation complexities—essentially coordinating the efforts of others and providing what's required for physical presence at trade shows. They are essentially cost managers. The Strohs and Finks of small business are value managers.

Reporting Structure.   In many companies, the exhibit function at the corporate level is a tagalong in the advertising department. It's considered support for field sales and top management. At the local level there is no formal exhibit manager. The function is combined with other staff work.

Exhibit Management Personnel.   Virtually none of us elected exhibit management as a career goal. Most meandered into the medium. For some young college-trained marketing communicators, it is a pass-through job in a marketing communications career path. A few, who become interested in the synergism of the medium, stay. Some are up-from-the-ranks employees or salespeople with little formal training in marketing communications. Exhibit management may be a final career-path step.

Each year the International Exhibitors Association conducts a survey among the managers and coordinators who attend its annual meeting. Until very recently, upward of one-half had less than 3 years' experience in the profession. Now, however, the experience level seems to be lengthening.

The Health Care Exhibitors Association has a similar experience record. A number of its members seem mired in lower-level exhibit coordination jobs with little room to move up. Many are up-from-the-ranks employees with little professional exhibit marketing training.

Top Management Perspective

The top-level corporate managers are not well versed in the use of the medium and are inclined to think of it as a necessary but costly evil.[1] And, as you know, the total cost is often far higher than what is revealed in formal exhibit budgets. Little do top managers know. They could double the national exhibit budget and get a more accurate picture of what exhibiting truly costs!

That's not all. The ultimate-cost iceberg includes dollars and time expended in local-office show participation as well as at large national events. Lots of local-office budgets for large companies do not even include exhibit lines so these expenses can be tracked. A sales manager may participate in two or three shows a year. The out-of-pocket and personnel time cost may not be large. Collectively, however, the investment is likely to be far more substantial than anyone realizes.

Instinctively, top managers think about exhibits as almost pure added cost. There is less value definition or understanding that a well-executed exhibit program lowers ultimate selling costs. This, however, is changing.

Small Computer Influence

Each exhibit marketing effort is like a small business operating inside its larger sponsor. But many of the functions have been diffused, with other departments taking on exhibit elements as secondary responsibilities. Now, however, it is economically feasible to concentrate exhibit marketing functions so that end-to-end responsibility can be assigned. In part, this feasibility comes from the development of new technology, essentially small computers.

Cost Tracking

Most companies operate with budget formats designed so that people and offices can be managed. Budget lines include salary, office expense, rent, training, travel, and the like. Projects are generally lumped into one budget line because the allocation is relatively small.

In advertising and exhibit departments, this single line can be huge. We have to know far more than the total to manage our jobs. Some of the large corporations, such as General Electric, have created formal project-cost-management accounting programs. They allow us to look at out-of-pocket expenses in ways that make them manageable. For the most part, however, we operate with two sets of books. One is for the company and the other, a homegrown system like the ones introduced in Chapters 3 and 8, are designed to serve our own needs.

Enter the micro or personal computer! We can assign our own item numbers to costs and track them while at the same time capturing data on how these costs are appearing on company budget formats.

For instance, personal travel costs should be debited to each show. The company books, however, may allocate travel to its own account, not to the project budget line. Using one of the off-the-shelf spread sheet computer programs, you may be able to make one entry and have it appear in both places. Another illustration: rent. Clearly, exhibit space rent is part of the cost of a show, but the company may insist on showing it on its own budget line. The same process can be followed.

Sales Lead and Order Management

If your company is small, you can keep track of exhibit leads and orders easily, sending them to the proper place and estimating their value. Larger companies, and especially those that must operate with sales leads rather than orders written at a show, have more problems. Many company sales lead distribution systems are designed to process advertising responses, providing only barebones information about the prospect. There is little opportunity to pass on the wealth of information obtained during live contact at a show. In addition, many of these systems do not provide an adequate mechanism for feedback on the quality of the leads sent.

Again, a small computer can help. It can be programmed to indicate where a lead or sales order should go, depending on territory or product. The information, once entered, can be printed out and sent to sales offices with return cards.It can be programmed to store evaluation reports from salespeople who follow up on leads.

Show Selection

In many industries, exhibit participations seem preordained. If you manufacture gift items, there are lists of wholesale gift shows around the nation to attend. Participation depends on how deeply you want to penetrate a given market. Life is not so easy, however, if you sell several different industries or are entering a new business.

A small computer may help. A number of computer software packages are designed to model. Most are sold as management tools for selecting new plant sites or making decisions on basic marketing direction. These same programs, however, can be used to evaluate and rank trade shows in terms of potential importance.

Internal and External Communication

Internal correspondence can be more extensive for exhibit marketing than for other areas. Implementing an exhibit marketing job requires paying attention to a lot of details—from gathering the home telephone numbers of key people to preparing hotel room lists. In addition, if leads are not followed up expeditiously, you gain time for the salespeople by sending prospects thank-you letters after the show. A small computer, again, can be used to do the job easily.

Exhibit Management in the Future

Look at the signals. We've traced the explosion in the number of trade shows taking place each year and the construction boom in new exhibit halls. We've pointed to the increasing body of periodical literature devoted to the subject. The first college-level courses on show and exhibit management are beginning to appear. This book is yet another signal that exhibit management is being taken far more seriously than a decade ago.

Management Responsibilities

Most people who carry the title of exhibit manager are primarily concerned with the exhibit itself, the physical presence. If you are a sales manager, you may have a coordinate—who is the exhibit manager—taking care of the physical aspect while you focus on show selection, staff recruiting and training, lead and order evaluation, and so on.

This is likely to change. The demands of exhibit marketing are unique. Many of the responsibilities absorbed by diffused work groups will be concentrated. The true costs and potentials associated with the use of the medium will emerge. There will be an understanding that critical exhibit management functions can not be well performed as secondary jobs in work groups with other primary responsibilities.

Budgets will be more concentrated. Personnel compensation will be tracked. The cost for display products will be identified. The dollars spent on hotels and travel for staff members will become part of the exhibit manager's budget, along with costs for preshow promotion, hospitality, and results tracking.

Manager's Skills

At the corporate level, some companies have used exhibit coordination as a training ground. A few have used the job as a corporate dumping ground, a place to put "good, old, reliable Charlie" so he can earn his pay and not do great damage.

William Mee, president of the Trade Show Bureau, says, "There is increasing understanding that exhibits are expensive and productive, marketing events rather than boards and plastic." Unfortunately, good, old Charlie *can* do damage and never know it. So can a trainee. So can a manager who worries only about graphics and structure. The exhibit stakes have risen. Managers in the future will have both a sales management background and solid training as marketing communicators. They will be somewhat older, more senior executives. They will earn more than they do today.

All the forms of "target marketing" have become increasingly important: booklets, brochures, direct mail, special events, and exhibits. They all reflect the increasing segmentation of our markets. The managers will emerge as equals with the advertising director, instead of reporting to that person.

Exhibiting is a marriage between advertising and direct selling. It is a medium driven from the bottom up, by individual salespeople—not top down from the president's office. Many corporate leaders do not even know how many times a year their company exhibits. Managing this expense, and ensuring that exhibits are used effectively by all, requires managers both sophisticated in the use of the medium and highly regarded inside their companies. They will be value managers. They are emerging. Today.

Appendix

COST TRACKING		
	Estimate	*Actual*
1. Space rent	$_____	$_____
2. Structure and graphics	_____	_____
3. Transportation for exhibits	_____	_____
4. Services at the site	_____	_____
5. Traffic stimulation promotions	_____	_____
6. Customer hospitality	_____	_____
7. Personal expenses for the staff	_____	_____
Total	_____	_____
8. Contingency and miscellaneous at 10 percent of above	_____	_____
Total show budget/actual	$_____	$_____

Figure A.1. Cost-tracking form. (Duplicate of Figure 2.1.)

EXHIBITOR'S TOOL KIT

With knowledge of exhibit and products, you should edit this list.

- Hammer
- Selection of nails and nail puller
- Pliers and wire cutter
- Screw assortment and screwdrivers, regular and Phillips head
- Scissors
- Tape: rug, strapping, masking, double-faced, Velcro (fabric loop)
- Staple gun, staples
- Tape measure (25-foot)
- Flat extension cords (25-foot)
- Waber strips, 4-way electrical outlet boxes
- Indelible marking pens
- Shims (wooden, for leveling)
- Fire extinguisher (ABC type)
- First-aid kit
- Hot-wire tester
- Touch-up paint for exhibit colors, small brushes
- Cleaning solutions (lighter fluid)
- Plexiglass repair kit and polish
- Spare light bulbs (same size and "color" as used by exhibit)
- Saws (small, wood and metal)
- Allen wrenches and a ratchet set
- Flashlight, utility light
- Wire (bailing)
- Chalk, string, plastic sheets to cover carpet during setup
- Cleaning cloths, spray cleaner, and a portable vacuum cleaner
- Spare fixtures, unique to a manufactured system

The list is extensive, suitable for a large exhibit installation. If there is any question of whether or not an item should be packed, take it along. Expect the unexpected, especially when stores are closed or you are in a strange city.

Figure A.2. An exhibitor's tool kit checklist. (Duplicate of Figure 3.4.)

EXHIBITOR'S SALES AND OFFICE SUPPLIES

Office supplies and company forms can be forgotten. Start with:

— Sales lead forms and carbon paper, order and contract blanks
— Office letterhead and notepaper
— Folders for temporary files
— Inexpensive paper staplers (several) and staples
— Staple remover
— Business cards
— Ballpoint pens (several) and marker pens
— Calendar
— Leather-bound appointment book to use for formalizing customer appointments at the booth
— Leather-bound guest book for VIP sign-in at a hospitality suite
— Cellophane tape and paper clips
— No. 10 standard office envelopes and 9 by 12 envelopes
— Traveler's checks and cash for on-site payments
— Note on where copying service can be obtained near the show
— Portable typewriter or note on rental sources near the show

In addition to general supplies, specific show items can include:

• Bills of lading for commercial transportation
• Exhibitor kit, including contract and order forms, and copies of orders sent in advance
• Telephone set (if a line was ordered)
• Travel tickets, hotel and rental car confirmation numbers
• List of all staff members, complete with home telephone numbers
• Copies of product brochures and fliers, press releases
• Name badges if sent to you in advance by show management
• Show tickets left over from those provided in advance by the show

---

Figure A.3. An exhibitor's sales and office supplies checklist. (Duplicate of Figure 3.5.)

HINTS ON PROSPECTING AT THE BOOTH

- Wear business dress standard for the industry and region, even if attendees will visit the trade show floor informally clothed.

- Wear older, very comfortable shoes.

- Arrive at the booth 15 minutes before start time each day.

- Never start a conversation with, "Can I help you?" Instead, create an open-ended question that encourages visitors to indicate a bit about who they are and what they do. Rehearse openings. Don't memorize, but do have a stream of conversation in mind.

- Use the first minute of conversation to "qualify" a true prospect before starting demonstration or discussion. Then make a conscious decision to continue or back off.

- Ask about buying interest within 5 minutes. Try to complete contacts as quickly as possible while remaining polite, friendly.

- Speak clearly and slowly. Show floors are noisy.

- Do not carry on conversations with other booth staff members, even during quiet periods. Stay on the alert, at the edge of the aisle, giving attendees an impression of your willingness to help.

- Do not sit, smoke, eat, or drink in the booth.

- Body language is important. Stand with hands at sides or cupped below the waist. Folding arms across the chest looks defensive. Hands in pockets imply, "I don't care."

- Wear your name badge on the *right* side, so that it can be seen during hand-shaking introductions.

- Use care in writing down particulars about the prospect and what is of interest for follow-up. Don't depend on memory.

- Remain professional and businesslike. Exhibits are not for the shy, but at the same time a huckster's approach does not work.

- Avoid indiscriminate distribution of sales literature or giveaways, unless a goal is education or overall awareness.

We suggest this list be copied and distributed.

Figure A.4. A list of selling dos and don'ts. (Duplicate of Figure 3.6.)

<u>Audience Analysis</u>

Total estimated audience	_____
Deductions	
Spouses _____	
Other exhibitors _____	
Press _____	
Students _____	
Total deductions	−_____
Total buying audience	_____
Percent of market served	×_____
Target audience	_____

<u>Exhibit industry average (alternate method)</u>

Total estimated audience	_____
Average percent interest in a single product line	×____.16
Target audience	_____

Figure A.5. Planning form—audience analysis for goal setting. (Duplicate of Figure 5.1.)

Waste Factor Calculation

Target audience (from Figure 5.1)   ———

Waste factor $\times$ 1.33*

Total exhibit contact goal   ———

*From a study of 40 exhibits by one large company.

Figure A.6. Planning form—waste factor projection. (Duplicate of Figure 5.2.)

```
┌─────────────────────────────────────────────────────────────────────┐
```

Sales Goal Projection

Sales lead goal

Total exhibit contact goal (from Figure 5.2)	_____
Less: waste contacts	_____
Target audience contacts (from Figures 5.1 and 5.2)	_____
Percent buyers and purchasing influences	✕____.50*
Total interested *and* buyers	_____
Lead generation rate in this group	✕____.50†
Sales lead goal	_____

Current customer show order goal

Number to contact	_____
Percent of them to place orders	✕_____
Current customer show order goal	_____
Sales lead goal (from above)	_____
Percent sold within 1 year	✕____.50
Total sales goal from sales leads	_____
Plus: current customer show order goal (from above)	_____
Total sales goal	_____

Dollar sales projection

Product _____	
Total sales goal (from above)	_____
Percent of sales orders for this product	✕_____
Sales goal this product	_____
Average value each sale this product	$_____
Sales goal this product (from second line above)	✕_____
Dollar sales projection this product	$_____

(Repeat for each product and combine for dollar total. Percent of sales orders for all products combined should total 100.)

Dollar sales goal for the exhibit	$_____

*Rounded up from an average of 45 percent.
†Research from 40 exhibits sponsored by one company.
  Cross-check by estimating 20 percent of all projected contacts at the booth.

Figure A.7. Planning form—sales lead and dollar goals. (Duplicate of Figure 5.3.)

Exhibits open	From–to	Hours	Deduct*	Active hours
Day 1: _____	to ____	_____	_____	_____
Day 2: _____	to ____	_____	_____	_____
Day 3: _____	to ____	_____	_____	_____
Day 4: _____	to ____	_____	_____	_____
Day 5: _____	to ____	_____	_____	_____
Total		_____	_____	_____

*Deduct estimated slow periods. These can include:
  - First and last hours each day
  - First afternoon if opening is on a weekend afternoon
  - Last afternoon of an out-of-town show for attendees
  - Times when seminars take place or there are general assembly meetings

Target Audience (from Figure A.5, "Audience Analysis")   _____

Divided by _____ active hours = _____ Contacts per active hour

Figure A.8.   Planning form—time factor analysis.

Day	Active hours	Contacts per hour	Contacts per day	Leads per hour	Leads per day
Total					

Figure A.9. Goals per hour and day.

1. Total sales contact goal	_____
2. *Divided by* total active hours	_____
3. Total contacts per active hour	_____
4. *Divided by* contacts per active hour per salesperson	___10___
5. On-duty sales staff (rounded)	_____
6. *Times* people-space factor (49 square feet)	_____ square feet
7. *Plus* one-third of people space (49) for product display	_____ square feet
8. Total required	_____ square feet
9. Rounded to nearest rentable space amount	_____ square feet
Booth spaces to rent ___	

Figure A.10. Space size estimating. (This is a blank form of Figure 6.1.)

1. Square feet of exhibit space
2. *Divided by* average space per selling station   _____65*
3. Number of selling stations (rounded ____ from ____)
4. *Times* selling contacts per person in an active hour   × _____10*
5. Number of selling contacts in an active hour   _____
6. Total hours open   ____
7. *Less* slack hours   ____
8. *Times* active hours   × _____
9. Total selling contacts for the show as a whole
10. *Less* .25 percent waste factor (.25 × line 9)   _____*
11. Target audience   _____
12. *Less* 50 percent (not decision makers)   _____
13. Decision makers or purchasing Influences   _____
14. *Times* sales lead conversion (20% of total contacts)   _____*
15. Qualified sales leads to take at the booth   _____
16. *Times* sales conversion ratio   × _____.50*
17. Sales to close during or after the show   _____
18. Average value of sale for ___ percent (#___) @ $_____   = $_____
19. Average value of sale for ___ percent (#___) @ $_____   = $_____
20. Average value of sale for ___ percent (#___) @ $_____   = $_____
    Note: Repeat for each product.
21. Total projected revenue $_____

*Based on research. Can be adjusted based on experience or on your own research.

Figure A.11.   Goal setting with space fixed. (This is a blank form of Figure 7.1.)

Budget item	Exhibit manager's current budget	Another budget contribution	Show cost allocation
1. Space rent			
a. Space (current year)	$	$	$
b. Deposit (last year)			
c. Deposit (next year)			
d. Total space	$	$	$
2. Exhibit structure, graphics, and display products			
a. Design	$	$	$
b. Building/ refurbishing			
c. Graphics			
d. Total structure	$	$	$
e. Display products	$	$	$
f. Total structure, etc.	$	$	$
3. Promotions and presentations			
a. Direct mail creative	$	$	$
b. Production/ printing			
c. Postage/ handling			
d. Advertising creative			
e. Media buy			
f. Premiums/ giveaways			
g. Special literature creative			
h. Production/ printing			
i. Handling			
j. Product literature			
k. Live audivisual show writing			
l. Preshow production			
m. At-show production			
n. Talent/host/ hostess			
o. Room/seminar/ writing			
p. Preshow slides, etc.			
q. At-show (rent, etc.)			
r. Preshow press relations			
s. At-show press package			
t. At-show press conference			
u. Preshow slides, etc.			
v. At-show (rent, etc.)			
w. Total promotions	$	$	$

Figure A.12. Exhibit budget form.

4. Customer hospitality

 a. Suite/room rental $ _____ $ _____ $ _____
 b. Food/beverage (day)
 c. Food/beverage (day)
 c. Food/beverage (evening)
 d. Decor/flowers
 e. Host/hostess
 f. Local transport service
 g. Entertainment/sports tickets
 h. Spousal program
 i. Invitations
 j. Formal dinner food
 k. Decor
 l. Entertainment/talent
 m. Outside management fee
 n. Total hospitality $ _____ $ _____ $ _____

5. Transportation

 a. Shipping to, truck $ _____ $ _____ $ _____
 b. Air freight
 c. Sea freight
 d. Shipping from, truck
 e. Air freight
 f. Sea freight
 g. Administration fee/commission
 h. Total transportation $ _____ $ _____ $ _____

6. Field service on site

 a. Drayage into hall $ _____ $ _____ $ _____
 b. Drayage out of hall
 c. Labor up
 d. Labor down
 e. Electrical
 f. Telephone
 g. Rentals (plants, etc.)
 h. Photography
 i. Security
 j. Booth cleaning
 k. Other services/ miscellaneous
 l. Management fee/expense
 m. Total show service $ _____ $ _____ $ _____

7. Staff personnel

 a. Time value of staff $ _____ $ _____ $ _____
 b. Personal out of pocket
 c. Sales training/clerical
 d. Total staff expense $ _____ $ _____ $ _____

Figure A.12. *(Continued)*

Budget item	Exhibit manager's current budget	Another budget contribution	Show cost allocation
8. Research			
a. Informal	$ ____	$ ____	$ ____
b. Professional			
c. total	$ ____	$ ____	$ ____
9. Total	$ ____	$ ____	$ ____
10. Contingency (10 percent)	$ ____	$ ____	$ ____
11. Grand Total	$ ____	$ ____	$ ____

Figure A.12.   *(Continued)*

Budget item	Exhibit manager's current budget	Another budget contribution	Show cost allocation
1. Space rent			
a. Space (current year)	$	$	$
b. Deposit (next year)			
c. Total space	$	$	$
2. Exhibit structure, graphics, and display products			
a. Design/ graphics	$	$	$
b. Construction			
c. Display products			
4. Preshow promotion/direct mail			
a. Total	$	$	$
5. Exhibit-related advertising			
a. Total	$	$	$
6. Live show, audiovisual, at-show promotion (giveaways, literature)			
a. Total	$	$	$
7. Transportation			
a. Trucking	$	$	$
b. Other	$	$	$
c. Total	$	$	$
8. Show services			
a. Drayage	$	$	$
b. Labor	$	$	$
c. Other	$	$	$
d. Total	$	$	$
9. Hospitality			
a. Total	$	$	$
10. Exhibit staff			
a. Salary	$	$	$
b. Expenses	$	$	$
c. Total	$	$	$
11. On-site staff training			
a. Total	$	$	$
12. Research			
a. Total	$	$	$
13. Total	$	$	$
14. Contingency (10 percent)	$	$	$
15. Grand total	$	$	$

Figure A.13. Exhibit budget short form.

Show: _____   *Opening date:* ___ / ___ / ___

Item status	Week 10	Week 9	Week 8	Week 7	Week 6	Week 5	Week 4	Week 3	Week 2	Week 1	Week 0

- _____
- Start ____ ____ ____ ____ ____ ____ ____ ____ ____ ____ ____
- Check ____ ____ ____ ____ ____ ____ ____ ____ ____ ____ ____
- Check ____ ____ ____ ____ ____ ____ ____ ____ ____ ____ ____
- Complete ____ ____ ____ ____ ____ ____ ____ ____ ____ ____ ____

- _____
- Start ____ ____ ____ ____ ____ ____ ____ ____ ____ ____ ____
- Check ____ ____ ____ ____ ____ ____ ____ ____ ____ ____ ____
- Check ____ ____ ____ ____ ____ ____ ____ ____ ____ ____ ____
- Complete ____ ____ ____ ____ ____ ____ ____ ____ ____ ____ ____

- _____
- Start ____ ____ ____ ____ ____ ____ ____ ____ ____ ____ ____
- Check ____ ____ ____ ____ ____ ____ ____ ____ ____ ____ ____
- Check ____ ____ ____ ____ ____ ____ ____ ____ ____ ____ ____
- Complete ____ ____ ____ ____ ____ ____ ____ ____ ____ ____ ____

- _____
- Start ____ ____ ____ ____ ____ ____ ____ ____ ____ ____ ____
- Check ____ ____ ____ ____ ____ ____ ____ ____ ____ ____ ____
- Check ____ ____ ____ ____ ____ ____ ____ ____ ____ ____ ____
- Complete ____ ____ ____ ____ ____ ____ ____ ____ ____ ____ ____

- _____
- Start ____ ____ ____ ____ ____ ____ ____ ____ ____ ____ ____
- Check ____ ____ ____ ____ ____ ____ ____ ____ ____ ____ ____
- Check ____ ____ ____ ____ ____ ____ ____ ____ ____ ____ ____
- Complete ____ ____ ____ ____ ____ ____ ____ ____ ____ ____ ____

- _____
- Start ____ ____ ____ ____ ____ ____ ____ ____ ____ ____ ____
- Check ____ ____ ____ ____ ____ ____ ____ ____ ____ ____ ____
- Check ____ ____ ____ ____ ____ ____ ____ ____ ____ ____ ____
- Complete ____ ____ ____ ____ ____ ____ ____ ____ ____ ____ ____

- _____
- Start ____ ____ ____ ____ ____ ____ ____ ____ ____ ____ ____
- Check ____ ____ ____ ____ ____ ____ ____ ____ ____ ____ ____
- Check ____ ____ ____ ____ ____ ____ ____ ____ ____ ____ ____
- Complete ____ ____ ____ ____ ____ ____ ____ ____ ____ ____ ____

Once this chart is complete, you may wish to copy items to your Job List for the Week sheet.

Figure A.14. Show production time line. (Duplicate of Figure 11.1.)

Show: _____	Opening date: _/_____/___

Week starting on Sunday, _____. There are ____ weeks to opening.

Jobs to start

- _____ Check date: ___/___ Complete date: ___/___
- _____ Check date: ___/___ Complete date: ___/___
- _____ Check date: ___/___ Complete date: ___/___
- _____ Check date: ___/___ Complete date: ___/___
- _____ Check date: ___/___ Complete date: ___/___
- _____ Check date: ___/___ Complete date: ___/___

Jobs to check

- _____ 2d check: ___/___ Complete date: ___/___
- _____ 2d check: ___/___ Complete date: ___/___
- _____ 2d check: ___/___ Complete date: ___/___
- _____ 2d check: ___/___ Complete date: ___/___
- _____ 2d check: ___/___ Complete date: ___/___
- _____ 2d check: ___/___ Complete date: ___/___

Jobs to complete

- _____ Check okay: ___/___ If not: ___/___
- _____ Check okay: ___/___ If not: ___/___
- _____ Check okay: ___/___ If not: ___/___
- _____ Check okay: ___/___ If not: ___/___
- _____ Check okay: ___/___ If not: ___/___
- _____ Check okay: ___/___ If not: ___/___

Figure A.15. Job list for week. (Duplicate of Figure 11.2.)

		Estimate	Actual
1. Room charge			
Room			
Tax	_____ =	$_____	$_____
2. Food per person	$_____		
Times number of people	×_____		
Base cost			
Times 15-percent gratuity	×___.15		
Total before tax			
Plus tax on base cost	+_____ =	_____	_____
3. Liquor, wine, beer, soft drinks			
Bottle cost			
Mixers	_____		
Condiments	_____		
Supplies	_____ =	_____	_____
4. Personnel (host, hostess, bartender, etc.)			
Hourly cost	$_____		
Times hours open + 1½*			
and setup, cleanup	×_____		
Base personnel cost			
Plus 15 percent gratuity	+_____ =	_____	_____
5. Leather-bound guest book and pens		_____	_____
6. Decorations—flowers, etc.		_____	_____
7. Entertainment			
Fees			
Production (sound, lights)	_____		
Personal expense	_____ =	_____	_____
8. Audiovisual equipment			
Slide projector			
Sound system	_____		
VCR	_____		
Easel	_____ =	_____	_____
9. Miscellaneous gifts, delivery service, etc.		_____	_____
10. Total		_____	
11. Plus contingency (10 percent)		+_____	_____
12. Total		$_____	$_____

*Presume suite will be open longer than anticipated.

Figure A.16. Hospitality budget checklist. (Duplicate of Figure 14.1.)

Trade Show Bureau
P.O. Box 797, 8 Beach Road
East Orleans, Massachusetts 02643
Telephone: (617) 240-0177

International Exhibitors Association (IEA)
5103-B Backlick Road
Annandale, Virginia 22003
Telephone: (703) 941-3725
Telex: 628605 IEA HEADQUARTERS

Health Care Exhibitors Association (HCEA)
5775 Peachtree-Dunwoody Road, Suite 500-D
Atlanta, Georgia 30342
Telephone: (404) 252-3663

National Association of Exposition Managers (NAEM)
334 East Garfield Road
Post Office Box 377
Aurora, Ohio 44202
Telephone: (216) 562-8255

Exhibit Designers and Producers Association (ED&PA)
1411 K Street, NW, Suite 801
Washington, D.C. 20005
Telephone: (202) 393-2001

Exposition Service Contractors Association (ESCA)
1516 South Pontius Avenue
Los Angeles, California 90025
Telephone: (213) 478-0215
Telex: 181149 WEST LSA

International Association of Convention and Visitors Bureaus (IACVB)
Post Office Box 758
Champaign, Illinois 61820
Telephone: (217) 359-8881

Convention Liaison Council (CLC)
1575 Eye Street, NW
Washington, D.C. 20005
Telephone: (202) 626-2723

Tradeshow Week Publications
12233 West Olympic Blvd., Suite 236
Los Angeles, California 90064
Telephone: (213) 826-5696
Telex: 194351 SHOWCOINT

Exhibitor Magazine Publications
745 Marquette Bank Building
Rochester, Minnesota 55903
Telephone: (507) 289-6556

Figure A.17. List of selected exhibit industry associations, publications, and reference sources. (Duplicate of Figure 21.1.)

Exhibit Builder Magazine
Sound Publishing Company
Post Office Box 920
Great Neck, New York 11022
Telephone: (516) 466-5750

Successful Meetings Exhibit Schedule
1518 Walnut Street
Philadelphia, Pennsylvania 19102
Telephone: (215) 546-3295

Tradeshow and Convention Guide
Billboard Publications: Amusement Business
Post Office Box 24970
Nashville, Tennessee 37202
Telephone: (615) 748-8120

World Convention Dates
79 Washington Street
Hempstead, New York 11550
Telephone: (516) 483-6881

Figure A.17.   *(Continued)*

Notes

Chapter 1

1. Jerry Lowery is general manager of the Convention and Exhibition Centre of Hong Kong.

2. Exhibit Surveys Incorporated. No research specifically aimed at delineating the relative impact of an exhibit's various elements has been completed to the satisfaction of the firm. Based on two decades of exhibit audience research, however, its principals offer a subjective opinion that three-fourths of an exhibit's sales impact can be traced to the action of the salespeople. Although product display and demonstration are important, what visitors remember is conversation.

Chapter 2

1. The Trade Show Bureau is an industry-supported research and educational organization funded by major exhibit industry associations and by corporate contributions. Its research is frequently referred to, not only in this book but in periodical literature as well. The cost for sales call figures we cite come from an annual study. The most recent, for 1985, was $106.80 per contact at an exhibit on the show floor. This is compared to McGraw-Hill Lab of Advertising Performance 1985 studies of the cost for an industrial sales call in the customer's office: $229.70 per call. Our specific source is the *Trade Show Bureau Research Report, Cost Analysis 2020,* July 1986.

2. In addition to the author's experience, several exhibitor kits were reviewed, including kits prepared for the National Association of Broadcasters convention, the high-technology Interface Show, and the National Wholesale Grocers Association meeting.

Chapter 3

1. *New York County Business to Business Yellow Pages*, 1986, New York Telephone, a NYNEX Company.

2. *Exhibitor Magazine*, vol. 1, no. 10, 1982, by Ina Feinberg and Michelle Neuman.

3. *Tradeshow Week's National Tradeshow Services Directory*, published annually by *Tradeshow Week*.

Chapter 4

1. *Trade Show Bureau Research Report Study Number 18*, April 1983. The study traces sales close activity. Because prospects see products at trade shows, and talk to salespeople, less time is required to close a sale after the show is over. In fact, over half the respondents in the study said that *no* personal sales call was required. Even when purchases were for products costing over $50,000, the average was only 1.8 postshow sales calls.

2. *Trade Show Bureau Research Report Cost Analysis 2030*, July 1986. This is the fifth in a series stretching back to figures reported for 1969. The year in this study is 1985 and the goal is to provide budget-building guidance. See note 1, Chapter 2.

   The Trade Show Bureau is reluctant to endorse this chapter's guideline on estimating the cost of personnel since there can be so many variables. It suggests that staff costs should be estimated by individual companies.

3. *Tradeshow Week* publishes, annually, a study of the 200 largest shows that take place in the United States and the top 20 in Canada: *Tradeshow Week's Tradeshow 200*. The average cost per square foot of space in 1985 was $11.65, up from $9.87 in 1984. The range was $1.27 to $26.50 per square foot in 1985. The average exhibitor rented 295 square feet. Over 131,416 exhibitors participated in these shows, up from 122,540 in 1984.

4. Ibid.

5. *Tradeshow Week* is a weekly newsletter. Annually, it surveys subscribers on exhibit spending.

6. *Trade Show Bureau Research Report Study Number 21*, May 1984. The study compares audiences at shows defined as *national* versus *regional*. Although there are differences, overall audience quality and sales potential are the same.

7. The audience interest factor (AIF) has been used as a show analysis tool by Exhibit Surveys Incorporated.

8. *Trade Show Bureau Research Report Study Number 22*, May 1984. The study included 13 regional and 15 national trade shows. At regional shows, 92 percent of the average exhibitor's visitors had not been called on by a salesperson from the company during the preceding year. At national shows, 84 percent of the average exhibitor's booth visitors had not been called on by the exhibitor in over a year.

Chapter 5

1. *Tradeshow Week* produces its annual reader survey to study trends in exhibit budget management. It provides information on percent allocation of marketing communications dollars to exhibiting. It also shows trends in space buying and goal setting.

2. *Trade Show Bureau Research Report Study Number 19,* June 1983. The study work is broader the *Tradeshow Week* reader surveys. An extensive amount of detail is presented on exhibit expenditures, objectives, and evaluation.

3. The 16 percent average interest in a single product line was produced through a large body of research developed by Exhibit Surveys Incorporated.

4. The waste factor study was reported in *Exhibitor Magazine* in a 1984 article by the author and Skip Cox, vice president of Exhibit Surveys Incorporated. The AT&T percentage was 20 percent. Over the years, other survey results indicate that 33 percent is a good rule of thumb.

5. *Trade Show Bureau Research Report Study Number 18,* April 1983. See note 1, Chapter 4.

Chapter 6

1. A number of exhibit designers and producers, and show management companies, have conducted research on exhibit hall traffic flow and space use, including stop-action film studies.

2. Ibid.

Chapter 7

1. Show floor interviews were conducted with exhibit professionals at Wang, IBM, AT&T, Northern Telcom, Sperry (now part of Unisys), and Digital Equipment Corporation.

Chapter 8

1. *Trade Show Bureau Research Report Cost Analysis 2020.* The costs identified in this study are updated. Survey information is evaluated on a 3-year rolling average. See note 1, Chapter 2.

2. This midwest Fortune 500 company provides exhibit structures for a number of product divisions on a central basis. We don't agree with the practice because it limits the degree to which local management can reflect individual audience needs on graphics.

3. See note 1.

4. The International Exhibitors Association address is listed in Figure 21.1. At publication of this book, the most recent of *Exhibitor Magazine*'s annual articles was in its December 1, 1985, issue.

5. *Trade Show Bureau Research Report Study No. 24, Exhibit Cost Analysis 1981–1983*, November 1984.

Chapter 9

1. *Trade Show Bureau Research Report Study Number 18*, April 1983. This research was compared with *McGraw-Hill Lab of Advertising Performance Report Number 8013.8*. The cost of exhibit and office contacts were updated with figures from the *Trade Show Bureau Research Report Cost Analysis 2020*, July 1986. It combines $106.70, as cost of the exhibit contact, with .8 of the cost of an office call, $229.70. That figure, $183.76, added to $106.70 yields $290.46 selling cost to close a sale starting from a booth lead.

For sales that do not start with an exhibit-demonstration-produced lead, an average of 5.5 office calls are required to "close," costing $1263.

Chapter 10

1. *Tradeshow Week* annual reader survey on exhibit budgets.

Chapter 12

1. William P. Muir, Muir Cornelius Moore, Inc.

2. Exhibit Surveys Incorporated. Most of this company's study work on exhibit performance is conducted *6 to 8 weeks after an event* has taken place. Remarkable unaided memorability results emerge.

3. Robert Dottinger, Dottinger Design.

Chapter 13

1. *Trade Show Bureau Research Report Study Number 27*, October 1985. The study measured exhibit traffic in conjunction with trade magazine advertising: with the Food Expo trade show audience and exhibitor advertising in an important trade magazine for that industry, *Food Technology*.

2. Two of these specialized convention city guides are: *National Conventioneer*, Publishers for Conventions, Inc., 1205 Main Street, Pittsburgh PA 15215, and

Pocket Survival Guide/PSG, Media Group Ltd., 11846 Ventura Blvd., Studio City, CA 91604.

Chapter 14

1. This is an interpretation of Michael Vance's description of the levels of knowledge. In addition to the three described, there is a fourth: the state of being unconsciously competent. Riding a bicycle is an example. We know how but can't explain it. Exhibits can not be run the way we ride a bicycle.

2. Much of the information in this chapter came from speeches by Theresa Bellinghausen, president, Events Management Corporation, Bellevue, Washington. Additional material came from hospitality management guidebooks developed by Events Management Corporation for the Weyerhaeuser Company and divisions of the Savin Corporation. The cost-of-time-at-a-meeting figure comes from a study done by the 3M company.

3. Ibid.

Chapter 15

1. The information gathered came from experience, lectures at meetings of the International Exhibitors Association, and interviews with a number of sources in the industry: exhibit transportation people, exhibit managers, independent and "official" show contractors, show labor union members, facilities managers, and exhibit builders. Additional background was provided by David Gold, of Exhibit Marketing Services, Long Island, New York, and Chris Walker from Giltspur Exhibits, Los Angeles.

2. Styrofoam crate models are used by Relocation Systems exhibit specialist Laurel Larson, a primary source of information on exhibit transportation pricing practices in this chapter. Additional sources were Rik Lowry, director of Special Transportation for Clark Transfer, and Bob Land, president of Showtronix. North American Van Lines, Fort Wayne, Indiana, gave permission to reprint portions of its exhibit tariff.

3. The exhibit builder involved with the Las Vegas case was Dutch Antonisse, president of Heritage Communications, Dallas.

4. The major news story, by Joyce Purnick, on Mayor Edward Koch's letters to New York State Governor Mario Cuomo, state legislators, and the Javits' Convention Center Board appeared in *The New York Times* "Metropolitan Report" on November 2, 1985.

5. Extensive background on show setup services was provided by Jack McEntee, Ellen Chapman, and Jim Wurm of Installation & Dismantle, Inc.

6. Our primary source of information on facilities management was Jerry

Lowery, general manager of the Hong Kong Convention and Exhibition Centre. See note 1, Chapter 2.

7. The exhibiting company is Rolm Corporation.

Chapter 16

1. *Trade Show Bureau Study Number 3*, April 1979, based on an analysis of the audiences at 22 national trade shows.

Chapter 17

1. "You . . . Make the Difference," published by and available through The Trade Show Bureau.

　　As the use of the exhibit medium becomes more expensive and difficult, a number of consultants now specialize in helping small and medium-sized companies, as well as the "giants." They provide a broad range of services, including sales briefing. Some of these people have experience as corporate exhibit managers. In addition to specialists in exhibit management, a traditional full-service exhibit designers and producers are starting to provide management and training services.

　　Many consultants are listed in an article by Chris Christman published by *Exhibitor Magazine*, no. 12, 1985. Additional sources for names include the Trade Show Bureau, the International Exhibitors Association, and *Tradeshow Week's National Tradeshow Services Directory*.

2. The information in this chapter comes from experience and exposure to a number of different sources, including consultants, a list of sales hints used by Gould International, a booklet called "20 Tips," distributed by Communique, of Englewood, New Jersey, and lectures at meetings of the International Exhibitors Association. Most important was an exhibit sales training program created by the S. W. Clow & Partners Company of New York with assistance from members of the psychology department of Fairleigh Dickenson University in New Jersey.

3. Diane Seymour, *Voice Power*, Actors Institute, 1985, New York City.

Chapter 19

1. Information was provided by Harrison Sherwood of the United States and Foreign Commercial Service of the International Trade Administration in the U.S. Department of Commerce.

2. *Do's and Taboos Around the World, A Guide to International Behavior,*

edited and compiled by Roger E. Axtell, Benjamin Company, Elmsford, New York, 1985, distributed by the Parker Pen Company, Janesville, Wisconsin.

3. The United States firm is Exhibit Surveys Incorporated. Its counterpart in the United Kingdom is Harry McDermott's Exhibition Surveys.

4. Much of the material in this chapter was garnered from a series of seminars presented at the International Exhibitors Association Meeting in San Francisco, August 13 to 16, 1985. Additional material was provided by Vredy Lytsman, from Holland, and Rik Lowry of Clark Transfer in Chicago. The International Exhibitors Association has published a comprehensive book, *The International Handbook and Guide*, that includes information on sites, show organizers, business etiquette, electrical requirements, sample freight forms, and a glossary of international terms.

Chapter 20

1. The show organizer was *The Wall Street Micro Investor*, a trade magazine with editorial and advertising offices in New York City.

2. The exhibit company was Alan Sitzer Associates. Although based in New York City, the Mitchell A. Fink Associates project was developed and supervised by Cindy Spuria, manager of the firm's Research Triangle Park Office in Carrboro, North Carolina.

3. The D. L. Terwilliger Printing Company, New York City.

4. The Exponents Company, San Diego, California. Specifications for its system, along with many others, can be found in *The Illustrated Buyers Guide to Exhibits*, Exhibitor Publications, Rochester, Minnesota, 1986.

5. The general contractor for the show manager was Exposition Service and Rentals, Inc., Clifton Park, New Jersey.

Chapter 22

1. Leslie Stroh, publisher, *Trade Data Reports* and *Rug News*.

2. Alvin Toffler, *The Third Wave*, William Morrow & Co., New York City, 1980.

3. *Tradeshow 200*, published annually by Tradeshow Week, Inc., Los Angeles.

4. Edward T. Hagen, the Gallery Hotel Management Group.

5. *Tradeshow Week*, April 7, 1986. According to the publisher's annual survey, 34 percent of the trade shows in 1986 were booked in hotel convention halls.

6. Joyce McKee, B. R. Blackmarr Associates, Dallas. An extensive survey of major technology buyers reveals that half send staffs to trade shows instead of

attending themselves. The quality of the educational program is very influential in show attendance decisions.

Chapter 23

1. *The Harvard Business Review*, January–February 1983, by Thomas V. Bonoma.

Index

About the Author

Edward A. Chapman, Jr., created the exhibit management system for the AT&T division that markets high-technology equipment. His concepts have been widely covered in the trade areas, including feature stories in *Tradeshow Week*, *Exhibitor Magazine*, and *Successful Meetings*. He has talked before business groups and presented seminars both in this country and abroad. Chapman, one of fewer than 100 people to hold the Certified Exhibit Specialist ranking from the International Exhibitors Association, is president of Sextant Communications in New York City.